The CAPE TOWN INTELLECTUALS

South African Library

Cape Town c1930

The CAPE TOWN INTELLECTUALS

Ruth Schechter and her Circle, 1907-1934

BARUCH HIRSON

THE MERLIN PRESS

The Merlin Press

ISBN 0 85036 500 7

First published in 2001

Typesetting and Cover Design: Sue Sandrock
Printed by: Clyson Printers, Maitland, Cape Town

CONTENTS

FOREWORD

About twenty years ago, Baruch Hirson noted that the process through which groups achieve political consciousness was subtle, and even mysterious: it did not happen as a consequence of 'an accretion of understanding'; it was not linear. Social processes were never simple, he added. Even so, he himself would have been surprised to learn that his three decades of 'activist' scholarship have culminated in the posthumous publication of a gentle narrative about an intellectual Cape Town literary critic and her equally cerebral friends. In this book Hirson makes a strong case, unlikely as it may seem, for The Cape Town Intellectuals to be early pioneers in a tradition of radical dissenting thought. To appreciate his arguments fully, though, and understand better his treatment of the subjects of this book, it is helpful to know something about the journey Baruch Hirson himself made before he encountered Ruth Schechter and her circle.

Baruch Hirson was born in 1921, the son of a Jewish electrician who had arrived in Johannesburg from Latvia two decades before. After an austere childhood in lower middle class white Johannesburg, Hirson's initial involvement with a Zionist youth club led him into revolutionary Marxist politics, first with the Hashomer Hatzair on the eve of the Second World War and then from 1944 as an adherent of a succession of Trotskyite groups. Between 1944 and 1946 he worked as the political organiser for the Workers' International League; subsequently he combined his politics with an academic career as a physicist at the University of the Witwatersrand.

Towards the end of the 1950s he joined the Congress of Democrats, the white arm of the ANC-led Congress Alliance. Highly critical of its leadership and policies Hirson, with other disaffected left-wing Congress activists, formed the Socialist League of Africa just before the Sharpeville massacre. Subsequently, Socialist League members were to help establish the first of several anti-apartheid sabotage groups – the National Committee for Liberation, later known as the African Resistance

Movement. Arrested and tried in 1964, Hirson was convicted of sabotage and imprisoned for nine years. Five days after his release in 1973 and confronted with a banning order he went into exile with his wife, Yael, and three children, Denis, Allen and Zoë.

For the next three decades, Hirson worked in Britain, as an historian, lecturer, and editor. Including his autobiography, *Revolutions in my Life*, he published five books before his death in October 1999. He received a doctorate from Middlesex Polytechnic. His journal, *Searchlight*, between 1988 and 1995 provided a lively platform for left-wing analysis of South African history and contemporary politics and published the first detailed exposure of the harsh regime which the ANC maintained in Angolan detention camps. His unpublished work as well as the papers he presented at conferences or published in journals constitute another voluminous body of writings.

In his exile vocations as scholar and teacher, Hirson reached and inspired many more people than he had ever influenced as a revolutionary organiser. A succession of meticulously documented and passionately argued books brought new depth and humanity to the scholarship of South African revolutionary history. It was a scholarship for which there was a growing readership. During the 1980s in his homeland, a radicalised generation of university students as well as the working-class intellectuals emerging from a huge new trade union movement helped to promote new popular interest in 'people's history'.

Hirson's first book, *Year of Fire, Year of Ash*, a powerful polemical chronology of the Soweto uprising, was published in 1979. It appeared to be about contemporary events. The appearance was deceptive, Hirson contended, for no events were completely modern. They were the product of processes that stretched over decades. One of these was a tradition of classroom rebellion which Hirson traced back in detail to 1920 when students in Kilnerton embarked on a hunger strike for more food. Another tradition was a lineage of political mobilisation around 'black awareness' which in *Year of Fire* Hirson documented from the gestation of the ANC Youth League. A final process which 'produced the climate which led to Soweto' was class struggle, and in particular the strikes which pulled 200 000 workers out of their factories between 1973 and 1976.

What renders Hirson's analysis of the events after 16 June 1976 distinctive is his insistence that these three genealogies of rebellion failed to combine effectively, a failure which he argued was chiefly attributable to the Black Consciousness Movement's preoccupation with cultural introspection and its conviction that for black South Africans there were 'no class divisions and no class struggles'. Both predispositions, Hirson argued, left Black Consciousness without a programme in 1976 and cut short the 'leaping movement of ideas' that flowed from the schoolchildren's rebellion.

His later work explored the unfolding saga of earlier generations of working class rebellion from its origins in the 1900s, a saga which for Hirson until his death remained the central theme in South African history. *Yours for the Union*, originally written as a doctoral dissertation, is a history of black trade unionism during the first phase of the development of South Africa's manufacturing economy between 1932 and 1946, a history in which in its later stages Hirson himself was a participant. This history was not the first in its field: as its author acknowledged, the narrative in *Yours for the Union* overlaps considerably with the events described in the much earlier volumes by Eddie Roux and Harold and Ray Simons. The latter writers, however, were engaged in documenting the 'prehistory' of 'national democratic' struggle; in both their texts the dialectic between class struggle and African nationalism was perceived to have generated a benign political synthesis.

The period covered by Hirson's history is itself significant; it starts after the destruction of the first generation of African unions in the Depression and ends with the collapse in 1947 of a much stronger movement in the wake of an ill-timed mineworkers strike. This history, Hirson noted, had lessons which should have been learned at the time and which retained relevance 'for the working class of South Africa today'.

These lessons are not spelled out explicitly in *Yours for the Union* but they are evident enough in its author's foregrounding of the history of various revolutionary socialist efforts to construct through trade unions a working class base for a socialist political movement. Hirson concedes that such efforts may have been premature: differentially incorporated into the urban economy, African workers in the 1930s and 1940s 'hardly represented a revolutionary crowd'. Even so their victories might have been more sustained if their leaders had been less affected by the vicissitudes of Communist Party policy, especially during the war when militant options were rejected by the Party's leadership. Nor was the ANC any more helpful with its prescriptions of racial self reliance (so as to exclude any left- wing 'dangerous elements') at wartime trade union assemblies. Despite such distractions, a tradition of struggle was established, a tradition which in his later autobiographical and polemical writing Hirson suggests was repudiated again and again by black conscious nationalists and national democrat Communists.

Not that Communists never had a place in this tradition. Before their subjection to the Comintern in 1928 they enjoyed an age of innocence and even virtue. South African party leaders receive an honourable mention in Baruch Hirson's and Lorraine Vivian's investigation of the 1925 seamen's strike, *Strike across the Empire*. 'Burrowing like moles' in the newspaper archives of three continents, Hirson and his collaborator managed to reconstruct a key episode – indeed one of the very few such episodes of working class internationalism – in which British and Dominion sailors struck against a wage reduction negotiated between a sweetheart union and ship owners.

Leading Communists at the time raised support for the strikers who came ashore in Cape Town and Durban and there were expressions of solidarity from both black and white labour, though no South African workers undertook sympathy strikes. One of the most intriguing issues arising from the strike is its absence from standard labour history, an absence which the authors attribute to its unofficial status and the conflicts it promoted in British and Imperial trade union organisations.

Hirson's next major book, *The Delegate for Africa*, also co-written, this time with Gwyn Williams, is a 'celebration' of one of the South African Communist Party's founding fathers, David Ivon Jones, whose political career began with his arrival as a tuberculosis invalid from Wales via New Zealand in 1910 and ended in a Russian TB clinic fourteen years later.

Hirson takes up the story from Jones's arrival in South Africa in 1910 after his Welsh upbringing and his short spell as a farm labourer in New Zealand. Gwyn Williams in his chapters on Jones's childhood and intellectual formation could draw upon a rich archive of personal correspondence in the University of Wales; this afforded exceptional insights into the emotions which helped prompt Jones's spiritual and political development, a development which took place in the heady milieu of Welsh national revival, industrial radicalism and Unitarian religious dissent. How these democratic impulses converted into revolutionary socialism is Hirson's part of the story. He had to work with more impersonal sources; in the later sections of the book Jones's voice mainly appears through his letters and reports printed in political newspapers. Even so, through a grittily emphatic evocation of white working class life on the Witwatersrand, Hirson supplies a persuasive account of Jones's 're-baptism' in the politics of syndicalist struggle, first among white mineworkers and later, more quixotically, embracing the cause of workers' combination, 'no matter what colour'.

What distinguishes Hirson's text from other histories of this period is the credit it gives to early Communist efforts to build black working class organisation. For Hirson, Jones was a pioneering figure who was absolutely correct in 'stressing class rather than colour' in his analysis of the prospects for building South African socialism. It was Dai Jones's advocacy of a class politics, in which 'colour is only an incident, one of the difficulties' which makes him represent, for Hirson, 'the most advanced thinking of the time' both then, and still, now.

Finally completed just before his death, after ten years of gestation, *The Cape Town Intellectuals* charts another tributary in the early history of the South African left. Despite its title, this is a biography of a single individual, the literary critic Ruth Schechter. In contrast to his assessment of David Ivon Jones, Hirson makes no claims for his subject's retrospective greatness. As he notes, this is a book 'not about the left groups, and not about the few working class struggles' of the times in which Ruth Schechter lived in South Africa, between 1907 and 1933. Not directly, anyway, though Hirson's interest in his biographical heroine is at least partly spurred by the conviction that movements begin with ideas, that in South Africa 'people equal in calibre to the leading socialist thinkers in Europe or the USA... must have been present' for a revolutionary politics to 'have come into existence, gain ground and continue for almost a century'.

In Schechter Hirson has discovered a personality who lived at the point of convergence of several overlapping social and intellectual networks. Through her reading, her writing, her heroes, her friendships and her loves, Ruth Schechter demonstrates the proximity and the interrelationship between what are conventionally viewed as different courses of South African cultural and political life. Ordinarily the well-springs of radical politics in South Africa are located in the harsh polarities of the Transvaal's capitalist revolution and the interplay between class struggle and rural populism, both black and white, which are the unsurprising accompaniments to a hurried and coercive industrialisation. This is the world described in most of Hirson's earlier writing. Here we are confronted with a quite different moral universe, one in which members of the political establishment like Schechter's husband Morris Alexander could express solidarity with such emancipatory causes as that represented by Mohandas Gandhi.

It was a world in which a radical humanitarianism reinforced by Zionism, anti-colonialism, Irish republicanism, feminism, various strands of rationalism, and most important of all, a sophisticated literary culture, could supply the starting point for radical politics. In Ruth Schechter herself such currents did not result in a life of political activism, though briefly, before her death in 1942, she belonged to the British Communist Party, an affiliation which Hirson views in this book as an aberration. Among others, such as Clare Goodlatte, the former Anglican nun who helped to found the Lenin Club, and Jean van der Poel, translator of the Communist Manifesto into Afrikaans, the milieu of Cape Town's intellectual life shaped as it was by the iconic status of Ruth's friend, Olive Schreiner, and the well entrenched conventions of liberal philanthropy, supplied an incubator for a dissenting socialism which continues to enrich our political landscape.

As social and literary history, *The Cape Town Intellectuals*, should influence any subsequent narratives about South Africa's political formation. As biography it is incomplete for only the most cryptic information was available to Hirson concerning long periods of Ruth Schechter's life. For a writer who had, through writing his own life, become increasingly sensitive to the methodological requirements of good biography, the limitations which arose from trying to understand his heroine's personal development through her journalistic commentaries could be very frustrating. Though Hirson was severely critical of his own shortcomings as a biographer his readers may be much less so: in his sensitive deconstruction of the most public kinds of literary testimony he has recreated a remarkable personality.

Hirson's explorations of alternative lineages to mainstream South African nationalist narratives represent a most formidable historiographical testament. They are the consequence of immense labour, all the more heroic when one considers the circumstances in which the later work was written: from 1989 he had difficulty walking and was affected by almost constant pain. An indication of the kind of effort which was needed to assemble the evidence he needed for his writing is supplied in the preface to *The Cape Town Intellectuals*, in which the author describes the process through which he collected his 'mosaic' of documentation, from scattered archives and attic mementos, from both chance and deliberate conversations with friends and acquaintances, from the files of long defunct newspapers and magazines, from encounters at conferences and fortuitous meetings.

It represents a research procedure which was also a social process, for Hirson's writing was the product of the intelligentsia to which he belonged and which he did so much to sustain, a community of passionate political beliefs, far reaching cultural literacy, and loyal, generous friendships. His books are luminous testimony to the philosophical complexity and intellectual richness of South Africa's liberatory politics.

Hirson had mixed feelings about the advent of liberal democracy in 1994. Unusually for a South African socialist, he was never contemptuous of civil liberties but he also never revised his conviction that social oppression was essentially economic and that it would persist after the attainment of universal enfranchisement. His later writing focused on biography and the history of ideas, both within and outside South Africa's Marxist left. It was informed by a strengthening perception that South African democracy was the product of a very complicated intellectual heritage, a democracy fashioned by the heroic idiosyncrasies of individuals as much as the collective endeavours of organisations.

Today his subjects may appear unfashionable and the stories they embody may seem to represent lost causes and forgotten times, to be about what might have been but did not happen. But Hirson was an historian, not a propagandist. His narratives of how modern South Africa was made may not offer much comfort to its new rulers but their angry honesty and their recognition of human potential still make sense in the world's most unequal society.

I first met Baruch Hirson when I was a student, twenty-five years ago. He summoned me to a meeting with him over a cup of tea at the Institute for Commonwealth Studies, to tell me that in my own researches I was looking in the wrong places for pointless answers to misconceived questions. In subsequent encounters with him I learned that there was always evidence (usually written down), that one only had to find it, and that one would never know the full story. Those were not bad lessons to learn at the beginning of one's training and they made a profound impression on me. Like his politics, his friendships were never superficial; he cared deeply about the people he knew, giving to them much more than he could ever demand. Ever critical and constantly kind, he could evoke affection and exasperation simultaneously. His closely typed letters always contained volleys of instructions, suggestions, reprimands, questions, and also flashes of gentle intimacy, though he all too rarely wrote about himself or about his daily experiences outside his work. Yet for him private relationships were as important as public commitments and through his friends and his family he lived out the revolutions in his life. In his final decade he lived in and out of hospital beds, afflicted by a series of immobilising illnesses. His letters and his published writing from this time are moving testimony to his courage and generosity of spirit.

Tom Lodge
Johannesburg
October 2000

PREFACE

An Approach to Cape Town

Cape Town, the mother city of the Cape Colony, is said to be one of the most beautiful towns in the world. Stretched out along the sea front, closeted by Table Mountain, and fronted by the warm Indian Ocean on one side and the chilly Atlantic on the other, it is ideal for bathers and surfers. Every summer holiday makers from across the country fill the town and swarm onto the beaches in an annual ritual of sun worship.

It has been like this ever since the railways were extended beyond the city into the interior of the country, stopping first at the diamond fields of Kimberley and then the gold fields of the Witwatersrand. The diggers and the prospectors, the merchants and the camp followers poured into the mines, lured by the new found wealth. To ensure control over that wealth the British annexed the diamond fields and engaged in a bloody war to wrest control of them from the autonomous Boer Republic. The country was united in 1910 – a triumph of British imperialism and white supremacy. The Cape Colony, the oldest region of white settlement, became part of the Union of South Africa, and Cape Town became the legislative capital of the country.

The people of Cape Town were not classless and never claimed to be. Though some whites lived in poverty stricken areas, the majority lived in houses set in large, well tended gardens in thoughtfully planned suburbs while the coloured people (or those of darker skins and mostly of mixed ethnicity) were packed into overcrowded hovels in areas such as the curiously named District Six, home too to clusters of Jewish refugees.

When disease hit, the casualty rate in District Six was high. Death struck frequently and the funerals – as lavish as the families could manage – ate deeply into savings that were kept for the purpose. Poorly nourished children suffered most, and parks and sport fields, which might have built better physiques, were absent. Football and other sports were played in the streets, while relaxation and entertainment over the weekends was often enjoyed on the pavements. It was remarked at the time, in all seriousness, that the mortality rate was kept down because there was a surfeit of sunshine and open air.

Some coloureds lived in districts outside this central reservoir of labour and their conditions were even worse, but irrespective of where they lived they had no access to the many amenities available in the city. They were excluded from tea rooms, cinemas and theatres; refused entry to public toilets and libraries and only allowed to attend segregated churches and schools. They were forbidden access to the main beaches and picnicked, if at all, in isolated coves that whites did not frequent. All in all the coloured people, without whom the city could not have functioned, were confined to an area that knew no repairs and no general improvements. They lived in poverty and served as labour for their white neighbours in the adjacent suburbs.

Cape Town provided the main port of entry to (and exit from) the country. Travellers and immigrants, students and teachers, sportsmen and tourists disembarked there and passengers on their way to the East stopped over while their boats were refurbished.

Passengers included tourists and refugees from eastern Europe, professional men, miners and engineers, skilled and unskilled workers, many hoping to make their fortunes at the diamond diggings or the gold mines. Most were single but others came with their families, some seeking a new, more remunerative life, others a more congenial climate and the possibility of a cure for their ills. Only a minority of new arrivals took up residence in Cape Town, the rest moved inland.

The more affluent of those who stayed in Cape Town found a place in the prosperous suburbs. Only the refugees straddled the 'two worlds' into which the town was divided and, finding rooms in District Six, were given trays and merchandise by their compatriots which they hawked in some chosen part of the city. They 'graduated' to barrows or small shops, and their wives sought employment or started small home industries until, eventually, they could move to other 'more respectable' suburbs.

This story also straddles the 'two worlds' of Cape Town. It centres on the life of a young bride, Ruth Schechter Alexander, who arrived from New York in 1907 with her husband Morris ('Alec') Alexander, a member first of the Cape Legislative Assembly and later of the South African Legislative Assembly, a King's Counsel, and President of the Cape Jewish Board of Deputies.

Her circle extended outwards from her husband's colleagues and university lecturers in the white 'world' to men and women in District Six. Her acquaintances in the coloured 'world' were probably a by-product of her electioneering for her husband, who was Member of Parliament for Castle (which included District Six). A talented young woman of nineteen, with the bloom of a beauty that was distinctly Jewish, she soon won the friendship of Olive Schreiner, then South Africa's most renowned writer and the only person on whom Ruth modelled herself. Schreiner's letters to her young acolyte display a warmth that arose from their intimacy

Olive Schreiner died in 1920, leaving as a legacy a new radicalism that grew in dimension in the years that followed. Ruth became the author's posthumous champion, writing in newspapers and journals in defence of her works.

It was in the year of Schreiner's death that Ruth met Benjamin Farrington, a newly appointed lecturer in Latin and Greek at the University of Cape Town. He came to South Africa a convinced Sinn Feiner, deeply involved in the politics of Ireland – then struggling to establish its independence – and was one of the founders of the Irish Republican Association of South Africa. A man of undoubted brilliance who was to achieve prominence in the late 1930s with his writings on the Greeks, Farrington was attracted to the vivacious and erudite woman who spent so much time at the University. It is not certain when Ben and Ruth fell in love, but together they were central to the set that dominated the intellectual life of Cape Town.

Ruth's circle of friends and acquaintance, catholic in composition, embraced people as diverse as the former principal of the teacher's training college, Clare Goodlatte, known colloquially as the 'Red Nun'; many of Cape Town's artists; members of the English Association of South Africa; Lancelot Hogben, the zoologist and populariser of science and mathematics; Jean van der Poel, the historian; writer Laurens van der Post; and bookseller Paul Koston. She was renowned as a personality whose voice could not be ignored and whose criticisms of South African racial legislation (published in New York) were incisive and demanded attention.

There can be little doubt that she was a person whose life should be commemorated but, at a stroke, the collective memory of Cape Town was wiped clean and, except among the people of District Six to whom she was dear, she was heard of no more. For Ruth, daughter of a renowned Jewish theological scholar, broke a deep-seated taboo – she divorced her husband to marry Farrington, an Irish Protestant. Many had known of their secret love and had condoned what was happening, but her divorce and remarriage were unacceptable. Nobody would speak about Ruth – and to this day the silence is impenetrable. She became a non-person and, accidentally or otherwise, most of her letters have disappeared from the family archives in New York.

Fortunately, her contributions to newspapers survived and it is partly from this source that her ideas and some of her activities have been reconstructed. Ruth also left in Farrington's hands her unpublished novel *The Exiles* and the beginning of what she hoped would be a history of the coloured people. These, plus her letters to Farrington in March/April 1932, placed alongside material left by others, provide the basis for a biography of an alluring young woman who gave so much to the society in which she lived, and whose writings are as relevant to South Africa now as they were to the Cape Town of the 1920s.

Another aspect of Ruth attracted me as I delved into the events of her life and I sketched it in my first essay on her activities. In *Searchlight South Africa*, No 9, August 1992, I wrote:

> It is not always obvious where this study should begin or subjects the investigation should cover. There seems to be no obvious thinker to whom the researcher can turn: few if any people equal in calibre to the leading socialist thinkers in Europe or the USA in the late 19th or early 20th century. Yet such men and women must have been present for the movement to have come into existence, gain ground and continue for almost a century.
>
> Other ideas, fed into the socialist movement by persons with no political affiliation, get bare mention or are

> overlooked. It is precisely to some such people, living in Cape Town in the 1920s and 1930s, that this paper is directed: to Olive Schreiner and her closest disciple, Ruth Schechter Alexander; and to the Cape Town academics of the 1920s and 1930s. There is a continuum before the Second World War that links these people: their criticism of racism, opposition to imperialism and war, defence of minority rights, and their rationalism and socialism. Then the thread was broken and new ideas were fed into the socialist movement by a new generation.
>
> The early luminaries and their traditions were forgotten in the events that followed the war. And for those who still remember names like Benjamin Farrington, classicist . . . Lancelot Hogben, zoologist . . . or Frederick Bodmer, linguist ... It is not generally known that they lived in South Africa, lectured in Cape Town and participated actively in the cultural and literary life of the town. They tended to be isolated in academic circles and had only peripheral contact with political bodies. Their ideas, even when they appeared in the journals of the day, or heard at learned societies, did not always appear relevant to the struggles being conducted in the country and, even when they impinged directly on political groups, the extent of their influence defies measurement. Nonetheless the potential impact of such people requires serious research. Of these none are more important than Ruth Schechter Alexander, whose name cannot be found in any of the annals of socialist history, whose essays are long forgotten and whose organization of a literary salon seems to be unrecorded.

Events have moved on since Ruth worked in District Six but that makes it even more important to record the lives and activities of those who opposed the growing shadows of segregation as it grew into apartheid and engulfed South Africa in a regime of terror.

The Author and the Book

I first heard about Ruth when I searched through the papers of Julius Lewin, one-time professor of African Government at the University of the Witwatersrand. He was a self-proclaimed Fabian socialist and, although we disagreed on many issues, I used to visit him in his office on the campus when I felt that the atmosphere in the Physics Department was stultifying. At his suggestion I read several books on race and class, but he never spoke of his past in South Africa, and never disclosed the fact that he was a cousin of Morris Alexander. Nor did he ever mention Ruth. After resigning his post in Johannesburg, he brought many of his papers to Britain – presumably because he wanted at some stage to use them for an autobiography. It was my contact with him and his wife Eleanor Hawarden that led, ultimately, to my reading his papers.

Julius had died and although I had asked Eleanor on several occasions what was happening to his papers, my questions went unanswered and I was certain that I had heard the last of those elusive documents. Then, in 1991, I received a call from Eleanor. She was ill and did not know how long she had to live. Could I please collect Julius's papers and arrange for them to be taken to the library of the University of the Witwatersrand? Together with my wife, Yael, I went to Eleanor's apartment.

I was shown five large cardboard boxes, previously used for transporting oranges, and was told that they contained all that Julius had left. It was understood tacitly that I could look through the contents before arranging to have them shipped to Johannesburg and, taking the boxes, we returned home.

I was working on another project at the time and planned to examine the contents of the boxes when my current task was completed. Curiosity decided otherwise and I went through one box, then another, and on until I had satisfied myself about the contents. There was very little to interest me: Julius had stored multiple copies of book reviews he had written over the years, some of them, with little alteration, to several journals. In a note he claimed that he had written more than a million words – a prodigious feat – but the reviews were of little interest to me and none of them was relevant to my work. I paged through in disappointment until I came across two files and one loose leaf notebook. The files were on Ruth Schechter and Olive Schreiner.

It was Olive's name that attracted me and I looked inside. The contents came as a surprise. I read about Dr Solomon Schechter – and in particular on his retrieval of documents from the Genizah of the old Cairo synagogue. There were cuttings from the *Jewish Chronicle* and other items relating to the Genizah collection, some articles from journals on Olive, a few reviews by Ruth of Olive's writings, and a five-part article based on her talk in Cape Town in 1929. There were also some penned appreciations of Olive.

Added to this were two letters from Ben Farrington to Julius which indicated that he had married Ruth after she had left Morris Alexander; and a memorial to Ruth when she was buried in 1942. In the loose-leaf notebook there were a few memoranda by Julius, indicating that he was related to Morris; that he had worked in Morris's legal chambers; and mentioning Ruth with obvious admiration. I made copies of the few items before sending the boxes to the library of the Institute of Commonwealth Studies which had offered to dispatch the collection to Johannesburg. They too looked through the contents of the boxes but decided that there was nothing they wished to have copied.

It was not my intention in writing this book to intrude personally but, as the writing proceeded it seemed correct to provide an account of how I came upon the story of Ruth, and how I discovered more about her until I thought that I had at least enough for a long essay if not a book. The elements that make up this account have had a lengthy gestation – some of them I found long before I thought of writing any history of South Africa.

I had always been intrigued by the fact that Farrington, whose book on Greek Science I had read in the 1940s, had been a lecturer at the University of Cape Town, but I had not been able to discover anything about his arrival in the country or any reason for his eventual departure. I knew that as an academic he had moved from one university to another. There appeared to be nothing remarkable about his coming and going – except, perhaps, that Cape Town had been too small to retain a man of his stature. But I was not a historian and had no incentive to delve any further.

I knew of Lancelot Hogben as the writer of popular books on both mathematics and science. These I had read and was perhaps less excited about them than other readers if only because I knew much of the subjects about what he had written. Nonetheless, he too was an academic of distinction, had been a leading Rationalist and had been infuriated by the racism that he had encountered in South Africa. I had been pleasantly surprised to discover that he too had been a lecturer for a short period at the University of Cape Town. As in the case of Farrington there was no cause for me, either as a political activist, or later as a lecturer in physics, to ask any questions about the role that Hogben might have played in South African affairs.

There was a long jump in time between my interest in Farrington and Hogben, and my search for the story of Clare Goodlatte. Here was another personality about whom I had heard in the 1940s, when I was active in the Trotskyist movement, but who remained almost unknown – in this instance because those who had known Goodlatte were not willing to talk about her. When I was reading archival documents in the 1970s I found reference to Goodlatte as secretary of the Cape Town Joint Council of Europeans and Natives, a distinctly moderate liberal body. I wrote to South African libraries asking whether they held material under the name of Goodlatte, or in the files of the Joint Council, but drew a blank. Some six months after my first inquiries I had a letter from the archivist at the South African Library saying that they had recently received a collection of letters, written by Goodlatte to a former student, John Chapman. It was a large collection and I was asked whether I was still interested in Miss Goodlatte. If so, what was I looking for? I asked for copies of any pages that dealt with her involvement in political movements. The papers arrived and I learnt anew what I had known and forgotten – that Goodlatte had been the principal of the Teachers Training College in Grahamstown.

I contacted Harriet Tunmer, a former colleague in the Physics Department in Johannesburg, with whom I had been writing a textbook of medical physics. She had long since departed for Grahamstown where her husband, Ray Tunmer, was professor in the Department of Education. The response was immediate. Goodlatte, known as Sister Clare, had indeed been principal of the Teachers Training College, now disbanded, and Tunmer occupied her former office. Harriet then found documents that had been deposited by the Training College in the library of the University. The next communication brought several items from the College journal with articles referring to Goodlatte. These were riches beyond my hopes and I wrote an article which appeared in February 1989 in *Searchlight South Africa*, No 2.

Later I obtained a file of papers that Goodlatte, as secretary of the Workers Party and editor of the journal *Spark*, had left in the loft of her house in Woodstock when she died in 1942, and which now stood, deserted and derelict. These had been found by a man who searched for anything of possible value in deserted properties. He sold the collection in two lots and I was able to secure copies of the papers for myself. These were not relevant to the events in this book but were invaluable in allowing me to write a history of the South African Trotskyist movement which appeared in *Searchlight South Africa*, No 10, in April 1993.

Other people or events relevant to Ruth's story had also been encountered many years before I heard of her. Firstly there was a meeting with Hermann Kallenbach in Johannesburg in the early years of the Second World War. I was a member of a left-wing Zionist group, one of whose members, Isa Lazar (later Sarid), was Kallenbach's niece. Knowing only that he had been associated with Gandhi during his South African days, I attended. I was young and had little knowledge of politics and I doubt whether I came away with anything substantial. Yes, he had been a friend of Gandhi in South Africa. Yes, he had a large library of books, many of them on comparative religion, and he was going to leave his library to the Hebrew University in Jerusalem. But why he should wish to leave his books to the Hebrew University I was not to discover until I read of his attempts, at Gandhi's request, to find points of contact between the Zionist movement – of which he was a leading member – and the Indian National Movement.

For me Kallenbach entered the story of Ruth when I read the biography of Morris Alexander and found that Gandhi, his wife, and Kallenbach had slept at the Alexander home the night before they left South Africa. Many decades after my original encounter, when I heard that Isa was writing a life of her uncle based on documents that had passed to her mother (then deceased) I asked to see a copy of her work. That only urged me on to find further details, and a search for literature led me to the works of Margaret Chatterjee and to Gideon Shimoni where I learnt that most of the whites who sympathised with and supported Gandhi were Jews, vegetarians and Tolstoyans, and were members of the Theosophical Lodge in Johannesburg. I had also heard that one of Kallenbach's brothers had married into the extended Lewin-Alexander family. This information was included in an account of the Indian community in the Cape – a topic that has been largely overlooked. A reference took me to a chapter on the Cape Indians by Edna Bradlow – a collection of essays that was not generally available but which David Blake, librarian at the Institute of Commonwealth Studies, London, found for me; and to the monograph on the Cape Jewish Board of Deputies by Milton Shain which provided the background that I needed.

There was also Hannah Kantor, whom I had met several years previously in London, and who had asked if I knew anything about her late uncle, Morris Alexander. I had to admit at the time that I knew little more than his name, his presence in the South African Legislative Assembly, and his membership of the Bar in Cape Town. She told me that she had a biography of Morris, written by his second wife, Enid Alexander, and would like to be better informed. I had not followed the fortunes, or misfortunes, of parliamentarians and could not assist. I later borrowed the biography of Morris from Hannah and, sparse as it was, it was important in my search for Ruth. But at the time nothing was further from my mind than such a search, and the strands that I mention did not even surface in my consideration of Ruth's life.

In some ways my ignorance was profound. Although I had read some collected colloquium papers from the University of Cape Town which centred on that town, and knew about isolated events that had taken place there, including the formation of the Industrial and Commercial Workers Union of Africa (ICU), I had no coherent knowledge of the history of the town. I had lived in Cape Town from 1940 to 1942 and had skirted District Six on my way to work and back. But I had no knowledge of what happened behind the doors of the houses of those slum properties.

Initially I had many reservations about writing about Ruth. This was not my usual field of study and I faced then what I tried to overcome in the months that followed – large sectors of Ruth's life about which I had no information. As an analogy I thought of the problems facing the artists who try to reassemble mosaic designs from which pieces are missing. The gaps can be filled with cement but the problem defies the best of workers if there is any uncertainty about where pieces should be placed. Several possibilities may be suggested but each will lead to a different portrait.

The writer, who is not working with a static picture but one in which the characters are changing, faces a more difficult problem: not only in determining what changes might have taken place but also how the characters might have adjusted to societal events outside their control. How was I to know which events impinged on them, and what their reactions were likely to have been? This was not a problem that was unique to me: other historians had to find similar solutions in their work, but usually with more material than I was able to acquire.

What I had found out about Ruth was fascinating, but there the matter might have ended if it had not been for a set of coincidences that made me feel as if I was being tugged, literally tugged, to write her story. Like Olive Schreiner I have no belief in the supernatural and have had no reason to question my belief system but I told friends as a joke against myself: 'Someone out there is saying "You must write my life story".'

Reconstructing a Story

This is how it happened. Firstly, on a visit to Israel in 1991, undertaken with some reluctance, I joined old friends to visit Nechama Genussow, whom I had last seen in 1939 when she had visited South Africa to assist the Hashomer Hatzair movement. She had played a crucial role in my joining the group and this was a nostalgic journey to Nir David, the kibbutz of which she was a founding member. We had not kept contact over the years and when we met the discussion was desultory. When we left Nechama gave me an extract from an article that she had written on her parents. I folded it and put it in my pocket where it lay almost forgotten, but before retiring that evening I took it out.

There I learnt that Nechama's mother, Tzipporah Schechter Genussow, was a daughter of Solomon Schechter's twin brother, Israel. She had come to South Africa in 1913 as the wife of Menachem Genussow, who had met her when he had taken greetings from Solomon Schechter to his brother in Palestine. Excitedly I called Nechama the next morning, but got a cold reply. She was not interested in Ruth and had nothing to say! She was the first of many who refused to discuss Ruth or the events surrounding her life.

I was booked to speak at the opening of a conference in Cape Town on 'Marxism in South Africa' – a remarkable and totally unexpected event that followed the lifting of bans on political parties in the country after four decades of repression. While in Cape Town I visited the library of the University of Cape Town to look at the papers of Morris Alexander. It was a cursory search and I probably missed some important papers. I was looking for anything written by Ruth, but found only one letter, written to Morris in 1913 from the ship in which she was returning home, after visiting her parents in New York. It was the letter of a devoted wife who gave an account of her journey and included mention of a concert on board ship at which she had sung. Ruth also wrote of the impending stay of the Genussow family in the Cape and her hope that they would see the family often.

I visited several universities in South Africa. It was a personal celebration of my return 'home' and allowed me to speak to many historians. None had heard of Ruth. I searched through books on Olive Schreiner found one or two footnotes on Ruth, one of which referred to her intention to publish Olive's letters.

Back in Britain I called the secretary of the Jewish Historical Society to find out whether there was any material on Solomon Schechter. She replied that the President of the Society, Dr Stefan Reif, had recently given an address to the society on Jenkins, Schechter and the Genizah fragments. The address was to appear in the next issue of the Society's annual journal – *The Jewish Historical Society of England* XXXII, 1990-1992. I also wrote to the librarian at the Jewish Theological Seminary in New York, asking if there were any papers ascribable to Ruth in their possession. Except for a few poems they had nothing. In my search I obtained the address of Raphael (Ray) Levy, a cousin of Ruth's in Yonkers, just outside New York. At this stage I must have become suggestible because I was excited by the fact that during my first visit to the United States I had stayed with friends who lived within a quarter-mile of Levy's house. The coincidence seemed significant and I wrote asking for information.

Levy was among the most helpful of my contacts. He sent me copies of a few letters written by Ruth when she reached Britain, together with articles by himself on the Genizah collection, and an article by Frank Schechter on his father. He later sent me comments on what I wrote and about the events that had overtaken Amy Schechter during the Gastonia strike in 1929. I had also found the address of Elsie Alexander, widow of Ruth's son, Solly, and she had photographs – photocopies of which were sent to me. She too had been looking for material on Morris and Ruth but had found very little.

My collection was growing slowly when, again with some luck, I was given the address and phone number of Jane Straker, Farrington's daughter by his second wife, Barbara Sell. An appointment was made and Yael and I set out for the country home to have lunch with her family. I could digress at some length about the warm reception we received, about the discussion in which I gave an account of my search for material, and so on. At some stage Jane asked her son to fetch the 'draw' and he soon reappeared with a long drawer that had been taken out of a cupboard or dressing table. In this there were letters tied together with tape, a typed and bound copy of Ruth's novel, and also the opening chapter of her history of the coloured people, with its cameo of District Six. I could borrow the contents of the 'draw' and use what I found useful.

The story of Amy Schechter only opened up after I met and discussed labour problems with Rick Halpern, an American who lectured at London University. He was about to travel home to attend a conference on labour history. I mentioned Amy and the strike with a request that he inform me of anything he might learn about the event. It was a request made with apologies and little hope of a positive outcome. However, as in so many of the events surrounding this story, Rick not only heard about Gastonia but met Professor John Salmond, a historian at La Trobe University in Victoria, Australia, who was gathering material for a work on Amy. Rick brought back some references and with additional books on United States labour history and a note from Ray Levy I was able to insert Amy's experience in the context of the book.

I had still to uncover the story of Lancelot Hogben in South Africa and this was solved in one of those unique ways that occurs when work is under way. I spoke to several colleagues about Hogben. When the name was known – and that was not frequent – his stay in South Africa was unknown. Then, one evening in a pub, after a meeting of left-wing socialists, I chanced to ask Cyril Smith, a lecturer at the London School of Economics (LSE) if he knew about Hogben.He did and he also knew that there was a team working on the history of the LSE (to which Hogben had gone after leaving Cape Town) and he would ask one of the researchers to contact me. This transformed the problem from one of great difficulty into a simple matter. The team knew about Hogben and also that Adrian and Anne Hogben (the son and his wife) were editing a voluminous autobiography to make it publishable. Contact was made and I was asked to read through the manuscript, and in particular the chapters on South Africa, to see if they needed revision. I thought they did, made many suggestions – particularly over Hogben's interpretations of South African history – and suggested that they look at *Rebel Pity* by Eddie Roux and his wifeWinifred, an autobiographical account that Eddie had started. He had died before the book was completed but Winifred, had completed the book for publication.

Roux had encountered Winifred (then Lunt) at open evenings held by the Hogbens, and his descriptions of those gatherings were full and entertaining. Roux also mentioned the political discussions during those evenings and spoke of Frederick Bodmer, the lecturer in German who was to write *Loom of Language* after he left South Africa and before he moved to Massachusetts Institute of Technology. I learnt from the Hogben autobiography about his contact with Ruth, and even more importantly, about the friction at the university dance in which the Hogbens were involved and which Ruth had fictionalised to provide the cathartic event around which her novel revolved. My collection of documents continued to grow. There were copies of Olive's letters to

Ruth, obtained from the South African Library, and also all the documents placed in that library by the English Association of South Africa. I obtained Bentwich's biography of Solomon Schechter, criticised by Ruth as the story of a frock-coated priest, but one which allowed me to sketch the background of his work – not an easy task for a writer who knew nothing of Talmudic lore or of the divisions inside the Jewish religious communities; and an essay on Mathilda Roth Schechter, which was part of work in progress by Mel Scult, a lecturer in New York, but not yet far enough advanced to lead me to her early encounters with feminism in Cambridge.

I had written several draft chapters when a communication from E S Reddy in New York informed me of the letter that Ruth had written to Gandhi in 1926[1], in which she had mentioned the three people who had made a particular impact on her. This made me rewrite sections to provide chapters on the three characters in search of a place in my history. In this the computer proved its superiority in shaping a document, cutting down an almost insuperable problem into a relatively minor operation. The manuscript was beginning to take shape but I still did not know if I would ever have enough for a book, and without having her comments on current events the book would be sorely deficient. I had started looking through South African newspapers and journals, and also the New York *Nation* for book reviews and articles written by Ruth. Although these were meant to appear as 'impartial' studies it was possible to read into many of them Ruth's views on literature and on local and world affairs. My visits to the library were halted by illness and hospitalisation but, by employing students to find the reviews, I received a collection of her writings that exceeded my expectations.

While I was in hospital in 1994 Jane Straker found a large scrapbook in her loft. In the front were newspaper cuttings, commencing in August 1920, which had obviously been collected by Ben and dealt exclusively with Ireland. Some were written in English, others in Afrikaans. A few were signed by Ben, others were not written by him. Some were taken from *De Burger* but others came from unknown papers. The cuttings at the back of the scrapbook were articles submitted by Ben or Ruth, mostly to the *Cape Times,* between November 1922 and December 1924 – but few were signed. The scrapbook was invaluable because the absence of bylines would have made it difficult, if not impossible, to identify many of the articles in a newspaper library. Unfortunately children had been allowed to play with the album and they had torn out many cuttings. My files were overflowing with cuttings, many of them unused, and I did not embark on a search for the lost bits.

I had to decide who had written what and, as a rough guide, decided that all reviews of Irish books or of Greek and Latin classics were by Ben and that many of the rest were by Ruth. Besides book reviews there were numerous articles and at least one editorial on Jewish themes or religious holidays. There were also 'snapshots' based on people or places in New York which indicated that Ruth had visited the United States in 1920 and again in April 1924. But I had overlooked the articles in Afrikaans. My knowledge of that language is rudimentary and I had conveniently put them aside. Only when the book neared completion did I turn to them and found reference to the Irish Republican Association in South Africa. This led me to the publication by Donal McCracken on *Ireland and South Africa in Modern Times*. Professor McCracken kindly sent me selected copies of *The Republic* and I was able to unravel Ben's involvement in the Irish Association. What had been a blank in Ben's life was partly filled and made my discussion of his early activities in Cape Town – of which I still know so little – somewhat more satisfactory.

Ruth's articles, many of them perceptive and of lasting interest, piled up in my files. She had written steadily during the war years and had subsequently reviewed several books a week for more than ten years in South Africa. The articles fell into several categories: reviews of the works of Schreiner and other South African writers; analyses of new legislation in South Africa that would be described at a later date as apartheid; discussions of political developments abroad; and reviews of biographies, novels and tales of travellers. I tried to fit these into different chapters to avoid reader-indigestion. But I was always caught between the desire to include as much as possible and the need to prevent the book becoming top-heavy with writing that might not be of interest to potential readers. The task was made more difficult because I was learning so much from the reviews. It was surely possible that other readers would be similarly delighted to have at least the summary of those writings of the 1920s.

I also had the reviews of articles written by Ben – enough for a chapter devoted to him. From comments in Ruth's letters to Ben it was obvious that she discussed the books she read with him and the two had clearly cooperated in planning and selecting the writings which should be highlighted by inclusion in the scrapbook. Their work, individually executed, carried the stamp of both their thoughts.

The background to Ruth's interest in South African politics seemed obvious. Her friends in District Six kept abreast of developments and Ruth saw parliamentary papers brought into the home by Morris. Ruth's other interests were catered for in the books she reviewed – on peace, on events in India and in the USSR, on feminism. Besides this, she both read and reviewed a wealth of good novels, some long forgotten. Through them she kept herself informed and, in turn, could advertise the better works to her reading public. Unfortunately, because of the absence of letters there was far too little available on those personal matters that make up the web of most lives. It was only for a brief period in 1932 that the daily accounts Ruth sent to Ben opened up a narrow window which illuminated the matters that concerned her.

Her departure from South Africa helped conceal the events of the next ten years. So much of what followed in her second marriage is lost to us. The pamphlet written by Ben as an appreciation of her life and made available at her funeral, together with copies of the few letters that Ben had written to Julius Lewin or to others, provide a glimpse of the last period of Ruth's life. She had lectured to a wide circle of workers and friends and to those whose interest in world affairs had been roused by the war in Spain and then across Europe. If she wrote for any British journals the articles have not been found, except for one item on Olive Schreiner which Ben had kept. It was an act of homage, even if pedantically critical, but above all it was a memorial to a great woman.

My restoration of the mosaic that is Ruth can never be complete. There are too many pieces missing, and it is possible that I have inserted some that would be more appropriate elsewhere. What I hope to have rescued is the essential outline of a woman who remained loyal to her friends, offered enlightenment to her ever widening circle, found a happiness in exile, and knew how to laugh when she was ill and in pain. I found my research illuminating. Hopefully my readers will feel likewise.

INTRODUCTION

In 1908, when Mrs Ruth Schechter Alexander arrived in Cape Town, she was struck by the difference between her new home and the towns in which she had spent her youth: Cambridge, the site of that ancient university in Britain at which her father had lectured; and New York, to which she had gone when he had been appointed President of the Jewish Theological Seminary. They were considerably older than the capital city of the Cape Colony and they were also very much larger in population and supported well established and universally known centres of learning.

Although it nestled at the foot of Table Mountain and was of breathtaking beauty, Cape Town was dwarfed by the mountain range - its buildings were modest and small and its population sparse and spread out along the arc that hugged the sea front. Within this arc lived two distinct and largely separated population groups - the whites who had come from Europe, and the 'coloureds', a group which included people from the Indian subcontinent, descendants of the original Cape inhabitants, and those of mixed ethnic origins. Although the separation of whites and coloureds was not yet as rigidly maintained as it would become in later years, there was little mixing across the colour line

It was probably only natural that Ruth, brought by her husband, Morris Alexander, into white-centred enclaves, was expected to find her friends within the small white population of Cape Town and more particularly among the Jewish inhabitants of the town. This might not have been a burden in her first years in the Colony, more particularly as she mixed with members of the Cape Legislature and the legal fraternity and was fully occupied in bringing up her three children. But whatever satisfaction she had from a busy existence, and from her marriage which, she declared, was a happy one, she lacked the intellectual stimulus that she had enjoyed in her parents' circles. The Jewish men of Cape Town, as described in *The Exiles*, were immersed in local community affairs, and the women were immersed in marriage brokering. It was an alienating atmosphere from which she sought escape and it was this as much as a desire for academic advancement that led her to the University College in Cape Town where she found new friends.

Ruth gave the appearance of intellectual and social independence: she sang, and occasionally gave recitals. She was said by Rabbi Bender, the spiritual leader of the Western Cape, to possess a voice that rang like a silver bell. She was to become the music critic for the *Cape Times*; she kept abreast of new trends in literature and was in demand as a lecturer on contemporary fiction at clubs and societies. Her book reviews and articles covering the minutiae of Cape Town life were published in journals and newspapers in Cape Town and New York. She was a prodigious letter-writer, keeping close contact with her family and writing to contemporary authors in Europe. One letter that has survived came from Romain Rolland thanking her for her offer to translate one of his books from the French, but regretting that it had already been arranged.

Ruth also involved herself in an area less well known to the people in her immediate circle. Probably through canvassing for her husband, she developed a close rapport with coloured community leaders in District Six and witnessed the extreme poverty of so many families in the area. Financed by Morris, Ruth set up playgroups for the children and brought them refreshments. She also assisted inhabitants of District Six with the self-help schemes they had established and administered and deepened her understanding of the misery that accompanied the policy of segregation in the Cape.

Through her contacts in the coloured community she met Mohandas K Gandhi. It was a brief encounter but Ruth was entranced by the young lawyer who had taken it upon himself to campaign against the discriminatory regulations directed against the Indian people.

There is no written record of her initial contact with Gandhi. It can be surmised that she read about the campaigns he led in Natal and the Transvaal against the Asiatic Bill designed to effect the repatriation of many members of the Indian community and to confine those who remained to ghettoes. When he came to the Cape in 1913, Ruth, who was acquainted with his host, would have been invited to meet him. Then, in an event that was to overwhelm her, Gandhi stayed in the Alexander home on the night before he left South Africa.

She did not communicate with him again until, in April 1926, she met the Reverend C F Andrews, a friend of Gandhi and of Rabindranath Tagore, winner of the 1913 Nobel Prize for Literature. She sent a letter with him to Gandhi in India.[1] She wrote in sympathy with the campaign he had conducted in South Africa and his more recent campaign in India against British rule.

It was a brave letter, one which would have brought embarrassment to her husband if it had been intercepted or disclosed. There was nothing in its contents that could be interpreted as being disloyal – except for its obvious disagreement with the policy of the government of South Africa, – but it was not the kind of letter that the wife of a member of parliament would normally write. In it Ruth said:[2]

> I am touched more than I can tell you when I look back at the time when you did me the great honour to stay with me and to talk with me, and remember how patient you always were with me, how uncondemning even of things you must have disapproved. It was wonderful of you.
>
> Let me tell you, for the pleasure it gives me, that you have always been, since I knew you, and always will be, until I die, one of the three great souls with whom I live from day to day, beyond those who speak to me from the printed pages. My father and Olive Schreiner are the other two. I am rich for having known you, and must be grateful always for your friendship and for your forbearance.
>
> Please remember me to Mrs Gandhi, whose gentle courage I have never forgotten.
>
> I hear that Kallenbach is gone to you, and am glad for him. His heart has hungered for that so many years.
>
> Stay with us as long as you can. It is not only India that needs you.
>
> Yours in love and homage
> Ruth S Alexander

Three of the people mentioned in the letter comprise a remarkable and unique trio. Gandhi was already the acknowledged leader of the nationalist movement in India; Solomon Schechter, Ruth's father, was renowned for the recovery and removal to Cambridge of the documents stored in the old Cairo Synagogue which had enriched theological studies; and Olive Schreiner, whose *Story of an African Farm* had been acclaimed both as the first truly feminist novel, but also as a unique study of life in a South African setting.

The trio were very different, suggesting that Ruth was able to accommodate very different opinions. With such people to inspire her, Ruth had a rich store of memories that stayed with her throughout her life. In 1926 she might have added a fourth remarkable name to her list – that of Benjamin Farrington, lecturer in Latin and Greek at the University of Cape Town, and later Professor of Classics. But perhaps it would have been indiscreet at that time to have mentioned the man about whom there were already whispers that went far beyond the corridors of the University.

One more factor in Ruth's life marks her letter to Gandhi as important. She had become a critic of events that were unfolding in South Africa, condemning in print the racism that permeated the society, and mixing increasingly in radical circles. It appears from the letter she wrote to Gandhi that he was one of the influences in her evolution yet it was written at a time when she was also finding new perspectives and embracing new ideas. Her book reviews took an increasingly radical stance, as can be seen in her praise for the South African poet, Roy Campbell, and the novelist William Plomer; in her criticism of Sarah Gertrude Millin's denigration of blacks; and in her praise of the black trade union – the Industrial and Commercial Workers Union of Africa (the ICU).

The person who exercised the greatest influence on Ruth's political orientation was, however, undoubtedly Olive Schreiner – admirer of Lenin and the Russian Revolution of October 1917 – and it was Ruth's increasingly intimate friendship with Farrington that provided the opportunity for her to strike out with confidence on her radical path. These influences were supplemented by the humanism of her father, even if she was to renounce the religion that had been the mainstay of Rabbi Solomon Schechter's life.

Ruth and Benjamin would become central to the intellectual life of Cape Town. Their erudition and the scope of their ideas shone out in this conservative (white-controlled) society and the many circles that formed around them were indicative of the influence they exerted. The names of many of their friends are not known, but those that are available show the extent of their contacts – in the university, among prominent personalities (white and Coloured), and with other intellectuals in Cape Town. The circumstances under which they found each other and their impact on each other are central to this book.

1
FATHER AND DAUGHTER

Solomon Schechter, 1847-1916

> [Solomon Schechter's] daughter, who loved him with understanding while he lived and honoured his memory with passionate devotion to the day of her death, bore throughout her life the visible impress of his exalted and generous character ... her best education was received in her father's study, where, as his unofficial secretary, she came to understand the ardour and the patience of the true scholar.
>
> – *Memorial Service for Ruth Schechter*
> *Farrington, 5 March 1942*

Ruth, the first child of Solomon and Mathilda Schechter, was born on 1 May 1888, into a household rich in humanity and learning. Schechter, savant and wit, seems to have left all domestic arrangements to his wife and to have gone about his intellectual preoccupations happy in his belief that all family matters were in capable hands. And Mathilda, for her part, put aside her previous profession as teacher and conducted a Jewish home as was expected of her at the end of the nineteenth century.

Because so much more is known of Solomon and because Ruth spoke so glowingly about her father, it is easy to forget the role that a mother played in the Jewish household. All the observance of customs and religious practice, the arrangement of food – so important in the family's lifestyle – the attention to the father's needs, were in the hands of the *mater familia*. That is only one side – the most obvious – of Mathilda Roth, but not the most important. She had come to Britain from Breslau and had been a teacher in London before she married

Solomon Schechter. Her early German education followed by her experience as a teacher gave her a grasp of language that was to play a significant part in her husband's many learned publications and she helped polish his essays.

She was also responsible for the upbringing of their three children. They were talented children, and whatever can be said for inherited ability, nurture must have added considerably to their talents as they grew up and emerged from this home of erudition. Moreover, she undoubtedly brought a sense of order into the household while leaving Ruth and her siblings a freedom that would enhance intellectual curiosity and allow them an independence that sustained them throughout their lives.

Frank was to become a successful patent lawyer, Ruth a leading literary critic, and both sisters were to find their way to the left-wing of politics that seems at first glance incongruous with the overarching religious philosophy of the home. Yet it was precisely the humanism of their parents that was to be reflected in the hatred of all discrimination, all repression and all injustice that inspired the members of the Schechter family.

Born into a Chassidic family in Rumania, Solomon Schechter absorbed the sect's humility, cheerfulness, enthusiasm for God and devotion to His teachings. At the same time he acquired a love of knowledge and scholarship and wove the enthusiasm and search for knowledge into a philosophy for himself.

He showed early brilliance as a student and was sent to a series of seminaries. He then went to Vienna where he entered a rabbinical seminary and, after being instructed in the ways of the great disciples, moved to Berlin, learning more about the mysteries of the Torah and the Talmud. He also studied secular subjects, including the new scientific study of Jewish history. Above all he acquired a delight in studying manuscripts – something that was to dominate his subsequent life. In Berlin he met Claude Montefiore who was seeking a teacher in Jewish lore and persuaded Schechter, then thirty-five years old, to accompany him to London in 1882.

Schechter only began writing after he arrived in London and his work soon established him as a man of talent. He lectured occasionally (on rabbinics) to the senior students at Jews' College but devoted himself, with the full backing of his wife, to research on religious issues. This was to be invaluable but left the family in financial straits which were only partially alleviated when he was appointed Reader in Talmudic and Rabbinic Literature at the University of Cambridge, in 1890.

Schechter was quite obviously a man who towered over most of his contemporaries but was happy in his peer group, which met regularly in London. The group included Israel Zangwill, the renowned novelist; Asher Myers, one-time editor of the *Jewish Chronicle*; Joseph Jacobs, future editor of the *Jewish Encyclopaedia*; Israel Abrahams, whose main interest was Medieval Jewish history and who later lectured at Cambridge; and Lucien Wolf, journalist and historian of the Anglo-Jewish community. These were the 'Wanderers', so named because they gathered at different homes for their meetings. There was also an anarchic streak which allowed any participant to wander off the given subject at any stage. Joseph Jacobs said of Schechter and the group:

> It is impossible to convey any adequate idea of the genial radiance and élan of Schechter's personality at this period. At the height of his physical and mental rigour, appreciated for the first time at his true value, surrounded by an ever-increasing circle of admiring friends, he burst upon us like a blazing comet in the intellectual sky. There used to be a gathering of friends in London who called themselves the *wandering Jews*, partly because they used to wander for their meetings, from house to house, and partly because they claimed the right to wander from the subject of discussion of each meeting. Into this circle Schechter burst like an exploding bomb and would tear down the rationalist or cynical comments that flourished there with his mixture of enthusiasm and indignation. I can see him in my mind's eye, at the height of a debate, rising from his chair, perhaps kicking it down, and pacing up and down the room, like a wounded lion, roaring retorts at Zangwill or Wolf, while Asher Myers as moderator, would attempt to calm the storm.[1]

The group also shared their enthusiasm over new publications. Ruth tells one story of particular interest to this history. She had longed to meet Olive Schreiner, partly because she had read her books,

> [A]nd also because of the passionate reverence with which my father and his friends spoke of her. When *The Story of an African Farm* came out, they were all young and all poor and all rebels together, and one of them rushed into my father's little study with the book so excited that they could hardly speak. They read parts of it aloud to one another, thrilling to the noble cadence of the prose, a prose that showed plainly the influence of the Authorised Version which, to the end of her life, she knew by heart as did few even of her generation.[2]

Schechter was the key member of this intellectual circle and inspired his fellows with his enthusiasm, his questioning and his erudition. This was acknowledged by the 'Wanderers' in the books they published long after the group had dispersed.[3] His agile mind found new ways of seeing problems which extended far beyond his learning on theological issues. Some of his comments on moral, social and political matters are to be found in his letters and were repeated by his son Frank in a short article in 1922.[4] They include comments on international events, which provide an insight into the way such topics must have been handled in the family home.

Schechter's position on war was stated in his comment on the Spanish-American conflict. In a letter to Dr Adler in June 1898 he wrote:

> I wish you all the success in your present war, but I can get as little enthusiastic over Pan-Anglo-Sax(on)ism as over Pan-Germanism, etc. The overemphasising of the racial principle will be the destruction of our people. They will as little forgive us our Semitic origin as they did in the Middle Ages our denial of the Son.[5]

And writing to Adler on 1 January 1900 on the South African War :

> We are now blessed with any amount of yellow papers, yellow sermons, yellow prayers (written in bad grammar) calling upon their yellow god to bless arms to the glory of his holy name and the Anglo-Saxon race.[6]

The 'Wanderers' did not survive Schechter's departure for Cambridge. He had been the central focus of the circle and without him the meetings ceased. Other social groups were formed but they lacked the stimulus and the excitement that had kept them together. As individuals the one-time members would visit Cambridge and spend the weekend at the Schechter home where the conversations were resumed.

After his appointment to Cambridge Schechter took small classes of advanced theological students, first as a university lecturer and then as Reader in Talmudic studies. Cambridge at this time was a centre for training clergymen and contained a group of scholars devoted to the restoration of texts of the Greek Testament to their original, Aramaic, form. There was an obvious place in this school for Schechter's work on rabbinical texts. But Cambridge also boasted a new school of analytical philosophy, of scientific advancement and of scholars who were in the forefront of historical and literary scholarship. The transition from his earlier centres of training and from Jews' College and the 'wanderers' could not have been more radical.[7]

He did not fit easily into Cambridge although he was able to find friends among the staff, including Sir James Frazer, Professor Maitland (the historian of English Law) and others. But he never found a sympathetic milieu. His style of speech and his acerbic remarks set him apart from other academics and his rough leonine features marked him as distinctly different. Norman Bentwich, who first met him in Cambridge, said that he remembered him looking

> Something like the popular conception of a great scholar – rather untidy, abstracted, too full of ideas to be ready in speech, and (like R Samuel) 'more familiar with the courses of the stars than with the streets of Nehardea'. When you came face to face with him you saw a rather straggling brownish-reddish beard and keen grey-blue eyes. My

> memory of him somehow suggested an eagle, but I find the general impression is that he is more like a lion. No doubt I was wrong; I suppose that what I remembered was an expression of keenness.[8]

In Cambridge Schechter found friends among men who were given scant recognition in the colleges within which they worked. So it was not surprising that his closest associate was James George Frazer, known as 'the recluse of Trinity [College]'. Frazer, author of *The Golden Bough* and recognised as the outstanding authority on comparative religion and anthropology, was never awarded a fellowship by his college and, being the shyest of men, had few friends. Yet his friendship with Schechter was instantaneous and warm. They used to walk together several afternoons a week and explore all topics, of heaven and earth. In a letter he wrote on Schechter's death he said:

> I am proud to have been recognized among the most intimate friends of such a man, great in his intellect and learning, greater even in the warmth of his affections and his enthusiasms for every high and noble cause. To have enjoyed his friendship is an honour which I shall always prize.[9]

Mathilda, along with his new friends, proved to be the mainstay of his work. She encouraged him in his researches, edited and revised his papers and maintained the growing household. But she also proceeded with her own work. Together with Mary Kingsley, who was to acquire fame for her work in West Africa, she started translating Heine from the German into English, but before the work had been completed a translation was published and she abandoned the project. She also translated some of Zangwill's work into German. In a letter to Zangwill she wrote:

> I am sure to put love into the translation of your work and I think that my German style is decently good to satisfy your publisher. Your English is difficult but beautiful. The

> translators abroad do not know the writer and the English spirit as I do.

Mathilda Schechter's literary work extends beyond these translations. She commented on and edited Eriker Magnusson's Icelandic songs and sagas, wrote fragments of a novel, and edited and typed her husband's volume of essays.[10] She also presided over a house that was always filled with women. The society of Schechter's women friends grew with the years united, as Bentwich says, in 'admiration for his humanity, sincerity and forthrightness'. Among other attributes, Mary Kingsley is said to have shared with Schechter pre-eminence in the art of swearing, while Alice Gardiner, lecturer in history, sat enthusiastically at his feet because 'of his devotion to scholarship combined with geniality and generosity'.[11]

Two of these friends – twin widowed sisters, Mrs Agnes Lewis and Mrs Margaret Gibson – were to play a decisive role in transforming Schechter's life and providing new impetus to the study of old biblical texts. The sisters were Hebrew and Oriental scholars who were devoted to the collection of manuscripts and made periodic visits to Egypt and Sinai in search of new discoveries.

In May 1896 they informed Solomon Schechter that they had acquired fragments of old documents in Cairo. He found one of them to be from the long lost Hebrew version of the Apocryphal Book of Ben Sirah (Ecclesiastes), written in the second century before the Christian Era and previously known only from a Greek translation. Determined to find the source of these documents, he obtained funds from Charles Taylor, the Master of St John's College, and travelled to Cairo. There he entered the depository of sacred texts (the Genizah) of the Ben Ezra Synagogue at Fostat (Old Cairo). Almost completely sealed off from the outside world, the collection was in an attic without windows or doors, its entrance a small aperture reached by a ladder. The Genizah contained one of the richest collections of biblical and secular documents found in the Middle East – a mass of fragments of books and documents collected since the 10th century and mostly untouched since then.[12] Schechter used all his wiles to obtain the documents while fending off others who had also hurried to the synagogue when news of its treasure reached them. In a letter to his wife he said that he had spent 'a fortune in baksheesh, carriages, etc' to secure the fragments that were in the Genizah.[13]

On 12 January 1897 he wrote to Francis Jenkinson, librarian at the University, without whose assistance his subsequent work would have been most difficult:[14]

> I am now here since three weeks. After making the acquaintance of the Chief Rabbi here and the president of the Jewish community I set to work on the 'Genizas' [*sic*] where I spend the most of my time in the dust of centuries.
>
> The beadel [*sic*] & other infernal scoundrels are helping me to clear away the rubbish and the printed matter. I have constantly to bakshish them, but still they are stealing many good things and sell them to the dealers in antiquities.
>
> I cannot possibly prevent it, but I found out the said dealers and bought from them the fragments which have interest for me.
>
> In the Genizah itself, which is dark, dusty and full of all possible insects, there is no possibility of examining the content of manuscripts. My policy is to take as much as I can (for which I have the full permission of the authorities).
>
> I have till now thirteen large bags of fragments, which though not examined, I am sure, contain many most important things.
>
> Now I have a great request on you. I do not consider it desirable to leave the MSS here and am anxious to send the first lot home to England. Will you give them a place in the University Library till I return?
>
> The MSS will probably belong soon to your Library. I want only to hear first whether you and the syndics will agree to certain conditions which I have to make.
>
> Money plays no important part in these conditions and I am sure you will find them *very fair* and *just. But till then I want the MSS to be considered as my private property; so that the boxes must not be opened before I have returned. For I am very anxious to be the first to examine them properly.*

> I feel fairly well and am rather thankful that it is cold. Otherwise it would be unbearable to live in this dus[t] & underground. How are you? PG I intend to stay here another three weeks as the Jews have here so many feasts and fasts in which I cannot work.

Schechter took thirty large bags containing approximately 140 000 fragments. With Jenkinson's assistance a place was found in the library for the collection and was accepted by the Senate of Cambridge University and housed as the Taylor-Schechter collection. Writing about his new-found treasure Schechter said in his *Studies in Judaism*:

> One can hardly realise the confusion in a genuine, old Genizah until one has seen it. It is a battlefield of books, and the literary production of many centuries had their share in the battle, and their *disjecta membra* are now strewn over an area. Some of the belligerents have perished outright and are literally ground to dust in the terrible struggle for space, while others, as if overtaken by a general crush, are squeezed into big, unshapely lumps, which even with the aid of chemical appliances [in the 1890s] can no longer be separated without serious damage to their constituents.
>
> In their present condition these lumps sometimes afford curiously suggestive combinations; as, for instance, when you find a piece of some rationalistic work, in which the very existence of either angels or devils is denied, clinging for its very life to an amulet in which these same beings (mainly the latter) are bound over to be on their good behaviour and not to interfere with Miss Jair's love for somebody. The development of the romance is obscured by the fact that the last lines of the amulet are mounted on some IOU or lease, and this in turn is squeezed between the sheets of an old moralist, who treats all attention to money affairs with scorn and indignation. Again, all these contradictory matters cleave tightly to some sheets from a very old Bible.

In the six years that followed before Schechter left Cambridge, 34 335 fragments – 7 762 of them on vellum – were cleaned and pressed. Nearly two thousand were placed between glass and another two thousand were bound. They consisted of Hebrew and Judeo-Arabic literature, letters and catalogues concerning relations with Muslims and Christians, plagues, police and prisons, warfare and welfare.

Among them Schechter found part of the original version of Ecclesiastes. Putting these together with portions that had recently been acquired from the same source by the Bodleian library in Oxford, he surmised that the document had originally been written in Hebrew and that the Greek version was a copy. Later discoveries would show that his assertion was correct. Also among the discoveries was an account of a sect led by the 'Teacher of Righteousness' who, it was believed by his disciples, would return after death as the 'Messiah'.

The discovery was described by Raphael Levy in the following terms:

> Schechter's account told of a strange, highly structured and unknown Jewish brotherhood of Second Temple times, given to a fierce piety, the communal ownership of property, and a belief in a Messiah. Their doctrinal differences with establishment Judaism, he surmised, 'led to a complete separation from the bulk of the Jewish nation'.[15]

To escape prosecution at home the sect had fled to Damascus where it adopted a 'New Covenant'. The group's existence was to be rediscovered a half century later in the Dead Sea Scrolls, but the first announcement of this existence dates back to Schechter's work on the Genizah fragments.[16]

Although the portions described here were of prime importance, there was, besides them, a treasure trove of knowledge hidden among the fragments. Schechter was well aware of this. Before his move to New York he said: 'Looking over the enormous mass of fragments about me, in the sifting of which I am now occupied, I cannot overcome a sad feeling stealing over me that I shall hardly be worthy to see all the results which the Genizah will add to our knowledge of Jews and Judaism.'

For the next half century the remaining fragments lay in crates in the library, neglected save for the researches of visiting scholars. Indeed, had it not been for the efforts of one particular librarian, they might have been destroyed. One study by Jacob Goiten provided an account of Jewish communities in an Arab world – of working people, merchants and brokers; of travel, piracy and war; housing, clothing, daily routine and the system of communal and institutional life.

In the 1950s new attempts were made to classify the remaining fragments but it was only in 1973 that the Taylor-Schechter Genizah Research Unit was launched under the direction of Dr Stefan Reif. He started afresh with a new comprehensive programme. When sorted, ironed, stitched into plastic envelopes and studied, many of the flimsy, torn scraps were found to contain 'letters and children's exercise books, illuminated verses and laundry lists, wedding contracts and bills of divorce ... A marriage contract states the bride's dowry and the value of each item ...The earliest biblical fragments are dated 905-906 and the section represents almost every chapter of the Old Testament'.[17] At the time it was thought that work on the fragments would be completed within five years. That was an underestimate and the work of unravelling the papers that were taken to Cambridge is still in progress.

The recovery of the Genizah fragments dovetailed with Schechter's belief that the reading of documents was the essence of research work. He said this in his own remarkable way in 1897 when, appointed (in addition to his existing post) as Goldsmith Professor of Hebrew at London University, he spoke in his introductory lecture about the need to return to original source material:

> Translations – it has been said – are the structures with which a kind Providence has over bridged the deeps of human thought caused by the division of tongues at the Tower of Babel. The remark is as humble in spirit as it is prudent in practice. It is certainly safer to walk over the bridge than to swim the flood. But in this case we must be satisfied not to express opinions about the nature of the river, its various currents and undercurrents, its depths and shallows, and the original formation of its bed. To form a

> judgment on these points one must learn to swim and dive, nay, one must immerse himself in the very element against whose touch the bridge was meant to protect him.[18]

Solomon Schechter was anything but single-minded, even if he did make the Cairo fragments central to his research work. He was a voracious reader of both fiction and non-fiction and his interests ranged wide. He appears to have read everything he could find – irrespective of the author's viewpoint – secular or religious, rational or mystical. When he was resting from work in 1901, he wrote to Judge Mayer Sulzberger of Philadelphia, saying:

> Now be good and provide me with some 'Lecture' consisting of novels, diaries, etc, bearing upon your civil war and Reconstruction period ... Of course I have read all the novels which have appeared during the last ten years and you will have to look out for productions of an earlier period.[19]

It is most likely that Sulzberger sent books on Abraham Lincoln, who seems to have been one of Schechter's heroes.[20]

Schechter was no pacifist. Indeed he could be most partisan in his appraisal of conflicts, and made his opinions known. One story illustrates this superbly. He was at a meeting in Britain during the South African War. Towards the end of the session a priest mounted the rostrum and called for prayers 'for our boys fighting in South Africa'. It is said that Schechter immediately walked out of the gathering saying audibly, 'the less the Good Lord knows about that matter, the better'.

Friends claimed that this *bon mot* was typical of the man and that it was a shame that nobody had recorded his many wisdoms. A letter dictated by Frazer in April 1939 and sent to Bentwich, declared:

> Schechter scintillated wit and wisdom, and it is a great pity that he never found a Boswell to chronicle the treasures he poured forth so lavishly in conversation. Though I walked with him regularly one day a week I never made

> notes of his conversation, and have now only a vague recollection of its brilliance and variety. You have done what is possible to preserve them for posterity, and have given what seems to me a very vivid impression of his very remarkable character and genius.

Frazer added a note asking for news of Ruth and wrote:

> It was she who arranged for a testimonial to Dr Schechter when the family left Cambridge for America, and the presentation of it at Christ's College gave him much pleasure.

Ruth, deeply devoted to her father, knew better than most what he would enjoy. She was reared in an atmosphere in which the Genizah fragments lay at the centre of her father's work and absorbed the climate generated by the interest in these ancient documents. Ruth's parents shaped her values and attitudes, her religious fervour and interest in Zionism, and the intellectual background that carried her through life. It could not have been otherwise: the family was imbued with the sensibility and culture of nineteenth century Europe and with a keen awareness of world events.

Her best education (it was said at her funeral in March 1942) was received in her father's study, where, as his unofficial secretary, she came to understand the ardour and the patience of the true scholar, and at her father's table where she met scholars, students, artists and leading intellectuals and 'acquired the delight in impersonal conversation about the things of the mind, in the absence of which she found all society insipid and dull'.[21]

Ruth's love for her father ran deep. Even when she altered course in South Africa and abandoned the religion in which her family was steeped, her admiration of him remained intact. When Schechter died in 1915, she wrote:

> My darling father, never while I live
> Your blue eyes smiling magic shall I see;

Into the darkness you are gone from me,
And though rebellious love may call and strive
It's mightiest, never again my heart will leap
For joy of happy phrase or splendid thought
I loved you so for. They and you are wrought
Into the changelessness of the long sleep.
Never again I'll touch your silvered hair,
And note its lovely wildness round the brow.
But when my loss is bitterest, as now,
It runs my seven-years' dearest bliss and care!
Gold hair that grows like yours, eyes speedwell blue,
And in their depths, the very seal of you.

It was obvious from her achievements that Ruth had learnt a vast amount from her father. She was later to learn to read with intelligent appreciation in the original tongues some of the great masterpieces in Hebrew, Greek, Latin, German, French and English. She had, besides, an encyclopaedic knowledge of literature, history and Jewish customs. She had also acquired her father's deep admiration for Abraham Lincoln, and learnt to admire the achievements of the American reconstruction after the Civil War.

Despite all the acclaim accorded Solomon Schechter (and this included an honorary Doctorate of Literature bestowed on him by Cambridge) he felt the absence in Cambridge of the study of the Hebrew language and the exploration of its mainly religious texts. Even in London there had been little enough of such atmosphere to satisfy him, although the 'Wanderers' had filled some of the gaps. In Cambridge the programme of studies concentrated on the education of an Anglican clergy, and the few Jewish students at the University came to read mathematics, the natural sciences or law. There was no rabbi in the town and whatever religious services were held took place only during term times.

When Schechter arrived in this university town he found a small Cambridge Hebrew congregation. By the time he left this had grown, partly through his inspiration, into a group of forty to fifty. The services were conducted by the members and Schechter would walk about the meeting place singing the tunes he loved while the men worked their way through the service. Saturday afternoon was 'open-house' to members of the congregation at the Schechter household. It was a place for discussion and debate – with Schechter holding forth against philistinism and laying down his conception of the Jewish creed.[22] The whole family was there and the children took part – expressing themselves freely and absorbing the ideas of their father.

Among the students who visited the Schechter household on these afternoons was Morris Alexander (b 1877). Alexander's education had been interrupted when his father's business had collapsed and he had taken jobs at the local branch of the National Bank and then on the railways, sold old paraffin tins and empty bottles, hawked chocolates and peanuts at the theatre, and bought and sold shares at a small margin to fund and complete his schooling. He had then enrolled at the South African College – later the University of Cape Town – from which he graduated in 1896, winning the gold medal in Arts and voted the senior gold medallist of the year. Determined to advance his career he sailed to Britain where he joined the Inner Temple, London, to secure entry to the Bar, and registered at St John's College in 1897 to read law.

In 1899, when the Schechter family was at tea, Ruth, then aged twelve, is said to have declared to Morris: 'I am going to marry you Morris Alexander. You must not engage yourself to any other girl when you return to South Africa. You must promise to wait for me'.[23]

This precocious declaration appears to have resulted from the fact that her father had been praising the young man. It seems that nobody had hushed her or rebuked her. Perhaps they had smiled or laughed good naturedly. Morris had apparently not considered marriage until then but, looking at an attractive young girl, he ignored the eleven year age difference, and henceforth thought of her as his future bride.

Soon after this Morris returned to South Africa where he practised law and took part in Jewish communal affairs. In 1902 Solomon Schechter and his family departed for New York. Schechter found satisfaction in his new role as Principal of the Jewish Theological Seminary, continued his researches, and trained young men for the rabbinate in the Conservative community.[24] He also established a wide circle of friends and disciples in the United States. I -n 1907 he travelled to New York to claim his bride.

A Father's Legacy

The education Ruth received from her parents exceeded anything she could have obtained in any institution, even though it meant that she never received a college certificate. She acquired a love for reading which she put to good use when she wrote articles and reviews. She also absorbed the religious atmosphere and the many stories of Jewish life in Europe which she heard at the family table.

The first occasion on which the fruits of this education appeared in print was in the *Cape Times* of 2 June 1923 in a review of *The Story of John Paul* by V R Emanuel. The story concerned an objectionable Jewish lad, nurtured in an equally obnoxious Jewish home and should have been dismissed in a cursory notice or in one of Ruth's 'Rhymed Reviews'. Yet Ruth had a full column providing her with space to discuss 'The Jew in Modern Society: The Vicious Circle of Anti-Semitism'. The review began with two quotations, the first by Achad Ha'am:

> Nothing is more dangerous for a nation or for an individual than to plead guilty of imaginary sins ... Our greatest need is emancipation from contempt, from this idea that we are really worse than all the world. Otherwise we may in the course of time become in reality what we now imagine ourselves to be.

The second passage came from a book of *Seminary Addresses* by her father in which he told of the wounds inflicted on him by Christian boys when he arrived home from *cheder* (religion school). His father had comforted him by saying that they were in exile, and that it was necessary to submit to God's will. This was only a passing phase in history, and as the Jews belonged to eternity, God would comfort his people. But when he (Schechter) had emigrated from Rumania to so-called civilised countries he had found 'what I might call the Higher Anti-Semitism which burns the soul though it leaves the body unhurt'.

These two pronouncements, wrote Ruth, both made within the last decade by Jews of unusual mental calibre and of markedly noble character, crystallised within their few words the depth and the extent of the tragedy of the Jew of modern times. 'The circle is vicious and complete; he feels himself disliked, knows himself despised, by the peoples among whom he lives.'

There were three obvious remedies, she wrote: 'assimilation to his surroundings so that in a generation or two he is rid of the past; return to Palestine to build a future, homogenous and free of problems'; or ' if he has the courage and the vision, come to grips with his own soul ... revere his own heritage, live in peace and freedom with the minority of the world which understands freedom and cares for peace, while ignoring or withstanding that inconsiderable majority which neither understands freedom nor cares for peace ...' She concluded her survey ironically: 'So living a man may easily be massacred in a pogrom, but he will not be blackballed in a club.'

The next contribution that owed much to her father was on Yiddish which, she wrote in the *Cape Times* on 11 August 1923, originated as a South German dialect written in Hebrew characters. It spread through Europe and America becoming a universal Esperanto of the wanderers among nations differing, as it spread, only in dialect. It could be heard wherever Jews congregated and there were newspapers and books written in Yiddish. In New York alone there were six daily newspapers, besides weekly or monthly periodicals, and a flood of novels, essays, poetry and plays, all published in Yiddish. It was the *lingua franca* of the Jewish workers and although thousands of rich Jews also spoke it, Yiddish was one of several languages at their command. Their children seldom used it.

Ruth's brief survey, which was similar to Morris's evidence in the Cape Colony in 1906, preceded her review of a touring theatrical company which had recently played to full houses in Cape Town. The company's repertoire included a bizarre translation of *Hamlet* and plays 'that were the rawest and frankest of melodrama' relieved with the broadest of farce, by singing and dancing, and 'by flashes of a mordant wit inseparable from the medium in which the pieces were played'.

On 11 September, Rosh Hashanah (the Jewish New Year), an editorial written by Ruth appeared in the *Cape Times*. She began with a recitation of the tradition: On this day, it was said, God and his angels 'inscribe in the Book of Life the fate of all living creatures. "Who shall live, and who die, whose appointed time is finished, and whose is not; who shall be at rest, and who wandering; and who shall remain tranquil, and who be disturbed ... who shall be cast down, and who exalted".' Ten days later, on Yom Kippur (the Day of Atonement), the decisions would be sealed and made irrevocable except that 'prayers, penance and charity may avert the evil decree'.

But, wrote Ruth, it was sometimes claimed that final decisions were only made five days after Yom Kippur, on *Succoth* – the Festival of the Tabernacle. With tongue in cheek she added that during those five days a rabbi would suggest to a beautiful lady that this was her chance!

Ruth described the finery that would be worn for the festivals and, as it was traditionally a time for reflection, she commented on the world situation over the past year. There was some cause for rejoicing, she wrote. In the USSR increasing numbers of Jews were taking to agriculture and in the Ukraine a newly established credit bank had made provision for loans for tools and clothes; in Petach Tikvah where there was now peace, the Arabs had paid reparations for the bloodshed during the previous year. A start had been made on the building of a Hebrew University in Jerusalem and, with the draining of swamps, orange orchards were being established and other produce was being grown.

Some time later, on 8 January 1930, when the depression was biting hard Ruth wrote a lengthy article for the *Cape Times* entitled 'Is Charity Over-organised – And Too Easy?' with a sub-title 'A Plea for the Older and Quieter Methods of the Jews'. Ruth decried 'the tortures of humiliation', of interrogation by over-worked, often callous, some times condescending organisers. Charity, she said, had been organised very differently in the small villages of Tsarist Russia where life was simpler and more self-contained. A small wooden box, a key to which was owned by every householder, was taken from house to house by the beadle on Friday afternoons before the onset of the Sabbath. Money was put into the box by those who were prosperous and taken by those who were in need. The system was discreet and dignified and, though nobody doubted who had put money in or taken money out, it was never discussed. The practice, she said, was traced back to the Temple in Jerusalem, where there was a room in which the rich left money and the respectable poor received support.

Published when the world recession was at its height, the article was a plea for a return to the older method. Undoubtedly first heard from her parents or their friends, the account was fascinating but the appeal was inappropriate. Indeed, Ruth recognised the impracticability of running across Cape Town, and called for a more personal response to the needs of the poor. There could be no return to the methods used in the small closed communities in eastern Europe and this appeal, together with several similar calls from Ruth, had little or no effect on the organisation of charity in the city.

Though her appeals went unanswered, her articles were read and contributed to the store of knowledge of her readers. Little was known at that time about life in the *shtetl* and the information acquired by Ruth and transmitted to a larger audience was not the least of her contributions.

2
THE MOVE TO AMERICA

As Principal of the Jewish Theological Seminary, Solomon Schechter had the opportunity to train rabbis and could make the Seminary a rallying point of Jewish life and learning in the United States. He could also create a Jewish environment for his family and gather around himself a band of scholars to lay the basis for a Jewish ministry based on Conservative Judaism. He was appointed Chair of the Board of Translators of the Bible, was a member of the editorial board of the *Jewish Encyclopaedia* and co-editor of the *Jewish Quarterly Review* (which he brought over from Britain).

Perhaps most precious of all, he brought a considerable portion of the unedited manuscripts and fragments from the Genizah collection. Some of these he edited himself, others were distributed for editing among staff members at the seminary.[1] Firm as he was in his beliefs in the Conservative creed, he made the Seminary a centre of unity and peace, preferring, it was said, to combat religious liberalism – which was anathema – with wit and humour.[2]

In his programme Schechter coupled the need for religious education with the acquisition of the Hebrew language. In this he adopted (and voiced) the view of traditionalists who maintained that Hebrew was 'not merely a language' but, to the Jew, a Holy Language 'a sacred monument of bygone times'.[3] Presumably it was not used in the household as a means of secular communication – which would be sacrilegious – but was used only when holy scripts were read.

There is no information about the three children. They went to school, but their connection with the Seminary is not recorded. Ruth's formal education ended at high school and she never attended college or university. Perhaps it did not matter overmuch: she was a voracious reader and there was no shortage of books. She also absorbed all that her father said in respect of Hebrew, religion and Zionism. She followed him in his admiration of writers and statesmen, including Ralph Waldo Emerson, Olive Schreiner and, above all, Abraham Lincoln, and undoubtedly adhered to the common belief that Lincoln had conducted the Civil War in America in order to liberate the slaves. This conviction stayed with Ruth and, at a later date, she thought of her husband as the statesman who would be the 'liberator of slaves' in South Africa.

Morris Alexander kept in contact through letters with the family in Cambridge and when they moved to New York. He took the initiative and pressed his claims to the hand of a young girl he barely knew. Ruth was growing into womanhood with her own ideas and her own strong personality, and in many ways acquired a maturity from contact with her parents and their friends. But it was a maturity in a young body and she still had a lot to learn.

Morris returned in 1900 to a South Africa at war. Although he lived in the western Cape, which was the part of the country least affected by the hostilities, the disturbances hindered his establishment of a legal practice, and it was by dint of hard application that he obtained briefs and started saving money. His plans for the future were clear – he wanted to acquire property and then to claim Ruth as his bride.

His legal practice flourished and he soon became active in local religious and communal organisations. One of his first concerns was the problems faced by Jews wishing to emigrate from Eastern Europe. The tiny Jewish community, which had numbered 3 000 in 1891 (when immigration from Tsarist Russia began) had increased to about 6 000 by the turn of the century and, absorbing refugees from the South African War of 1899-1902, had increased sixfold by 1904 to 19 537 (3,37 per cent of the white population). Many of them had few resources, were without their immediate families and had no stability.[4]

Morris's first step was to help establish the Roelands Street Synagogue (opened in 1900) to serve the immigrants. His most notable activity was to campaign on issues raised by the passing of the Cape Immigration Restriction Act of 1903, designed to exclude Asiatics from the Cape. It defined 'prohibited immigrants' as persons unable to write out and sign an application, to the satisfaction of the minister 'in the characters of any European language'.

One of the effects of the new law was to question the status of Yiddish. The Hebrew characters in which it was written had originated in the Middle East and were not considered European, and doubts were expressed about it being a 'European language'. With such criteria the vast majority of Jews would be denied entry to the Cape.

The more conservative sections of the Jewish community were in favour of accepting the new law, claiming that it could be left to the British sense of justice to rectify matters. Morris, together with Lionel L Goldsmid, editor of *The South African Jewish Chronicle*, and others mounted a campaign to have the restrictions on Jews removed.[5] To make their action more effective he and his allies, prompted by the recent steps to launch a Board of Deputies in the Transvaal, resolved to set up a parallel board in the Cape. The move was opposed by Rabbi Bender who tried to stop its formation. Morris was not deterred, and at a small meeting in Cape Town on 4 September 1904, the board was established and he was elected President.

In May 1903, while the launch of the board was being prepared, Morris led a deputation to the Cape Attorney-General to present the case for designating Yiddish a German dialect and consequently a European language. To prove their case a Yiddish expert read a philosophical tract to a sworn translator of German who knew neither Yiddish nor the Hebrew characters, but was able faithfully to translate what he heard.[6] When legislation was enacted as the Immigration Act of 1906 it was stipulated that for purpose of the Act 'Yiddish shall be accepted as a European language'. Consequent on their successful campaign the authorities asked the Board of Deputies to scrutinise applications made for naturalisation – a function that the Board undertook with some willingness, further establishing its position as an official body.[7]

In the early years of the century there can be no doubt that the Jewish leaders accepted their victory without giving much consideration to the problems that arose from aiding and abetting a discriminatory Act. They set out to assist Jews fleeing from pogroms and persecution in Tsarist Russia, and they set their sights no higher than assisting their co-religionists to enter the Cape. Indians in the Cape (who had arrived as traders) and had been protected by their British citizenship, also opposed the legislation, but there is no available evidence that, at the time, there was cooperation across the ethnic divide.

In 1904 Morris had joined the Zionist movement and became Secretary in August 1905 of the Dorshei Zion Society which supported Jewish interests, including relief of distress, support of national and religious institutions, war relief, and the cause of Hebrew education and Jewish culture.[8] In July 1906, in the aftermath of a wave of pogroms in Russia, he organised a mass meeting at the Good Hope Hall in Cape Town to protest against the 'frequent and inhuman outrages perpetrated upon Jews in Russia'. The resolution passed at the meeting was moved by W P Schreiner, Olive's brother. A copy was sent to the Governor of the Cape Colony.[9]

A further threat against minorities appeared in 1906 when a General Dealers' and Hawkers' Licence Act was passed, ostensibly to control trading abuses. Once again the language issue was dragged in: business records would have to be kept in a European language. The Bill was directed primarily against Asiatics, but when a £3 tax was levied on hawkers under the new legislation it was seen as a threat to new Jewish immigrants. It was only removed after intensive lobbying of members of the Cape Legislative Assembly by Morris and his supporters on the Board.

Morris added to his activities in Cape Town by becoming a member of the Town Council in 1905; helped to found the Progressive Club – of which the Prime Minister, Dr Starr Jameson, was elected President; and was chairman of the Imperial Union Club. He had established an impressive looking curriculum vitae to present to his intended bride in New York in 1907.

Some of the letters that Morris wrote to Mrs Schechter and to Ruth before the marriage are still available but the replies have disappeared. Then, as later, Morris's are stilted and dull. This might have been a reflection of his shyness and also of the incongruity of a man writing to a young girl he hardly knew. Yet on Ruth's instructions the correspondence continued at monthly intervals. Morris wrote at one juncture to say:

> I respect your wish that I am not to write you love letters. I shall be only too delighted to write to you once a month, and oftener, if you would reply regularly. I shall let you know as much about myself and my folk as I can find time to write about. By all means let us continue to be 'real good friends', you and I, as we have always been. Emerson says that there are two elements that go to the composition of friendship, one is truth, the other tenderness. Let me have the second element as well as the first, as the same writer says, 'Let the soul be assured that somewhere in the universe it should again rejoin a friend, and it would be content and cheerful alone for a thousand years'. [10]

In this way the 'romance' developed, peppered with quotations but with little real engagement of emotion.

There is no record of what members of the Schechter family thought about the match. It is inconceivable that the matter had not been discussed by Ruth or by her parents but, as in so many families, such matters were not recorded. Moreover, it is conceivable that in the fashion of religious Jewish families, there was a certain pressure for the oldest daughter to marry. This was the single most important event in the life of a woman when she reached a marriageable age. It did not matter that there was a large age difference between a potential bride and her spouse, nor was it important that a girl, in the bloom of youth, with the flush of beauty that is displayed in her photographs, should marry a man who was so distinctly plain.

By 1907 Morris was ready to sail for New York. Before he left he wrote a long letter to Rabbi Schechter giving an account of his achievements and of his financial situation. His savings, he wrote, would allow him to take extended leave of absence, sail across the ocean and bring his bride back to a substantial house 'in the best part of Cape Town'. He listed the sums of money he had invested in land outside the city and the value of his life insurance, and gave details of the cost of rates, taxes, electric lights, and so on.[11]

He arrived in New York to make final arrangements for the wedding. A day was set aside for the taking of the vows, invitations were sent out, and many important luminaries responded. The bare walls of the seminary were 'transformed by palms and cut flowers into a bower'. After the ceremony on 9 June 1907, about 200 guests attended a reception in the auditorium.[12] At some point an old friend spoke to Mathilda Schechter about Ruth's impending departure. The story was recounted by Ruth many years later:

> An old woman came and remonstrated with my mother, with tears, saying that she for her part would rather see her daughter dead and lying in her coffin than let her go off to such an outlandish place.[13]

Solomon Schechter was consulted and the matter resolved. He said: 'Well if you do go, perhaps one day you will see Olive Schreiner'. It was the kind of response that could be expected from him but it does raise one serious question. He had a high regard for Olive as a novelist and she came from the Cape, but why should she want to meet this young woman, even if she was the daughter of an eminent theologian? Had Ruth already tried her hand at writing? Were there any attributes that might attract a writer of some repute? In the absence of evidence the question is not readily answerable even though Ruth's precociousness is evident from three letters found in the Zangwill archives.[14]

On 11 December 1902, when she was fourteen and a half years old, she had written to Mr Zangwill:

> Once there was a Little Nobody. And also there was a Literary Lion. The Little Nobody had heard much of the Literary Lion; in fact she knew him. That is, she knew the outside and a little bit of the inside of the Literary Lion. But like the elephant in Mr Kipling's story, the Little Lion had 'satiable curiosity'. Also, she was fond of the Literary Lion. So she wrote him a letter asking him if she may tell him, from week to week what happened in her small world, and certain thoughts and fancies of hers, which she thought the Literary Lion might care to hear about. And the Literary Lion answered the Little Nobody, and said —

> Dear Mr Zangwill please tell me what he did say, – and soon. For the Little Nobody is *very* fond of the Literary Lion.
>
> With love,
> Yours waitingly, Ruth H Schechter.

On 4 January she wrote again, apologising for the delay in responding to his reply and giving as the reason the fact that the examinations, which would determine her chances of promotion, were due. She continued:

> Latin and English I am not afraid of for they are both pleasant and easy for me. Algebra is also fairly safe, and physiology, though its long list of names bore me, is also not dangerous, but drawing is a 'vexation of the spirit'.
>
> It is strange that my letter should have come on Christmas Eve. Was it not jolly that Hannucah this year just fitted into Christmas? It made a double holiday, physical and spiritual, so to say, for me.
>
> About a week ago I received a dainty little copy of *The Cricket on the Hearth* that sweetest story of Dickens. The gift has an incident attached to it, which I think you might like to hear.
>
> The month before we departed from England was spent in Ramsgate. We had lodgings on the West Cliff, and three doors away lived the hero of this little story. He was an invalid about thirty years old, and suffering from some spine-trouble which made his lot very hard, for he had to lie on a long kind of couch on wheels all day. But instead of being soured, taciturn, pessimistic, or atheistical, because of his hard fate, he is the sunniest mortal I have ever known. All day he lay there looking at the sea with a far-off look in his blue eyes, and a singularly sweet smile. He looked so tranquil and peaceful that I could not help smiling back as I passed him daily. I felt so pitiful for him in his loneliness

> that one day I smiled at him and paused a moment, too shy to speak first, and yet determined to try and be kind to him.
>
> He said 'Good Morning', and soon I found myself talking to him as if I had known him ever so long.
>
> After that I came every day to talk to the invalid. His soul was as tranquil and sincere as his smile. We had a mutual liking for Dickens, and talked much about him. On the day before which I went away, he gave me a small paper-covered volume containing that author's *Reprinted Pieces*. I hardly liked to take it for I knew that it had been a life long companion to him. This year as I have said, he sent me the *Cricket on the Hearth*.
>
> I did pull the other literary lion's tail, but he is very busy now...
>
> I shall certainly read *Blind Children* for two reasons: 1) because I read one poem bearing that title and liked it, 2) because you told me not to.
>
> I hope the bitter lines *never will be* finished. For it is my private opinion that quite enough have [*sic*] been written already on that subject, and the sooner someone begins to show, as Martha Wolfenstein did, that these people who have suffered so long and so much whose blood flows in your and my veins are good and true also, so much the better including the Jews – ourselves.

There are no other letters, nor any other written pieces by Ruth which testify to her abilities. That she was bright, precocious, and probably more than a bit brash seems obvious. Whether this provided a basis for meeting Olive Schreiner remains unclear. Ruth knew of her father's hope and when she eventually met Olive in South Africa her beloved authoress thought that she was the most intelligent young woman she had yet met.

But that is to look ahead. This was the day a marriage was formalised in traditional fashion and thereafter Morris and Ruth Alexander set out for Europe. They stopped first at the Zionist Conference in The Hague where Morris was accredited as the delegate for South Africa. Their agreement was obvious; they were devoutly Jewish and religious, and they were Zionists who believed in the need for a Jewish 'homeland'. For Ruth there was an extra interest. Solomon Schechter's twin brother, Israel, had settled in Palestine and with thirty-nine other families had established the village of Zichron Jacob.

Then it was time to return to Morris's home, to his legal career and his political ambitions. Once again the biographer must guess, but there is little need to stretch one's imagination: the Alexanders were greeted on their arrival at the Cape Town dock, and Ruth took her place as the wife of one of the leading Jewish personalities in the town. She had arrived in every sense of the word and there is no reason to doubt that she was proud of her new status and devoted to the establishment in which she now found herself.

Morris's political ambitions received fresh impetus in 1908 when he was elected to the Cape Legislative Assembly. This was the last election before Union and Morris won one of the seven seats for Cape Town. He also retained his seat in the Town Council and stayed there until 1913. Morris's approach to the franchise at this stage is known from his correspondence with a black nationalist. In December 1907, after his return from New York, he received a letter from Francis Zaccharius Santiago Peregrino appealing for assistance in extending the vote.

Peregrino, who achieved some prominence in the Cape, was born in Accra, educated in England and then, moving to New York, was influenced by WEB DuBois, the leading proponent of Pan Africanism.

Peregrino emigrated to Cape Town to win adherents to the African Methodist Episcopal Church (with which he had links) and to Pan Africanism. He published the fortnightly *South African Spectator* calling for black advancement in the Cape and the extension of the Cape's non-racial franchise to all blacks in South Africa. In his reply Morris said that he favoured 'a franchise as broad and liberal as that of the Cape, allowing for no distinction of race, colour or creed'. He also wrote (to another correspondent) to say that he favoured an imperial conference to lay down the free right of Indians to enter and settle anywhere in the Empire so long as they conformed to the laws of the country. Until then he thought that the *status quo* should be maintained.

In 1908 Ruth gave birth to a daughter, Esther. During the next four years she had two more children, Muriel (or 'Bobbet'), and Solly. This was a matter of joy and Ruth revelled in her new family. Yet, despite her duties as a mother, she was absorbed in her husband's world, and through him met leading members of the Jewish community, politicians, the legal fraternity and colonial officials. It was company that marked her status as a leading social figure in the Cape but the novelty soon palled.[15]

In the introduction to her unpublished novel, *The Exiles,* which is set in Cape Town, Ruth writes that the characters are imaginary but the events are real. The autobiographical overtones indicate that, within the boundaries of story-telling, she was the heroine and that Farrington, soon to enter my account, was the hero. In her writing she expressed her irritation at the pettiness of the life she had entered. It was actively anti-academic – a life of chatter and gossip – which she despised.

The marriage was, however, happy, at least at first. Ruth maintained a traditional home in which the Sabbath was kept and the many minutiae of religious observance were maintained. The happiness she found in her marriage was mentioned in a letter to Kallenbach (in October 1915), when she wrote of Morris:

> He really is the straightest soul I've met, in young mankind. I love him and respect him more now than when we were first married, and that is saying a great deal.

In 1910 her parents and sister Amy visited the Cape and were fêted at innumerable receptions. They toured the country under Morris's guidance and Ruth was proud to present her parents and sister to Olive Schreiner. Three years later Ruth returned her parents' visit, taking with her Solly, her youngest child.

On her return she wrote from the ship with accounts of how she had spent her Sabbath and told of the many Jewish societies and institutions she had visited. She also said:

> No one in all the world could ever have loved you as well as I. Wherever I go, it is to love and appreciate you the

> more, your sterling honour, your sweetness, your uprightness, above all your clear fineness in regard to sex. I could love you no better than I did, but I admire you ten times more than I did.[16]

It is not to be wondered that Morris experienced a period of domestic bliss and, it was said, was miserable when Ruth was away.

3

MORRIS ALEXANDER, GANDHI, AND THE THEOSOPHISTS

One of Ruth's 'Great Souls'

Ruth's reference to Gandhi in her letter to him as 'one of the three great souls with whom I live from day to day' is unexpected. Besides having met him on a few occasions in the company of several members of the Indian community, the only evening she spent with him was the night before he left South Africa. Yet his impact is not altogether surprising. Anyone who was sensitive to injustice and who found racism repugnant would have been interested in Gandhi's activities and intrigued by his tactics.

There were, undoubtedly, several factors that predisposed Ruth to admire Gandhi. He was so very different from other leaders of the community, so active in comparison to a seemingly quiescent people, and his campaigns against discriminatory regulations were so justifiable that the impact he made on her did not require extensive contact. Many people with whom she was intimate were also admirers of this remarkable man. One of these was Olive, whose respect and admiration for Gandhi were reciprocated: After she and friends came to bid him farewell as he boarded a ship for Britain in 1909, he wrote in a letter 'Fancy the author of *Dreams* paying a tribute to passive resistance'.

Morris and Ruth had a close relationship with Hermann Kallenbach, one of Gandhi's closest friends and an active participant in his campaigns. Born in 1871 in Europe, Kallenbach was educated in Germany and then came to South Africa. He became a well-known architect and was a prominent Tolstoyan. He was also said to have been related to Morris Alexander through the marriage of one of his brothers into the extended Alexander-Lewin family. I have not been able to confirm this, but related or not, he was a frequent visitor to the Alexander home. There he found pleasant company and would describe the progress of the Indian struggle, tell of his own participation, and undoubtedly receive financial contributions to assist the campaigners. He would also have explained Gandhi's philosophy and spoken with enthusiasm of the man and his activities.

Kallenbach's involvement in what was happening in the Indian organisations is itself remarkable and has only recently been told in works by Gideon Shimoni, Margaret Chatterjee and Isa Sarid. To put the story in perspective I must give an account of the Indians' entry into South Africa. It is a story that has been told in many books, but most exclude information about the Cape Indians and the role of Gandhi's white friends.

The Indians in the Cape

Indians were first brought to Natal between 1860 and 1911 as indentured labourers to work in the sugar cane fields. Their contracts stipulated a ten-year stay, the first five under indenture, followed by five years as free labourers. Thereafter they were to be offered a free passage home, or a plot of land in Natal, and more than half the labourers preferred to stay on in South Africa. Indians were also recruited to work in the coal mines and on the railways. By 1875 Indian merchants, having found outlets to provide provisions for the settled Indian population, began arriving in South Africa.

The indentured labourers were worse off than slaves. Their deaths might have been inconvenient to the land owner, but they were readily replaced and did not constitute a financial loss. In the driving quest for profits they were provided with the bare minimum of necessities: their housing, food, clothes and general upkeep were atrocious. There was also a shortage of women, and those who had joined their men existed under the most pitiable of conditions.

The whites in Natal, disregarding the conditions under which the vast majority of Indians lived, saw in them a cultural and social intrusion and, potentially, an economic threat. White workers objected to the competition of freed labourers in the work place, farmers objected to the competition of those who received plots of land, and merchants complained of a loss of trade. Populist politicians called for the repatriation of the Indians and termed this combination of complaints the 'Indian question'.

Inevitably, those Indians freed of indenture and able to move entered the Transvaal, until new laws prevented movement across colonial (and after Union, provincial) boundaries. Though regulations in the Transvaal closed avenues of employment, they hoped to better their conditions as traders or hawkers. The Orange Free State was even worse: it excluded all Asiatics, preventing settlement and even transit through the state.

In the Cape conditions were somewhat different. In both 1874 and 1879 motions were debated in the Cape Legislative Council that Indian indentured labour be introduced in the Cape. Farmers welcomed the possibility but the proposal was disallowed by the government. The last attempt to use indentured labour in the Cape was in 1902 when about 300 Indians arrived voluntarily to work on the Koffiefontein mines (south of Kimberley) but the project was soon abandoned. Those Indians who did settle in the Cape arrived during the 1880s. They came from Natal, Mauritius, or India, mainly as merchants or shopkeepers or their assistants. There were no restrictions on immigration and in 1891 they numbered about 1 500 – 915 of them in the district of Kimberley. By 1899 the numbers had increased to 3 471 (preponderantly men) – with 1 600 in Port Elizabeth, 600 in Cape Town, and 575 in Kimberley.[1]

The Indian population was divided, as in Natal, between a Muslim majority and a Hindu minority. The former was partly absorbed into the Cape Malay community, attended their mosques and married local girls. The Hindu minority mixed amicably with the Muslims, but maintained their own separate social existence.[2] Both Muslims and Hindus belonged to the same political associations and protested together against discriminatory regulations. However, they occupied different positions in the larger Cape society. The Muslims tended to go into business as general dealers and butchers; the Hindus became fruit and vegetable dealers or set up small workshops as shoemakers, and so on.

The number of traders was initially small, but with no restrictions on land ownership or on the right to trade, their number grew. By 1897,

137 Indians held licences to trade in the Cape; by 1905 this number had grown to 714, some of whom prospered and became affluent. But they were the exception: most Indian shops were in poor areas, where profit margins were small and insolvency rates were high. By comparison, 3 675 whites had trading licences. There were also 256 Indian hawkers, most of whom barely survived on small turnovers.[3]

During the South African War there was an exodus of Indians from the regions where fighting was taking place and some found their way to the Cape. By 1904 their numbers had grown to 10 242, spread over 72 districts, but with the majority in the three coastal towns of Port Elizabeth, East London and Cape Town, and in Kimberley. A hitherto barely concealed xenophobia was now openly expressed in demands that the immigration of Asiatics be limited or stopped and this gave birth to the Immigration Restriction Act of 1903.

Voluntary associations appeared, most of them responding to regional or local issues. Two political bodies, established around the turn of the century, were also to become active in the wake of discriminatory legislation introduced after 1903, to limit entry into the Cape and to limit the number of traders and hawkers permitted to operate in the Colony. These were the British Indian League, under the presidency of Adam H Gool, and the South African Indian Association, with E Norodien, the owner of several shops, as president. Both bodies were 'loyal', passing resolutions of condolence on the deaths of Queen Victoria, and then of Edward VII, and welcoming the arrival of Joseph Chamberlain in 1903 and the first Governor-General, Lord Gladstone, in 1910.[4]

There is no indication that Morris showed much interest in the plight of the Cape Indian community when the Immigration Act was first introduced in 1903. His concern was to protect the right of Jews fleeing from pogroms and it was only later, when he was approached by leaders of the Indian organisations, that he gave some attention to what was agitating the Indian people. There was no easy linguistic solution, such as that used for the Jews, because the Indians, and in particular the uneducated, spoke only Indian dialects, and these were obviously not European. Nor was Morris inclined to suggest extra-parliamentary methods of struggle. But he was one of the very few whites who succeeded in winning the confidence of the Indians as a man who would listen.

In April 1911 General Smuts, then Minister of the Interior, introduced an Immigration Restriction Act which gave an immigration officer the right to exclude any person who could not write fifty words satisfactorily in a language dictated by himself. Once again Morris took up the matter in Parliament and moved several amendments, including, once again, the right to use Yiddish in any such test. The amendments were of benefit mainly to Jews. Indians, who were the chief target of the Act, had no means of fighting the new restriction.

The General Dealers' and Hawkers' Acts, both of them further measures designed to restrict Indian rights, were amended, largely thanks to Morris, to delete clauses which discriminated against Cape Jewry. The Indians in the Cape resented the discriminatory regulations but their organisations were small.[5] Activity was confined mainly to organising petitions and meetings at which resolutions called for the repeal of obnoxious laws, and expressed solidarity with the Indians of Natal and the Transvaal. With little or no possibility of – and no heart for engaging in – open political activity the Cape Indian leaders appealed to Morris, first as a member of the Cape Council and, after 1910, of the Union Legislative Assembly, to oppose the offending legislation. Morris responded but, although he championed the Indians' cause and spoke in Parliament, he achieved little.

Gandhi and Passive Resistance

Active opposition came almost entirely from the main urban centres in Natal and the Transvaal. The story of this resistance in the colonies which were to become the Union of South Africa is popularly – if not always correctly – associated with the name of Mohandas Gandhi, a British trained barrister who visited Natal in 1893 to take up a one-year appointment with the firm of Dada Abdullah to assist in a law suit against a Transvaal merchant. Within weeks of his arrival he was assaulted in a racial attack and resolved to combat the discrimination to which Indians were subjected. These included their right to move across colonial borders, the annual tax of £3 they were required to pay, and the acceptance of the validity of the marriages they had contracted. Gandhi joined with the political groups representing the merchants, traders and more privileged workers in the colony and because of his legal training he provided a focus around which more organised activity became possible.

From 1904 Gandhi called on merchants in the Transvaal to oppose the regulation requiring them to prove that they had traded before the war of 1899-1902 before they could be licensed.[6] There was little response to his call that they defy and go to jail, but the regulation fell away after leading traders appealed to the legislature. Pressure on the Transvaal Indians continued. Act 2 of 1907 required them to register, and allowed only those who complied to remain in the country. Gandhi, with the support of local associations, called on members of the community to remain without registering.

Although the Cape Indian leaders sympathised with Gandhi, his campaigns did not include the Indian community of the Cape. In a lengthy letter written on 23 January 1897, J M H Gool, a fish curer and basket manufacturer of Cape Town, expressed his admiration for Gandhi's campaign in Natal.[7]

> Your single-hearted efforts and fearless representations of grievances under which the unfortunate Indians ... in Natal suffer.
>
> We are deeply grieved that you should have been subjected to the cruel treatments reported in the papers here ... at the hands of a mad mob in Durban, but let us assure you that the eyes of thousands are on you and are watching with sympathetic appreciation on all you have done.

When Gandhi was arrested on 10 January 1908 for defying an order to leave the Transvaal there were nationwide protests and Indians in East London wrote to Lord Elgin, the Colonial Secretary, and to the Viceroy of India asking the Imperial government to protest. All Indian businesses stayed closed.[8]

Gandhi had adopted his eclectic philosophy – with its Hindu roots – when studying in London. It was during that period that he attended meetings addressed by Annie Besant and other Theosophists[9] and sympathised with some of their tenets. He consolidated his concepts of personal self-reliance and moral duty and made this the basis of his outlook. At the turn of the century he was introduced to and met adherents of the Theosophical Lodge in Johannesburg, probably at the vegetarian café to which members repaired after Lodge meetings. Whatever the basis of his attendance at some of their gatherings he found people of like mind and established close friendship with some of them. Yet, despite the fact that he agreed with some of their tenets, Gandhi differed with the Theosophists on essential points. In a talk at the Lodge he reportedly said:

> There were many admirable works in Theosophical literature which one may read with the greatest profit, but it appeared to him that too much stress had been laid upon mental intellectual studies, upon argument, upon the development of occult powers and that the central idea of theosophy, the brotherhood of mankind and the moral growth of man, had been lost sight of in these.

He continued, saying 'they must cultivate absolutely pure and truthful lives, they must learn to control their passions'. The Real Life 'was to be lived in the world around them, in the real practice of the little teaching that they might have been able to grasp'.[10]

Finding it necessary to clarify his own views and to refine his own moral stance he turned to Hindu religious tracts which he felt he had ignored.

Contact with the Theosophists allowed Gandhi to recruit whites who could win support for the immigrant Indians and provide administrative personnel for his organisation. He also found people who could take his messages to Europe and raise funds there and in India. The whites mentioned in the literature were mainly Jews. However there were non-Jews who receive less attention for their service to Gandhi's cause. These included men who worked in the Natal settlement, 'Phoenix', and some remarkable women – Emily Hobhouse, Alice M Greene, Betty Molteno (a keen Theosophist) and Olive Schreiner. These women had all opposed the war waged by the British against the

Boer Republics in 1899. They were among the first to reject the racism that permeated white society, and Hobhouse had agitated against the confinement of Boer families in concentration camps although she overlooked or ignored the similar plight of thousands of Africans.

Several members of the Johannesburg Theosophical Lodge assisted the Indian movement in an official, or semi-official, capacity. They included Louis Walter Ritch, who had launched the appeal for the formation of the Theosophical Lodge, and was subsequently secretary of the British Indians' Defence Committee; H S L Polak, a subeditor on the *Transvaal Critic*, who assumed the editorship of *Indian Opinion*, became a lawyer and helped organise the volunteers from Natal in the 1913 passive resistance campaign; Sonja Schlesin, Secretary of the Indian Women's Association (1906-14) and private secretary to Gandhi; and Kallenbach who had joined the Theosophical Lodge in Johannesburg (c 1904). He found a social home in the Indian movement, became an intimate friend of Gandhi, and acquired an outlook on life – which included celibacy – that was in close accord with Gandhi's philosophy. In 1908 he became Secretary of the European Committee of Sympathisers for Satyagraha (passive resistance) in Johannesburg.

By mid-1912 the Indian movement had rallied behind Gandhi and illegally crossed from Natal to the Transvaal in protest against the £3 tax and restrictions on travel. Whether by design, or by chance, Gandhi had found men and women who would assist him actively in the campaign. He had assembled a team of assistants from outside the Indian community, some of whom were to play an important role in the campaign, and he acknowledged their importance.

In his autobiography Gandhi wrote of Polak:

> Mr Polak's candour drew me to him. The same evening we got to know each other we seemed to hold closely similar views on the essential things of life. He liked simple life. He had a wonderful faculty for translating into practice anything that appealed to his intellect. Some of the changes that he made in his life were as prompt as they were radical.[11]

Of his encounter with Kallenbach Gandhi wrote:

> When I came to know him I was startled at his love of luxury and extravagance. But at our very first meeting, he asked searching questions concerning matters of religion. Our acquaintance soon ripened into very close friendship, so much so that we thought alike and he was convinced that he must carry out in his life the changes I was making in mine.[12]

But that is looking ahead. Twice before 1910 Gandhi had led 'passive resistance' campaigns against the government in an attempt to secure the ending of discriminatory laws. Gandhi and his fellow resisters went peacefully (even willingly) to jail, but promises extracted from the government were broken and there was little or no amelioration of the conditions of Indians. By mid-1908 Gandhi had formulated the major elements that came to be associated with his name, both in South Africa and, later, in India. His campaign against particular discriminatory measures became a moral as much as a political challenge which aimed to prevent the further erosion of the status of Indians in the Transvaal, without altering the social structure of the country. Eventually, in 1910 there were new calls for action against discrimination.

Kallenbach, who played a central part in the events that followed, bought a farm 32 km south of Johannesburg to provide a refuge for the passive resisters and their families who had become destitute as a result of their previous imprisonment.[13] The farm was called Tolstoy Farm.

The Campaign of 1913

Morris Alexander had kept contact with Cape Indian leaders and his solidarity with the Indian community became most visible in 1912 when, on Gandhi's invitation, Gopal Krishna Gokhale visited South Africa, the first Indian nationalist leader to do so. Gokhale addressed meetings in the main centres of Indian residence where he laid stress on the dignity of the individual, and concentrated on the vulnerability of Indian merchants and on the £3 tax imposed on every Indian. In her biography of Morris, Enid, his second wife, records that he attended all the gatherings and, on occasion, took the chair, but his participation was probably confined to meetings in Cape Town. Kallenbach hosted Gokhale and would have been brought into further contact with Morris during the tour of the Cape.

In 1913 Gandhi called on volunteers to cross the border from Natal to the Transvaal. The response exceeded his expectations as his band of resisters was joined by hundreds of women, some carrying their babies; by miners from the Natal coal fields who came out on strike; and by large numbers of workers who walked off the sugar fields in protest against working conditions. The latter included many who had previously earned their release from indenture but had been forced to return to servitude during the recent depression. Besides Gandhi, who assumed the leading role, Polak assisted in organising the volunteers in Natal and Kallenbach did the same in the Transvaal. All went to jail, an event which Polak and Kallenbach, in particular, treated as a token of purification. There were also acts of bravery. In his autobiography Gandhi described an incident in Volksrust in which whites had threatened Kallenbach with physical violence. When challenged to a duel he had said:

> As I have accepted the religion of peace, I may not accept the challenge. Let him who will come do his worst with me. I am here to inform you that not all Europeans are ready as you are to lay violent hands upon innocent men. The Indians are not out to challenge your position as rulers. They do not wish to fight with you or to fill the country. They only seek justice pure and simple.[14]

He continued, declaring that the protest was against the unjust tax demanded of Indians. They would not fight with those who had gathered in Volksrust, but would enter the Transvaal even in the face of bullets. This, wrote Gandhi, left the audience abashed, and the man who had challenged Kallenbach to a duel became his friend and protector.[15]

Ruth was obviously impressed by Kallenbach's stance and on 18 December 1913 she wrote to him:

> Yesterday my husband and I talked of you, and now comes the news of your release. I do not think you will consider it a matter for congratulation, and yet those who admire and love you as we do cannot but be glad that a strenuous physical trial was not very long prolonged. I wrote to Gandhi weeks ago, just before his arrest, telling him how proud we were of you and him, and how entirely our wishes were with you in your splendid battle. I hope he got my letter.
>
> Indeed we admire you and are with you. And now we want to know cannot you come to us for a while, and rest, now or whenever you choose? We have taken this little comfortable house here [in St James] and put our own things into it. You can do exactly as you will, and be as quiet as you please. We should consider it an honour to have you.

Kallenbach's involvement in the Indian movement undoubtedly played a significant part in Ruth's political awakening. An impressionistic account of the memorable evening on which the Gandhis had stayed in the Alexander home appears in Enid Alexander's biography of Morris:

> During the evening, he spoke long and earnestly of his mission for his fellow men, and begged that his small band of supporters should continue to defend their interests. On retiring, Morris offered Gandhi the best bedroom in the house. He refused it and chose instead to sleep on the hard wooden floor of the front stoep [verandah]. He refused mattress, blankets, pillows, in fact anything which would make for his bodily comfort.[16]

On that evening Gandhi spoke at length to Ruth and expounded on his *ahimsa* or moral creed. Much of it was known to her and she found it in accord with the ethical standpoint of her father. The moral purity of the individual was all important in the Judaic philosophy – and only the moral man could intervene to help others. Gandhi undoubtedly spoke about *Satyagraha* and of the recent campaign in Natal. He might even have spoken of the strike called by the Indian labourers in the sugar fields and the Natal coal mines. It is obvious that Ruth was enthralled and it was this account to which she referred to in her letter to Gandhi in 1926.

Another Gandhi supporter with whom Ruth was acquainted was Betty Molteno. One address, by Betty, at a meeting of Indians in Durban in January 1914, to welcome the Rev C F Andrews, was minuted and published:

> After the Boer War I saw that Boer and Briton would have to unite, but would they try to do it the cost of their dark brothers? Broken-hearted I went to England. For eight long years I remained away from South Africa – in body – never in soul and spirit. And England and Europe have sent me back with this message to white South Africa: 'Open your hearts – your souls – to your brethren of colour'. We are in the 20th century. Rise to the heights of this glorious century. Try to comprehend the words of DuBois – that grand and sympathetic soul: 'The 20th century will be the century of colour'.[17]

Ruth had already heard DuBois's words, now they dovetailed with her sympathetic acceptance of Gandhi's philosophy.

After Gandhi left South Africa there was nobody capable of providing leadership for the Indian people and their political organisations languished. During the First World War problems of discrimination receded into the background for the Alexanders. Morris and Ruth, saddened as they were by the massacres in Europe, were patriotically pro-war, and their attention was given to providing soldiers' comforts. Olive Schreiner was disillusioned when she heard that Gandhi was providing an ambulance corps for the Allies, but Ruth had no such qualms: she undoubtedly approved of his action.

After the war there were several calls on Morris to intervene to protect Indian interests in the Transvaal and Natal. In 1919 Indian traders in the Transvaal petitioned Parliament complaining about their conditions and Morris was able to secure a select committee of the House to investigate their disabilities. Among the telegrams he received was one that expressed the feeling of the traders:

> We look up to you as champion of justice and fair play. Crave protection as voiceless citizens. Your timely assistance shall never be forgotten.[18]

In 1921 Muslims in Natal asked Morris to present a petition to the government about a lengthy dispute over the solemnisation of marriages under Muslim law. Syed Ali El Edroos, the religious officer in Gujarat, had written to General Smuts about the seriousness of the matter, saying:

> The Indians here have repeatedly petitioned the Government for the removal of the unwarranted stigma placed upon their religious and social customs, without avail. In some instances, the validity of their marriages have also been tested in courts of law, and with no better results.[19]

Ruth wrote most forcefully in the New York *Nation* in June 1926 about proposed legislation that would have a deleterious effect on Indians. Her article is presented more fully in Chapter 9. An extract is apposite here to indicate Ruth's new radicalism.

> The government aims to diminish, ultimately to eliminate the Indian population; it has proposed a measure restricting the areas in which Indians may live, thus establishing virtual ghettos; taking away the right to buy or lease land except in narrowly limited districts in Natal.

The future of the Indian community hung in the balance. Then on 23 April the governments of South Africa and India announced that they had agreed to hold a round-table conference, pending which the Asiatic Bill would be postponed. The South African government claimed that public opinion would demand a settlement which would safeguard the maintenance of 'Western' standards of life: the trend of the current government being directed to a harsher declaration of white supremacy. The position of the Indian community 'in the Transvaal and Natal remains pitiable enough,' Ruth wrote. 'The restrictions and the uncertainty of their future rests heavily on them.'

She went on to say that pitiable as the position of the Indians might be, that of the Africans was far worse. Ruth had widened the scope of her criticisms of South African whites and from there there could be no turning back. There were no further articles by Ruth on the problems facing the South African Indian community. Instead, she turned her attention to the new Bills that threatened the African people.

The Indians had by no means overcome the problems they faced. Their leaders turned to new tactics: deputations and petitions were sent to India; and mass meetings were called, although these were symbolic rather than practical. The Indian organisations had to maintain a position of leadership and impress on the various governments the seriousness of their complaints. It is doubtful whether Morris did very much for the Indian community in this new period of compromises, and this would have affected Ruth's ability to pursue the issue.

4
RUTH AND OLIVE

> In the twenty-two years I knew Ruth she lived in the continual awareness of Olive Schreiner's personality. This awareness lay at the deepest level of her thought and feeling, and above all, was present when hard decisions had to be made. Nor was it dependant on Olive's books, but on their friendship. This needs to be remembered in estimating the importance of anything Ruth has said about Olive. I saw Olive only twice, in the weeks before her death, both times at Heilbron [the Alexander home]. The only thing I remember of any importance is the fact of their friendship. I stress this because the hardest job for any biographer of Olive will be to get the feel of her very unusual personality, and in this respect anything that Ruth has said is first-hand evidence of an exceptional validity. They were close to one another from the time they met till Olive's death. I have written this, not only for yourself, but for anyone likely to handle the material.
>
> Ben Farrington[1]

The Meeting

Olive Schreiner (1855-1920) was in her fifties when Ruth first met her. She had behind her a successful novel, *The Story of an African Farm*, and her *Women in Labour*, a milestone in the writings about working women. There were also a somewhat less successful novel which had nevertheless won acclaim, *Trooper Peter Halket of Mashonaland*; several allegories; and a vast unfinished work in two parts, eventually published as *From Man to Man*.

Before she sailed for South Africa Ruth knew of some of this work – the rest she read later, some of it only after it was published posthumously.

A solitary child, Olive was reared by missionary parents in the Eastern Cape. She had no formal schooling but was taught to read at an early age by her mother, a facility which she built upon from readings in the ever-present Bible. It was said that she could recite large sections of biblical texts throughout her life – despite her rejection of its veracity – and her acquaintance with its language was reflected in all her writings.

Olive's novels contained much that was autobiographical. The story of childhood – and her early rebellion – is told in her earliest work, *Undine*. Her solitariness and her childhood experience, including the overwhelming impact of the death of her young sister, Ettie, were integral to her novels. The events in her life that appeared in her writings were summarised by the Cape Town writer, Dora Taylor:

> Olive Schreiner remembers early experiences with remarkable vividness. The 'wicked' queer little child, Undine, of her first novel, is herself. The woman Undine is a saintly shadow. The spiritual travail of the boy, Waldo, in *The Story of an African Farm*, is exactly her own; Lyndall, also in the same book, is herself. Most visible autobiography of all is the Prelude to her third novel *From Man to Man*. In it she relived her passionate maternal affection for her baby sister, Ettie, whose death when she was only ten, did so much to crystallise her religious doubts.[2]

There were few books at the mission station and Olive's secular readings only began when she was engaged as a governess at the age of fifteen. It was soon seen that she could not supervise the children's lessons and she was left to her own devices. Among the books she found there were Herbert Spencer's *First Principles* – which underpinned her agnosticism; Charles Darwin's *The Origin of Species;* Buckles's *History of Civilisation in England*; the writings of John Stuart Mill; and Carl Vogt's *Lectures on Man: His Place in Creation and in the History of the Earth*.[3]

It was during these long periods of solitariness that she began to write *The Story of an African Farm*, which so impressed London's literary world. Olive was lionised when her novel was published and it brought her into contact with people with whom she maintained ties throughout her lengthy sojourn in Europe. Among her closest friends were Eleanor Marx (Aveling), Havelock Ellis, Edward Carpenter and Karl Pearson. Ellis, with whom she had a particularly close relationship, was to play an important part in her own development and was the recipient of her letters – at times arriving daily – over many years. The contact brought her new ideas in contemporary scientific work, in literary developments, and in radical thinking.

From her new friends she derived a better-informed understanding of what was happening in Europe – an understanding which she applied to events throughout her life. A rebel since childhood, Olive learnt to hate all oppressive systems. With an astuteness that was rare she was also able to understand the shifting nature of oppression, allowing her to move her focus of concern as circumstances altered. The most crucial change in her views came a few years after the end of the war in South Africa when she ceased to sympathise with the Dutch and pointed to the colour question as central to the future of South Africa.

Her published works were few. There was no one simple reason for the tardiness with which she completed her books. Illness and pain were restricting and cannot be underestimated, but when confronted by injustice she found the energy to proceed immediately, as she did with *Trooper Peter Halket* – her allegorical condemnation of the rape of Mashonaland. Her one major failure, *From Man to Man*, was left incomplete not only because of illness, but because her didacticism conflicted with the story she aimed to tell. Instead of allowing her characters to act, Olive used them as vehicles for discussing the sexual role of women and for her condemnation of all injustice – and she could not find a way to combine message and narrative. Perhaps, as she said, she was searching for perfection and that stopped her completing what was projected as her *magnum opus*. She wrote in a letter to her husband, Cronwright (S Cronwright-Schreiner – the name he assumed when they married), in 1898:

> When you look at my hand when I am dead, you will be able to think that that hand never set one dot or one stroke

> on paper for the sake of money, and that, of all I have given to the world (poor as it is), there is not one word that stands there, which, if it had been in my power to better it, would not have been bettered. If I feel I have not expressed the exact truth that is in me in any line or sentence or book, it shall be destroyed.

In a talk on Olive Schreiner in 1929, Ruth maintained that all her works contained deficiencies. She was not a great novelist, but she was a great writer. *The Story of an African Farm*, and *From Man to Man* were great books which would inspire men and women in years to come.

Referring in that talk to the 'Wanderers' who had gathered around her father, Ruth said:

> When *The Story of an African Farm* came out they were all young and all poor and all rebels together, and one of them rushed into my father's little study with the book, so excited that they [he?] could hardly speak. They read bits of it aloud to one another, thrilling to the noble cadence of the prose, a prose that showed plainly the influence of the Authorised Version which, to the end of her life, she knew by heart as did few even of her generation. But there was more than the manner of books to enchant them; in much of its matter they of the later nineteenth century found the echo, only more articulately and more intensely voiced, of their own inner agonies, their own inner rebellions, so that in joyful wonder and gratitude their spirits cried out as they read, like Rebekah in *From Man to Man*, when she thinks of Socrates and Euripides, 'My own! My own!'

It is not known whether Solomon Schechter had also heard of Olive's radical defence of the Boer Republics against the British provocation that led to the South African War, about which he had been so caustic. But he might have heard of her defence of the Jews in 1905 and 1906.

In February 1905 Olive had written to the Social Democratic Federation of Cape Town, attacking the Russian state for encouraging the recent pogroms. One year later she sprang to the defence of the right of Jews to be in South Africa when she referred to the recognition of Yiddish as a European language. Morris had known of her interventions, which must have caused a stir in the Cape, and it is possible that he discussed them with the Schechter family when he touched on his own role in getting Yiddish accepted as a European language. It is also possible that his success in the battle for the acceptance of Yiddish had brought him to Olive's attention.

Olive had expressed herself in radical terms in her letter of 1905:

> Absent bodily, I shall yet be with you in thought, and yet more with those in far off Russia who are today carrying on that age-long war of humanity towards a larger freedom and a higher justice – a war which has been waged through the ages now by this people and then by that, now a small nation against one that would subjugate it, then by a class, then by a race; now for religious freedom, then for the right of free thought and free speech; but which, when looked at from the highest standpoint, has always been essentially one battle fought with one end – now with success and then with seeming failure, but always bringing nearer by minute and imperceptible degrees that time in the future when for a free and united humanity a truly human life shall be possible on earth.
>
> I regret especially that I cannot be at your meeting, because I should meet very many of our Russian Jews – members of that great race which has given to Europe its religion and the world some of its finest sons.
>
> As a South African, it is a matter of pride and joy that we have been able to give refuge and to accept among our citizens many whom oppression drove from their birthplace. If the great struggle of our fellows in Russia tends only to diminish their sufferings, then it will not have been in vain. I believe that in this movement in Russia [the revolution of 1905], we are witnessing the beginning of the greatest event that has taken place in the history of humanity during the last centuries.[4]

Her concern about the Jews in Eastern Europe and her contempt for Tsarist Russia was reiterated in an address in 1906 in defence of the right of Jews to enter the Cape.

> ... The colossal nature of the outrages now being perpetrated on the Jews in Russia, make it inevitable that vast numbers will seek to leave their native land, not singly, but almost in bodies; and it would be of incalculable benefit to them, if, instead of having to force their way into the already overpopulated countries of Europe, a free land of their own was open to them for their immediate settlement.
>
> ... But it is not only the exile Russian Jew, fleeing from the land of his birth who demands our thoughts today; rather it is that vast body of Jews remaining in their land and at this moment exposed to tortures and wrongs, which would have stood out [as] a blot on the very darkest page in the history of the middle ages.
>
> With regard to South Africa, I can only say that I am grateful that in the Bill now before our Parliament the language of the Russian Jew was not made a ground for excluding him.
>
> I have no higher ambition for my native land than this – that it should be truly said of her now and for all time to come, that no man, of whatever race, or colour, or creed, fleeing from religious or political persecution had ever failed to find a refuge and a home in her. I have no loftier ambition for her than this.[5]

'A Genius for Friendship'

Ruth met Olive before the end of 1909. From the outset the acquaintanceship blossomed into intimate friendship. They met as frequently as possible and their conversations – unfortunately unrecorded – brought them ever closer together. When Olive sailed for Europe, she was to declare that Ruth was the brightest person she knew in South Africa – a statement that must stand as a summary of their conversations.

A brief reference to Olive by Louis Herman, writing of her visits to his wife Ethel and himself, draws a vivid picture of the writer and gives an indication of the personality that Ruth would have known.

> An exceedingly vivacious little old lady who charmed and delighted us for hours at a time with her amusing narratives of personal experiences made more lively in the telling by sprightly gesture and humorous mimicry.
>
> She would make brilliant comments on public affairs and on famous persons whom she had met. Sometimes, in the course of our discussions of current topics, her old rebellion would blaze up with her championship of some unpopular cause and she would flash defiance of tyranny.
>
> I can picture her sitting in the lounge of our little house in Oranjezicht [Cape Town], thumping her knees with her clenched fists and declaring with all the energy of strong conviction: 'I'm a free thinker! I'm a Bolshevik! I'm a Sinn Feiner!' These bold declarations of partisanship with unpopular groups and unconventional ideologies bear a slightly different connotation today than when they were uttered fifty years ago.[6]

An account of that visit also appeared in the New York *Nation* in 1924, written by E.H. [Ethel Herrman]:

> She [Olive] talked the whole day amazingly on politics and art, literature and persons, world problems and famous people. She told tales of her experiences in London where she was always being suspected by boarding-house and hotel-keepers of being a German spy. She imitated comically all manner of people that she had come across.
>
> We enjoyed a remarkable sample that day of the charm of a vivid personality, her humour, her sprightly intellect, her broad sympathy and her attractive vivacity.[7]

Ruth was unreservedly a disciple and devotee . Her profound knowledge of Olive's writing was matched by a personal intimacy with this most outstanding of South Africans. Two years after Olive's death Ruth penned a personal tribute lamenting the sense of 'irreparable loss' felt by Olive's friends. The world had 'become infinitely poorer, shabbier, less splendid, since she had gone':

> The high privilege of her companionship, the liberal education of her conversation had become too vital a part of their lives, too real an inspiration for that. They learned more from her than from her books; she had a genius for friendship greater even, perhaps, than her genius for writing. To be much in her company was to grow ever more conscious of so rare, so rich a personality, so inexhaustible a courage, so beautiful an honesty, so noble a scorn of baseness, so all-compassionate a love, that a readjustment of values, a setting of one's whole spirit to a loftier harmony, becomes imperative to one's self-respect.[8]

The Radical Commentator

> Before and during the Boer War we were in cordial agreement. I sat on the platform with four other Englishwomen when she made her magnificent speech of protest against the annexation of the Transvaal and the Free State ... Much of her prophesy has since come true and South Africa is far more Dutch today than it was in 1902 ... Wherever she was she dominated the room. She was a born hater of shams and lover of liberty and truth, her passion for freedom dominated everything. She loathed the 'shoddy Imperialism that started about 1887 and continued till after her death but she saw vengeance coming.
>
> Julia F Solly,
> 'Notes on my Recollections of Olive Schreiner'
> Written for Ruth Schechter Alexander,
> [date unknown].

After years in which a stuffy conservatism had prevailed in Britain Schreiner's thoughts met with a response from a public that sought new views and perspectives. From her earliest days her thoughts had centred on the rights of individuals to self fulfilment. In her books Olive asserted the right of women to full independence and to work productively on equal terms with men, as well as the right of every person to religious freethinking. These were the messages she wished to transmit and her novels became the medium through which she transmitted them.

When he first encountered *The Story of an African Farm* at the turn of the century, wrote Louis Herrman in his reminiscence, he was not encouraged to read it and, since it was 'considered improper reading for young people' it was banned from some British provincial libraries. At the time the book was considered:

> A powerful plea, in the form of a simple, quiet story, for independent belief, thought and action, on the part of youth, against accepted conventions, moral, religious, social and domestic.[9]

In the book Olive explored the experiences of her childhood, among them the deep depression she had gone through when her baby sister had died. The book also reflects ideas she absorbed from her reading and made her own, but there were no boundaries to her thoughts and on some issues she expressed views that were far in advance of contemporary thinking.

Although her *Thoughts on South Africa* was only published posthumously as a book, chapters had been published in the closing years of the nineteenth century. It revealed a strong bond of sympathy for the Boer Republics in their stand against Britain's demands which led inexorably to the South African War.

Olive and Cronwright had campaigned on behalf of the Boer cause and railed against the British government's provocations which had led President Kruger of the South African Republic – or Transvaal – to declare war. Might, and capitalism, had prevailed, and the former Republic was incorporated in the larger South Africa. However it soon became clear that the one-time enemies would work together to rule the country and that there would be no dispensation for the Africans or Indians. Olive wrote to Cronwright saying that she no longer cared for the Boer cause. 'They are more than able to take care of themselves. But the Natives are always with me.'[10]

Despite an early ambivalence in her attitude to blacks, she looked ahead before the war and saw potential disaster. In a letter to John X Merriman in 1897 she wrote:

> It is the far future of Africa during the next 25 or 50 years which depresses me. I believe we are standing on the top of a long downward slope. We shall reach the bottom at last, probably amid the horrors of a war with our native races, then not the poor savage, but generous races whom we might have bound to ourselves by a little generosity and sympathy ... but a fierce, much-brutalised race, who will have their own.[11]

By 1906 her attitude was undergoing a decided change. Emmeline Pethick Lawrence, a British suffragette, gave her a copy of W E B DuBois's *The Souls of Black Folk*[12] and, like Betty Molteno, she responded to its message. This became obvious in 1908 when the editor of the *Transvaal Leader* submitted twelve questions to Olive for her consideration. On 22 December the answers were printed in the paper. On the 'Native Question' she wrote in terms that must have seemed revolutionary at the time:

> I hold the Native Question to be the root question in South Africa, and as is our wisdom in dealing with it, so will be our future. The Natives are the makers of our wealth, the great basic rock on which our State is founded, our vast labouring class. If to us he is not a man, but only a tool; if dispossessed entirely of the land for which he now shows that large aptitude for peasant proprietorship for the lack of which many great nations are decaying; if we force him permanently in his millions into the locations and compounds and slums of our cities, obtaining his labour

> cheaper, but to lose what the wealth of five Rand would not return to use; if, uninstructed in the highest forms of labour, without the rights of citizenship, his own social organisation broken up, without our having aided him to participate in our own; if unbound to us by gratitude and sympathy, and alien to us in blood and colour. It is before all things imperative that the rights and liberties of the Native should be fully safeguarded ... If we reduce this vast mass to the condition of a great seething, ignorant proletariat – then I would rather draw a veil over the future of this land.[13]

Wherever she saw poverty, exploitation or repression Olive spoke out publicly, or in writing, for the victims. In September 1899 just before returning to South Africa, she wrote to Carpenter excited over the strike of the dockers demanding the right to unionise, and commenting on the new spirit of hope on the faces of the workers. 'Isn't the strike splendid? You ought to see the East End now.'[14]

Her support for the workers continued in South Africa. Asked for a message in support of shop assistants, she sent a letter which was read to a demonstration (c1905).

> I am glad to hear of your meeting in Johannesburg ... because it shows that at last, we, in South Africa are ... waking up to take our place among other civilized nations in the great struggle for healthier and sounder conditions of labour. I am glad that in your meeting men and women are combined ... I am especially glad that women workers are taking their place ... because as a most poorly paid and heavily pressed section of workers ... it is especially necessary that women workers will learn solidly to combine.[15]

Then came the shooting, in 1913, by the (British) Dragoons, of men and women who gathered to hear the announcement of a general strike on the Witwatersrand. As a consequence some twenty men and women were killed and between two hundred and four hundred left wounded. Olive's most stringent attack on the government was made in a message sent to a protest meeting in Cape Town:

> [The massacre] should have served to show the mass of our people in this country the true conditions under which we are living. The death of those innocent persons will not have been in vain, if we make the light it has shed on our position as citizens of South Africa one which will dominate our future actions, political and social.

In a prescient letter to Carpenter she wrote:

> If they shoot us down in this way the moment *white* labourers strike, what will it be whenever the natives move? And they are bringing in more and more oppressive laws against the latter. We have just passed a terrible native Land Bill – the worst bit of work we have done for years.[16]

In line with her new understanding Olive adopted a radical approach to the demand for women's suffrage because it was intended to extend it only to white women. In December 1910 she had stormed out of a meeting of the Women's Enfranchisement League to which she had been invited. To explain her action she sent a copy of the movement's leaflet to Ruth with the words 'the vote to them [the women] on the same terms as men' underlined. She doubly stressed 'them' and wrote across the text: 'It was *not* a personal matter that made me leave the society. The [vote for the] women of the Cape Colony *all* women of the Cape Colony. These were the terms on which I joined.'

With no space for more on the face of the leaflet Olive wrote on a clean sheet: 'And no one had the right without letting me know, or giving me a *hint* so that I might either come down and fight the matter or resign.'

Ruth accepted Olive's lead on this question and during her trip to the United States in 1913 spoke at several meetings on the suffrage question. Three newspaper cuttings in the Morris Alexander papers record Ruth's participation. On 6 June 1913 the *New York Tribune* reported her contribution at a meeting at which, in contrast to the opinion of a Mrs Harriot Blatch that 'women should waylay every man and with sweet, gentle, persuasive methods win him over to their cause' Ruth was trenchant:

> I am sick, dead sick, of indirect influence. I believe that for her own sake, for her child's sake, a woman should be fearless and direct. I have canvassed for my husband and I know that queer things must be done in politics sometimes, but I do think we women should avoid the danger of the lie – the white lie, to which we are too much given – and what does indirect influence mean if not a lie?

Ruth had begun her talk with a refutation of 'Mrs Something-or-other Dodge, I can' t remember her first name', who had misquoted a statement of Olive's on bottles for babies. Indignantly she said it was ridiculous to make such assertions. She then continued:

> It is my good fortune to know Olive Schreiner well, and a more absolutely selfless, a more entirely good woman I have never seen. Quite unconsciously she is all the things the rest of us are striving to be. Though she has had more than most people of suffering, both physical and mental, she is the serenest being I know.

Ruth then described the fight for the women's franchise in South Africa, but the report carried no reference to the rift on the colour question. The second report was in the *Newark Morning Star* of 8 June which carried an account of Ruth's talk at the Miriam Verein of the Oheb Shalom Congregation. This time she remembered Mrs Dodge's first name, and voiced her contempt for a speaker who could say 'that suffrage would unsex women' and then declare that the present suffrage question 'was only a mere excuse for the women to carry on a flirtation'.

Ruth spent a large part of her address showing that a woman's interest and involvement in politics would not be detrimental to the family, and that it could even cement relations between husband and wife through shared interests.

The *Newark Evening News* that day also covered the meeting and devoted its report to Ruth's answers to questions that were raised. She handled issues such as religious instruction for children, duties in the home, and so on, if and when the franchise was granted. Inevitably the question of the vote for Negro women was raised. Ruth's decisive answer, which echoed the sentiments of Olive Schriener, earned applause from the audience:

> Since we here are nearly all of the Jewish faith, I am sorry that this question has been asked. We who know what social ostracism is perhaps more than other races would hardly hesitate about extending to the negro woman equal rights with ourselves. If the negro man is intelligent enough to vote, so is the negro woman.

Olive and the War

Olive was in Germany at the spas, finding some relief from the pains that left her prostrate, when the war broke out. She managed to get back to Britain where she remained a staunch pacifist, isolated from fellow thinkers. She broke from most of the suffragist movement because of their ardent support for the war, and was angry with Gandhi when he recruited an Indian ambulance corps for the British war effort.

Here too Ruth reflected her opposition, condemned the newspapers for the 'lies' they published, and bemoaned her isolation. Added to her general opposition she also condemned Britain for its alliance with Tsarist Russia, the most anti-Semitic of all European powers. She welcomed the defeat of the Russian army and believed that the persecution of the Jews would be halted. The revolution of 1917 gained her approbation and she was enthusiastic when British dockers refused to load ships taking arms to stifle it. It seems doubtful whether Ruth accepted Olive's anti-war position, but one episode in 1920, a few months before Olive's death, remained with Ruth throughout her life. She described it in the printed version of her talk on Olive in 1929. Summoned to meet her mentor early in the morning because something had happened that 'made her very happy', Ruth hurried across Cape Town:

> 'Well?' I said. 'Haven't you seen the papers?' she answered. 'Didn't you see that Denikin is out of Russia? Don't you see what it means?' And then for an hour, with flashing eyes and in full tones she told me what it did mean – the lifting of the blockade, the ability of the Russians to get hold again of food and medicine and machinery, and to begin to get their house in order.

Two further messages were quoted in that talk by Ruth. The first referred to a letter Olive had written to her in 1916 (which has apparently been lost). Her subject was the Jews – from the prophet Isaiah, to Jesus and Spinoza – who were the great teachers of peace and internationalism, and most of the great international Socialists of Europe, from Karl Marx up and down; the Jew who had suffered torture but had stood firm in his ideals and his own sense of right – why should he forsake his part today?

The last message that Ruth quoted was taken from a posthumous article, 'The Dawn of Civilisation', which was to have been the introductory chapter of an anti-war book. Printed in the London *Nation and Athenaeum* on 26 March 1921 it summed up, said Ruth, 'as no words of mine could', Olive Schreiner's consistent attitude to life:

> You cannot be willing to alter the vast world outside of you; you cannot, perhaps, cut the lash from one whip; you cannot stop the march of even one armed man going out to kill; you cannot, perhaps, strike the handcuff from one chained hand; you cannot even remake your own soul so that shall be no tendency to evil so the great world rolls on, and you cannot reshape it; but this one thing only you can do – in that one small, minute, almost infinitesimal spot in the Universe, where your will rules, there, where there alone you are as God, strive to make that you hunger for real! No man can prevent you there. In your own heart

> strive to kill out all hate, all desire to see evil come even to those who have injured you or another; what is weaker than yourself try to help; whatever is in pain or unjustly treated and cries out, say 'I am here! Little, weak, feeble, but I will do what I can for you'. That is all you can do; but do it; it is not anything! And then this feeling came to me, a feeling it is not easy to put into words, but it was like this: You are also part of the great Universe; what you strive for, something strives for; and nothing in the universe is quite alone; you are moving on towards something ... somewhere, some time, some place – even on earth.

It is not possible to exaggerate the influence of Olive on Ruth. Her many reviews in the South African press and the New York *Nation* show again and again the convergence between her position and that of her friend. This was a meeting of like minds in which the warmth and wisdom of the older woman met with the spontaneity and growing understanding of the younger. Ruth visited Olive, confided in her, and in those days conveyed the happiness that she had found in her domestic affairs. They were friends socially and in their strong convictions. The letters that are available indicate the empathy between them. Ruth responded warmly to the growing friendship. Verse she wrote was sent to Olive for her pleasure and, hopefully, for approval.

The values shaped in the thirteen years of their friendship became the touchstone of everything Ruth did after Olive's death – although it led to an adulation on Ruth's part that seems excessive and *gauche*. The essays Ruth wrote on Olive, and the reviews of her posthumously published works, must be understood against their close relationship.

First Encounters

Ruth's activities as writer, singer, and lecturer brought her renown in Cape Town. With the wide knowledge of Jewish lore acquired from her father, as a keen observer of local conditions, and with her insatiable search for the latest novels, she always had something new to say. Her talks were so stimulating that she drew people to herself. It is said that

Olive heard her speak and, fascinated, arranged a meeting. If that is true – and there is no other account of how they met – it is not certain when this might have happened. Olive's first letter to Ruth was dated December 1909 but they may have met many months earlier. Whatever the date of their first meeting, their mutual friendship was remarkably short. Olive left for Europe in 1913 and only returned in mid-1920, just months before her death.

During that brief period, however, she directed Ruth to new problems and supplanted the powerful influence once exerted on her by her father. In an introduction to three of Ruth's longer articles, including her 1929 talk on Olive, prepared for publication but never published, Ben Farrington wrote:

> If her father had hitherto been the main influence on Ruth's development Olive Schreiner was now to become so. Both were outsize personalities with something dynamic, not to say demonic, about them in the moral fervour by which they were driven. In this atmosphere, which frightened some people, Ruth breathed freely. But the role to which his genius and circumstances cast Solomon Schechter, namely to recall world Jewry from the shallows of modern civilization to the spiritual treasures of three thousand years of Jewish history, was not for Ruth. She was a child of her own age. Its problems – the emancipation of women; the struggle against colour-prejudice, race-prejudice, and particularism of every kind; the overcoming of poverty; the pursuit of peace – were those to which her spirit turned; and in all of these she found guidance, where so many others of her own generation had done, in Olive Schreiner.

Ruth also paid tribute to Olive in an article, published posthumously in *University Forward*, March 1942, which she completed just before her own death:

> There are those who, though it is almost a generation since her death, still feel grief for her loss, love of her personality,

> a sharp pity and anger for the avoidable pain and frustration of her life, an awed and continuous recognition of her unique quality ... The quality of greatness is not easy to define; but it is unmistakable when encountered. In the case of Olive Schreiner one was always aware that the little stumpy woman with the magnificent eyes was possessed of a dynamic force, an invincible courage, a code of cast-iron as regards her own actions, an understanding though not condonation of other people's codes and their translation into daily living, that set her apart. So likewise did the fact that her actions and her writings followed inevitably from convictions, no matter what the cost. This was often extremely heavy, since in the course of her life it happened over and over again that the price was her isolation from those she specially loved, and a resulting isolation dangerous as well as agonising to herself.

Letters

Ruth's first letter from Olive contained instructions for getting to the residence of Betty Molteno where they were to meet. The letter concluded with the words 'I enjoyed my evening with you so much. I wish I had known you before. Now perhaps I shall not be [?].' There was no reference to what they might have discussed, nor are there available references to the discussions that took place when they met at Miss Molteno's.

The first page of the next letter (including the date) appears to have gone astray. Starting on page 2, Olive wrote about her niece Dot. 'She's just 22; all life and intellect and sympathy and charm. I am sure you will care for one another ... She is my special treasure. I wish we could go together on Tuesday, but I'll be there waiting for you when you come.'

Then came a special communication. On 30 November 1910 Olive wrote from Graaff-Reinet, exclaiming enthusiastically over photographs sent by Ruth of one of her daughters and of Solomon Schechter. She wrote that she was much better and added a note that proved to be significant in shaping perspectives over the coming years:

> I am going down into the town of Graaf Reinet this week to attend a large woman's suffrage meeting. I'm not going to speak, but they've asked me to be present. I will send you a report of the meeting.
>
> I wish I could see you and have a long talk with you, darling Ruth. It will be very long before I see Cape Town again I think. Good bye.

If the report of the meeting was ever sent to Ruth, there is no copy available. But among the letters is the printed leaflet (not dated) from the Women's Enfranchisement League with Olive's statement of refutation on it. Olive stood almost alone in her insistence on the enfranchisement of black women – the few who sided with her were isolated and unable to influence the course of events. Ruth was one of those who took the matter up in 1930 when the vote was given to white women.

There is a gap of more than eighteen months between this letter and the next in the collection. But it was not a period of neglect. Ruth thought constantly of her 'mistress, sister, friend' to whom she penned a poem of adulation which is preserved in the South African journal, *The State,* of July 1911.[17] Olive wrote again on 11 June 1912 (from Newlands, Cape Town). First came news of deaths of her husband's mother and two of her sister's step grandchildren.

> I seem to have been living in such an atmosphere of suffering that I'm not good company I'm afraid.
>
> I was so glad dearest to see you looking so bonnie. You and that dear fine little son are the brightest things I've seen here since I came.
>
> If I can I'll come and see you again.

Referring to deaths (unspecified) Olive seemed to have put behind her some of the racist remarks that tripped so easily off the pens of writers in South Africa:

> It was very sweet of your husband to say he wanted to send a contribution to that cot in the hospital which some temperance people speak of. But all of *us* feel that if anything were raised in her memory it ought to be something connected with natives and Coloured people she loved so and had worked for since she was a little girl, or for temperance work among them. I think she had rather my horror of hospitals.
>
> But of course those people who propose it mean very well and kindly. But none of us like the idea.

Olive concluded by advising Ruth to rest for a lengthy period after childbirth. Women who took long rests 'kept perfect health'.

On 16 July 1912 Olive wrote from De Aar (in the Cape), asking about Solly (Ruth's son), and wanting to know if Ruth was still going to America in 1912. Cron was away at Brits, and she was alone in the house with the animals. Miss Greene had informed her that she and Miss Molteno had both visited Ruth, and had said (ironically) that the abilities of Ruth's two daughters were laudatory.

Olive's next communication, dated 14 February 1914, came from Le Grand Hotel et d'Alissio on the Italian Riviera. In it she described the excruciating pains she had experienced – a repetition of those she had had in Muizenberg a year before 'when you [Ruth] were so sweet and good to me'. Doctors in London had diagnosed kidney stones, and the local doctor had said the same. The pain had lasted for six days and during that time: 'The dear women visitors in this hotel were so good to me. For six nights they took it in turns to sit up with me ... The agony has been something indescribable like the worst labour pains and he said he was afraid of giving large doses of opium on account of the heart being so weak'.

Olive had been given 'strong medicines to try to dissolve the stone'. She had now recovered and gone downstairs, where she was 'quite touched by the welcome everyone gave me even the waiter'. She had 'met nothing but kindness and love' since she had landed in Europe. A German lady had hired a carriage and taken her for a long drive. 'It is wonderful they should all be so kind when I think that a month ago I had not seen any of them. I shall go on to Florence at the end of the month. But while I feel weak I shrink from leaving Alissio where I have so many kind friends.'

The next letter, written from the Hotel Augusta Victoria, Bad Nauheim, in mid-June 1914, conveyed praise that must have heightened the regard Ruth felt for her friend and mentor: 'Darling Ruth', it began, 'it was just lovely to get your letter yesterday.' Olive, obviously replying to Ruth, said she should send any poems that had been written, to her. Continuing, she wrote:

> Will [Schreiner] and I were talking about Jews with some people here, who like many Germans are not fond of Jews – and Will said 'Well the most gifted ... person we have in South Africa is a Jewess ['meaning you' said Olive in a marginal note] – which delighted me. I don't think your mother or sister could rejoice as much – I'm sure they couldn't rejoice more than I do when I see people appreciate you. And you are going to develop so much still, intellectually and in other ways. I think you will go on developing all your life. Quite the most refined and good looking people in this hotel are Jews, and yet they talk about our hotel 'swarming with Jews', as [if] they were a source of evil.

The letter reported on consultations with three doctors and their gloomy diagnoses of Olive's ailments.

When Olive wrote, in July or August 1915, it was war time and there were no safe havens on the Continent of Europe. She had moved to Llandrindod, 'a quiet little health resort on the hills in the centre of Wales'. 'I like the air here, and am feeling most wonderfully stronger since I came, and so thankful to be out of London. It's not got a little little bit left of the old London.'

After writing about friends who were ill, Olive spoke with great concern about the dreadful news emanating from the warfront in Flanders: 'One dreads day by day as it passes for the terrible news that may come.'

> I wonder how the election is going to go at the Cape? One learns so little from the newspapers here, and that principally lies. I am glad to hear from the newspaper that at least Andrews [of the International Socialist League][18] and some of the working men and [are?] for peace and not playing into the hands of those who work to plunge South Africa deeper into the war in Europe.
>
> I am so thankful the Russian autocracy is not doing well. It may mean freedom at last for the Jews and the Russian people if there is again a great demonstrative uprising.
>
> I hope I shall have news of poor old Kallenbach soon.[19]

Olive wrote again from Llandrindod on 22 August 1915. It was a letter in two parts – the beginning (and most of what was written overleaf) written as is usual, horizontally down the page, leaving a fair margin on the left hand side, then filling the margin and written at right angles to the main text abutting on the main body of the letter, and then written abruptly at the top of the letter, still perpendicular to what had been written already and almost obscuring the previous writing.

The main body of the letter was about Ruth's children. Olive wrote that the boy *must* be 'trained in unselfishness' because 'all life teaches him he is a superior being'. Then overleaf she commented on two of Ruth's poems which she had enjoyed, and wrote in the margin that 'I think your verse has greatly gained in music'.

Accompanying the letter was a note from Mrs Havelock Ellis to whom Olive had sent the poems for comment. In her reply Mrs Ellis said:

> Thank you for sending us these charming poems to read. H[avelock] likes No 1 best & I like No 2 – partly because it is the idealistic description of a friend of mine. The No 1 is like a soft smooth breeze and has a lilt of Yeats at his best to my mind.

The marginal note that was appended might have been an afterthought, but it was one which was so central to Olive's thoughts about Russia that she felt it had to be included. What Olive wrote (in 1915) displayed a prescience that must have been rare.

> I am so glad Russia is being beaten. It may mean freedom for Russia, but I fear England and France will come to the autocracy's help again as they did after the Japan war and crush down the movement for freedom. If only Finland would rise and just proclaim herself freed.

There were no letters in the collection for 1916 – although Ruth received at least one which she quoted in her 1929 talk – nor in the first eight months of 1917. There were three postcards sent from London, short and devoted to family affairs. On 30 September 1916, Olive said she had been feeling better since she had returned to London. She asked if there was any chance of Ruth coming to England soon and requested to be informed if Ruth's mother came because she would like to visit her. The second card, sent in January 1917, spoke of a bitter winter which was worse than anything she had ever experienced 'in all my long years in England'. She also said that Kallenbach had written to say that he was leaving for the continent. He had asked after Ruth.

The card of April 1917 was not very informative, but it referred to plans that Ruth had mentioned in a letter, the nature of which is unknown:

> I thank you for the poem and your dear letter. I hope all you wish and plan will come to pass.
>
> Oh, Ruth, how beautiful it would be to see you, even for a few hours. I often see Miss Molteno she's almost the only person I ever see. It is a great joy to me that she is here. My nephew Oliver has gone to India, the girls are still nursing in France.

In a letter written on 22 September 1917 from London Olive wondered why Ruth had been silent for such a long period. Was it because of the death of Ruth's mother – of which she had heard – or was Ruth expecting another child? In the note that followed Olive expressed fear that her letter, written without a date, might not reach its destination. She sent instructions that Ruth should address her reply to a London bank with an enclosed envelope addressed to her residence. They were living under martial law and this required caution.

From Olive's final marginal comment it seems that Ruth had written a pro-war letter. Olive commenced with no reference to family matters and none of the usual inquiries about the children. She began abruptly and some of the sentences seem incomplete, indicating that she was in pain or in great distress.

> My darling Ruth, it is all so awful. Oh Ruth it's not the fighting it's the lying – the injustice. That is the worst of it all & you in South Africa hear no truth only the lying news they send out to the papers there. Oh the wickedness of this league of ours with Russia. We have just carted through England from northern Russia a *vast* body of Russians to fight in France because we and the French together are only able continually to retreat
>
> Ruth is it coward[ly] for one wishes so one died before one saw this day. For three years England has been in league with the Russian government, the oppressors of their own & all other peoples. I feel so utterly alone here.
>
> Oh it is wicked so wicked, and people of whom one would expect better things are countenancing all this wickedness because they are *afraid*. We ought never to have made a league with France and Russia.
>
> Good bye dear, Olive.

In the margin Olive wrote: 'Ruth, *you*, can't think it right we should aid Russia in this terrible war?

A letter followed on 3 December 1917, wishing Ruth and her family a happy new year. Ruth had not written for a long time and, because she had been unwell when last she had written Olive was concerned. She asked about the possible death of Ruth's mother and raised one further matter. Had Ruth seen her 'little allegory [on war] in the

Fortnightly Review of November'. Before closing Olive asked whether Ruth's husband would like her to see his mother [then on holiday in England]. If so, could she have her address.

A postcard without a date, but probably written during war time, does throw some light on the long gaps between available letters: 'I long for just a word from you Ruth, my darling child. I wrote to you *but the letter was in the ship that was lost* [my emphasis]. Do tell me about yourself. I wish I were near you. The cold dark winter is beginning to close in about us.'

On 1 April 1917 Olive wrote on a card that she was expecting a visit from Frank [Schechter]. Besides commenting on appalling weather, Olive said she hoped 'it goes well with your studies'.

In July 1918 an urgent card was sent by Olive to Ruth in which she wrote that she was feeling anxious. 'I never hear from you nor of you ... I've never heard from you since you sent me that lovely little poem so long ago.' There was also concern about the health of Ruth and her family. A second card in November 1918 was even more urgent: 'How does it come I never never hear from you. The last letter I had was when you sent me that lovely little poem – the best thing you ever wrote. Do write and tell me about you all. I never forget you.'

Ruth must have responded but Olive's replies were either lost at sea, or she was silent because she was unwell.

On 14 December 1918, having just heard from Ruth, Olive wrote again. In the previous letter Ruth had said that she was without power or energy, and not having heard from anyone else, she had been worried. She wrote about friends and family but complained about her isolation:

> I'm leading a strangely solitary life here, seldom see any one, often for six or seven days exchange a word with no human creature but the girl who brings up my coals. I sometimes see Miss Molteno but she is very absorbed in her theosophy. She's a dear creature.

There was one sentence in the letter that is important in trying to follow what Ruth was doing, but such is the difficulty of having only one side of this lengthy correspondence that it remains unexplained. Cryptically,

Olive wrote: 'I am so glad that you are working at the University[5]. I am sure it is so wise.' Without further elucidation it is not possible to ask whether Ruth was studying for a degree, writing a dissertation, or just meeting members of the staff.

After another long silence Olive wrote in September 1919. Ruth had informed her that she would be stopping in London, presumably on her way to New York. It was an excited letter at the top of which there was a 'post'-script: 'I long to see my friends in Africa, but you most of all.' Then came the main body of the letter:

> Darling Ruth, It will be so beautiful if you come. It seems to (*sic*) good to be true. Don't wait too long or you mayn't see me. I will do all I can to get you a room in the house in which I am, & if that can't be, near by. Rooms are almost impossible to get in London now. *Let me know as soon as you can when to expect you.*
>
> I have written to Mrs Rostowsky at the address you gave.

The remainder of the letter was given over to news of younger members of Olive's family.

On 2 May 1920, in response to a cable from Ruth, Olive wrote;

> I do hope you have had a nice companion in your cabin and that you will enjoy your clear sea. You don't know what your visit was to me Ruth, & you gave up so much time to me that you could have spent in other more enjoyable ways in your short stay here. I seem always looking for you to come back. The lilacs you brought the last day are as lovely and fresh as if they had just been picked.

Ten days later Olive wrote again:

> It was a joy to get your letter from Madeira [where ships to South Africa stopped briefly]. When you went I felt as if

> the sun had gone down. Your brother-in-law sent me some lovely prints: I'm sure I would like him and understand him.
>
> I have been much worse since you went dear. It sometime seem[s] doubtful to me whether I shall ever get to the Cape – but oh I want to try. I meant to be so brave when I came over & die here quite alone where I could trouble no one.
>
> I can't face another winter here – I *can't*.
>
> I shan't trouble any one in Africa. If I get bad I'll go to that nursing home in Tamboers Kloof [a suburb of Cape Town].
>
> If there was any chance of my getting to Italy I wouldn't go out [to South Africa] – but I can't travel alone now & they are going to have endless revolutions here [in Italy] & now I can't walk, I can't manage things. Otherwise I would just go to Alasio (*sic*) & stay there to the end.
>
> My one terror is that any of my dear fellow humans should feel me a burden before I go – but one can't determine when your life shall end you must fight it through. When there's nothing else left you can still defy fate quite to crush you.
>
> I am so glad the working men here have refused to load the ship with guns to fight the Russian Republic. The Poles are not doing it of themselves, poor things; the French & we are urging them on. I am so thankful the English liberals have taken the matter up. Through all the dark and agony of this time I see far, far off a better & brighter day arriving.

Ruth did visit and seems to have sent Olive a jacket after the visit. A card was duly sent in June 1920.

> My lovely long jacket has come. Such a priceless comfort it will be to me. I am sailing on August the 13th. But its [I'm?] nervous. I have such a horrible foreboding feeling

> about the voyage and about going out. A kind of *horror*, but I *can't* stay here another month and there are your dear faces shining in South Africa. My dear love to you.

The two remaining postcards and two letters (all undated) were written after Olive returned to the Cape. The cards related to visits and, besides their customary warmth, do not add to our knowledge of Olive. In one letter, written when Ruth and Morris were on holiday, Olive wrote:

> I hope you are having a lovely change and that your husband is rested. Give him my very kind regards.
>
> I am missing seeing you so. There are always a lot of people coming and going here, but when I go to see sister – in [?] – one can have real nice long chats on her verandah. I want to have a real long talk with you about so many things.
>
> What was the name of the young man I met at your house. He seemed such a delightful person. A young student was talking about him here yesterday. Says he is so remarkable. The students seem impressed by him.
>
> What is Mrs Moskowitz [Movsovis?] address? I don't feel I can do anything more for her or him in the way of finding work. I could never find anything as good as that post in the Standard Bank. I think the best thing they could do is to go home to England. Life here is only good for people who have the strength to rough it for the past years...
>
> I expect I shall have to go and live here in the end as I can't get rooms at Tamboers Kloof.
>
> *Do come* and see me *here* as soon as you can spare time.

There are four remaining pages, without any obvious beginnings.

> I am influenced not at all by any ambition for you. Every year as I grow older fame and success in the usually

appraised manner seems to me of less and less value. And the ambition I have not for myself I have not for those I love. If any other man seemed more likely to lead to the ends we desire …

After I had finished *Peter Halket* I spent three days and nights almost entirely without sleep pacing up and down my verandah, trying to decide whether I should publish it or not. I believed that Rhodes and the Chartered Company would proceed against me; and I felt sure that the matter would kill me, as it did to a very large extent.

There was all the other possible future work I might do; my box of manuscripts lying unrevised, and on the other hand the great doubt whether whatever the book meant to me, it might have any effect in increasing justice at all commensurate with the price I was paying. At last the matter decided itself within me. Don't think I meant anything supernatural takes place; though that decision which one's nature gives where one tries to silence the lower and purely personal interest and to allow the higher elements in it to adjudicate among themselves *is* what the ancients called the 'voice of God', and *is* so to a certain extent; because it is the highest and for each soul within itself, the most ultimate injunction it can ever receive, It was Socrates' little demon, and is undoubtedly in every one who lays himself open to be guided by it. And this one thing is certain, that when one acts in obedience to it, one never regrets even though absolute failure in the eyes of the world follow in it. A man may be mistaken, but when he has acted under such guidance: he knows he has followed the highest course open to *him*: and he never looks back.

Ruth's Writings on Olive Schreiner

The search for Ruth Schechter Alexander has become, in part, a search for her published writings. That information, lost with the disappearance of her letters, could, hopefully, be partly replaced by the many articles that appeared in newspapers and journals in South Africa and the US. Those discovered in libraries present some of Ruth's ideas through her years in South Africa.

In selecting extracts from some of her articles, and particularly her reviews of Olive's works, I have had to resist the temptation of reprinting whole articles. There is so much wisdom and understanding in her writing, more particularly after 1920, that it has not been easy to decide what should be excluded. To have included more would have made the book top heavy, and yet I had my regrets when confronted by whole paragraphs that seemed so worthy of inclusion.

Olive's impact on Ruth was revealed in the publication of a poem in an early period of their friendship. Ruth, obviously overwhelmed by this renowned writer and conversationalist, must have spoken about Olive, privately and publicly, but there is no indication that she wrote about Olive, or her publications, until after her death. This poem was the one exception. Entitled 'To Olive Schreiner', it was printed in *The State,* in July 1911.

> Sometimes of evening when that God is good,
> In that still wonder-hour that comes between
> The sunset and the lighting of the stars,
> I sit and watch the pageant of the skies.
> Then when the last rose-flush has come and gone,
> And all the world is violet and grey
> Save where a yellow light dies slowly down –
> A sudden glory in the purple air,
> And lo! the evening star.
> Three times or four
> Within the passing of a hundred years
> A soul is born, serene, light-bearing, pure,
> Even as the evening star. One such art thou:
> And even as the lonely mariner,
> Steering a fragile bark through unknown seas,
> Looks up and sees a comfort and a hope
> In the soft radiance gleaming from the sky,

So all the silent band of lonely souls
Groping in darkness through age-frozen seas
Of prejudice and ignorance and wrong
To purer air and freedom, light and truth,
Look up to thee, their mistress, sister, friend.
Olive, beloved, we have drained thy strength,
Thy fresh, best years, thy wondrous heart and brain,
Thy very life-blood, for our help and need.
What gift is great enough to render back?
Ah! What but this – that even I may bring
A humble offering for love of thee;
Ah! But what this – to work our whole lives long
And never cease, that justice may prevail,
That truth and mercy may yet be the law,
That womanhood and manhood may be free
To live and grow and make their destinies
Even as the Lord who made them meant they should.

The Posthumous Publications

From February 1923 to March 1929 Ruth wrote reviews of Olive's posthumously published books. The first of these (*Stories, Dreams and Allegories*) alerted her readers to the carelessness with which the books had been edited, and indeed to the way in which Olive was being belittled by Cronwright's failure to follow out her instructions. By the time the *Letters* and Cronwright's *Biography* appeared Ruth was alarmed by the selectivity, the omission and the additions that could not, in her opinion, be justified. There is no doubt that Ruth's reviews would have been critical, irrespective of the offending editorship, but she went further and set herself up as the guardian of the writings that Olive's reputation deserved.

Ruth had an advantage in writing the reviews. She knew Olive's work as did few others in the land. She could add details about Olive as a person, could compare texts, could detect errors in the selection or omission of material, and was able to set the record right when other reviewers failed to recognise gross errors. In Ruth, Olive had more than a friend; she had a critic who could act as a champion and a watchdog against an unscrupulous editor, a disloyal 'friend' (Havelock Ellis) and an unwary readership.

Stories, Dreams, and Allegories

The first collection of works published by Cronwright after Olive's death was a set of five stories entitled *Stories, Dreams, and Allegories*. In her review in the *Cape Times* on 24 February 1923, Ruth commenced with a tribute to 'a personality so rich and noble':

> For those who loved her ... the passage of time has done nothing to minimise their sense of irreparable loss. Love so tender and so clear-sighted, courage so unfaltering and honesty so deep and stainless, standards so splendid and tolerance so exquisite, none of us had known before or are like to know again.

Continuing, Ruth wrote that the collection could only be read with 'a sense of chilling disappointment'. The five stories added little to Olive's lustre.

'Not that there are not beautiful passages in these hundred and fifty pages ... but the pieces here published were not of the first quality, two of them having been written by Olive as a girl. Yet, she argued, 'The Dawn of Civilization' with 'its lofty conception, its lyric imagination, its noble anger', was not included in this collection.

Thoughts on South Africa

The review of *Thoughts on South Africa* appeared in the *Cape Times* on 23 July 1923. It was more a eulogy to Olive than a review of the book. In the first paragraphs there is information on the genesis of the book. The chapters were written between 1890-1892 and the first seven had been carefully edited by Olive before publication in English or Cape papers. Olive had not wanted the eighth chapter published because some passages contradicted what had previously been written. To have included it was the betrayal of a trust.

Ruth noted the fact that the articles included had been a tribute to the Boers – written at a time when Olive was opposed to British machinations – and the 'review' went off on a tangent:

> But whether we agreed with her opinions or not, we were sensible, as always in conversation with this rare woman, of being in touch with a personality honest, fearless and truth-loving to a degree so far above ordinary human kind that we can only wonder and look up, hardly even comprehend.

There followed Ruth's usual apologia for Olive's restricted output, her failure to publish more than a small portion of her writing, and so on. Returning to the book Ruth praised it for providing the 'most vivid and beautiful pictures of South Africa we posses'. It was essentially a period piece, and Ruth suggested that it could be used for classroom reading to evoke memories of the country as it had been.

> The bush at night, seen through the eyes of a child from the ox-wagon; the Karoo, at sunrise, midday, and sunset; the life of the voortrekkers; and above all, the life of the Boers of the backveld – the Boer untouched by present-day modes or speech other than the Taal [literally language, usually referring to Afrikaans] – all these are described for us with a passionate love and in a nervous and powerful English.

Cronwright's Biography

Ruth's review (or demolition) of Cronwright's biography of Olive appeared under the title 'Olive Schreiner', in the New York *Nation*, on 4 June 1924, and in The *South African Nation*, on 9 August 1924. The American review is probably the more caustic. Ruth wrote that a reading of an earlier publication by Cronwright (who held copies of all Olive's writings and papers) of *Stories, Dreams, and Allegories* which contained 'a curiously heterogeneous assortment of pieces' did not inspire confidence in him as a biographer. None of them approached the standard of 'The Dawn of Civilization' ... and as Cronwright admitted, some Olive did not wish to have published.

Misgivings about the 'Life' were not groundless, wrote Ruth. Cronwright had begun by saying that Olive would have preferred that no biography of herself be written, but feeling quite sure that some unauthorised life would appear, incomplete and certainly incorrect, he felt compelled to take up the work. He added that he was the only person 'who ever had adequate opportunity of knowing her completely'. This 'almost childish, almost pathological vehemence,' Ruth wrote, would cause anxiety in those who knew both Olive and the biographer, and 'that does not disappear when this man who professed love, profound admiration and deep reverence proceeded to the biography'.

Cronwright might have found his wife eccentric, undependable and hard to live with, but that could be no excuse for the pages of details, so selected, that the publication was a crude caricature. The reader is told by Cronwright that Olive banged the doors at night, walked up and down in their house, so that he had frequently to remonstrate with her. But not one word about her innumerable acts of kindness 'which made of her friendship a thing different in kind as well as in degree from that of more ordinary folk'. We are told that she did not mingle in the social life of De Aar – 'which is laughable'; and Olive's resignation from the Enfranchisement League ('about which' Cronwright said, 'she wrote some wild letters') was condemned without the reader being told that the League proposed to introduce a 'colour-bar' clause.

Ruth found the book so painful that she did not want to linger upon it, but she felt she had to protest against Cronwright's denial of Olive's story that her larger work, of which *Women and Labour* was a rewrite of only its first chapter, had been destroyed in an act of vandalism by soldiers during the South African War. Cronwright had no evidence to contradict Olive's story. As Ruth wrote: 'I speak not for myself alone when I protest against this unproved statement and take my stand on her word rather than on his'. [Olive was vindicated by fresh evidence at a later date – BH]

Ruth added that despite its lacunae, 'intentional or unintentional', the book gave glimpses of the Olive we loved and marvelled at. In the text is included, justifiably, the words of Arthur Symons, about the afternoon with her in 1889: 'The day of days, I can now realize all that can be told of woman, of a great woman, and I feel that Olive Schreiner is the greatest of them all'.

Ruth's review in the *South African Nation* – which repeated many of the points made in the New York journal – began with a criticism of other reviewers who praised the book without stopping to question the accuracy of Cronwright's portrayal. Furthermore, Cronwright and Ellis subscribed to the thesis that Schreiner, 'though an undoubted genius':

> Was in the business of daily living, a child, 'a divine child' it is true, but for all that so wayward, so restless, so irresponsible, as to make 'close personal intercourse almost impossible'. She chewed her railway tickets; she slammed the doors at night when her husband wished to sleep; she hid from people she did not like; she flew into violent rages; she 'imagined' things, among others, the writing of the big book on women, destroyed in a raid on her house during the Boer War, both the writing and the loss of which she describes in detail in the preface to *Women and Labour.*

The 'divine child' theory, said Ruth, as applied to persons of spiritual genius, has always been popular. It did away with 'that involuntary compulsion to reverence' which was distasteful to many people, and implied an uncomfortable admission of inferiority to those 'whose conception of love, honour, justice and beauty is higher and more perfect than our own. But where it can be shown that the pinnacled soul, attuned to the music of the spheres' is clumsier than us in everyday living, the feeling of inferiority was diminished. 'Complacence and pitying patronage, replaces the feeling of inferiority. Olive Schreiner had her idiosyncrasies, but Cronwright's 'emphasis on them turn his careful portrait into a caricature'. He gave supposed details of household impracticabilities – but gave no details of the order and neatness which made her house in De Aar exquisite. Ruth explained Olive's restlessness as the consequence of her illness and pain, and spoke in contrast of her 'radiant loving-kindness, her utter absence of pose ... her infectious gaiety.' Once again she came to the defence of Olive's account of her book *Woman and Labour*. Contrary to Cronwright's contention that the larger work existed only in her imagination:

> We have his account and we have hers; we may choose, he compels us to choose. Those who have personal knowledge of her high, unfaltering truthfulness, her utter lack of vanity, her clear selflessness, and who have heard the story of her book from her own lips, will not find the choice difficult.

In her acerbic attack on Cronwright's biography Ruth called it an 'ill-balanced, ego-centric book' and rubbished Cronwright's characterisation of Olive as a child, divine or otherwise. 'She was an adult born, to her continuous suffering, into a world some centuries behind her in evolution and composed mainly of grown-up children'. In her talk in Cape Town in 1929, Ruth once again demolished many of the points made by Cronwright. However, a full understanding of that talk needs, as an addendum, these reviews. Without them some of the allusions are easily missed.

Ruth's reviews gained widespread endorsement. Among the letters she received was one, dated 10 March 1925, from Alice M Corthorn, who had been encouraged by Olive to study medicine. She wrote: 'Indeed I agree with all you say of this hateful biography. It is an outrage that we who loved her can never forgive.'

Letters

The title of 'Mr Cronwright's' book (*The Letters of Olive Schreiner: 1876-1920*), wrote Ruth in a review in *The Nation*, 14 October 1925, was a shocking misrepresentation. Leaving aside altogether the letters which Cronwright had not included, there were hundreds of letters, covering the same space of time, the existence of which must have been at least suspected by him and of which he had taken no steps to avail himself. She was furious at Cronwright's purported collection of Olive's letters. He had selected about 950 from a collection of six thousand and had only published extracts of these, hardly ever quoting a letter in full and frequently using a single line. About 100 letters were addressed to Cronwright, 200 to various friends and acquaintances and the remaining 600 to Havelock Ellis.

Most of the letters to Ellis were written between 1884 and 1890, commencing when Olive was new to London, new even to her own fame. People she did not know were pestering her with visits and letters seeking her acquaintance. First among them was Ellis. He was sympathetic, their friendship ripened rapidly, and it is clear from the letters that he wished to marry her. Olive loved him tenderly but she did not envisage marriage. She wrote to him almost daily, sometimes oftener, pouring out to him her thoughts, or how she suffered. For the first time in her life she felt 'secure of an understanding and loving hearing on all matters: of her physical pain; the ugliness and misery of a big city; of the sorrow of her friends; the wrongs to this or that people'.

The correspondence continued when she returned to South Africa. But in 1917 she began to beg him to return or destroy her letters. Ellis finally agreed to burn 'her later letters'. Her further, persistent pleas that all her letters be destroyed were ignored. After her death the letters were handed over to Cronwright and these were included in the collection. The title of Cronwright's book, wrote Ruth, who knew the story of the letters to Ellis, 'is a shocking misrepresentation'. Reviews in the British press showed that there was no understanding of the background:

> Some found the revelations extraordinarily interesting, others found it disconcerting and lamentable. All seemed perfectly satisfied that the actual letters contained in this volume were a fair and representative collection and reflected truthfully the personality as a whole of the writer. The English writers were gravely mistaken …
>
> In an earlier review of the book which appeared in the *Cape Times* in December 1924 Ruth made many of the same points as she would later make in *The Nation*. What she added was a note on Cronwright's biography of Olive in which he had promised a complementary volume of her letters. 'These have now appeared, and to that first disconcerting volume they are indeed disconcerting.'

> In the *Life* Mr Cronwright drew for us a genius who was also an untruthful, inconsiderate, scarcely responsible human being. Over this hapless and helpless figure he, 'the only person who can be said to have known her', as he informs us in his introduction, looms very large indeed. Having read the *Life*, we cannot remain unaware of Mr Cronwright's difficulties and sacrifices in their life together; indeed long before the end we have become oppressively well versed in them. Nor have we been able to avoid an embarrassingly complete knowledge of Olive Schreiner's love for her husband ...

It was a book about Cronwright with just so much of Olive Schreiner ... 'for the highlights and deeper shades of the portrait'. In the *Letters*, wrote Ruth, Cronwright had been at pains to do nothing to disturb the false impressions made by the *Life*.

It is interesting to note that Virginia Woolf, in her review of the letters, without knowledge of Cronwright's perverse editing, spoke of the letters as careless, egoistical, 'of her health, of her sufferings, of her beliefs and desires, as if she were talking in the privacy of her room to a friend whom she trusted'. Woolf also referred to Cronwright's lie and his assertion that he had 'sacrificed a livelihood so that she might pursue her work with the utmost favourable conditions'.[11] Thus was the misinformation spread!

Subsequent to Ruth's review she received a letter from Olive's niece, Katie Stuart:

> It's just as well I am far away and not nearby – else I might be tempted to do what you might resent – give you a loving hug and kiss – for my heart is overflowing with gratitude to you for your beautiful article on Olive Schreiner's letters.
>
> God bless you for it dear loyal heart!
>
> ... You are the first one outside of our family to voice some of the overwhelming dismay and indignation most of the family members feel! And there is no one but me – poor little me – to defend our dear noble dead. Mr

> Cronwright would never have dared to publish what he did had any of the four been alive. He waited till they were in their graves to malign them but he reckoned without me ... Cronwright's whole record is a tissue of half truths and half lies – I know even of our beloved Aunt Olive what he evidently does not know – for she evidently never *trusted* him wholly though she loved him so passionately ... He was the evil genius of her life – who killed her genius by his ambitions for her and his plannings for her to write. Could you? Could I? Write a word if someone was ceaselessly planing, arranging and cajoling us to do so? And then bitterly disappointed because we couldn't ...

Julia F Solly, having discussed the matter with Mrs John Brown and Mrs Herrman, wrote to Ruth on 9 February 1925 suggesting that those disgusted with Cronwright's presentation of Olive and 'who knew and loved Olive Schreiner, and admired her genius and appreciated her sympathy and wide interests, should bring out a book of recollections'. She added:

> Mrs Brown tells me that the story about the burnt papers which Cronwright now pretends is imaginary, is true, and that *she has letters both from Olive and Cronwright to prove it.* [My emphasis].

From Man to Man

Reviewed in the *Cape Times* of 28 October 1926 under the headline 'The Most Womanly Book that Ever was Written', this previously unpublished work had been known to Olive's friends who had waited patiently for it to be finished – but never saw its completion. The work, wrote Ruth, consisted of two well marked parts, 'The Prelude' or 'The Child's Day' – a long short story complete in itself, and the first thirteen chapters of the unfinished novel *From Man to Man* – about two-thirds of what had been conceived. 'The Child's Day' had been named in Olive's will as one of the two writings (the other being *Thoughts on South*

Africa) which she wanted published after her death. *From Man to Man* had been pieced together laboriously and carefully from the rough drafts held by Cronwright. Olive's handwriting was often indecipherable and sometimes words or even phrases were substituted. Unfortunately it was not known what Cronwright had done with the original manuscript, for a comparison of that with the published text would be interesting.

However there could be no difficulty with 'The Prelude', which Olive had 'revised and re-revised' with 'religious care':

> 'The Child's Day' is a flawless thing. In all the arts there appear, now and again, certain splendid and beautiful achievements which instantly, and for all time, take their proud place among the very greatest, become part of the immortal loveliness in which the spirit of mortal man puts on divinity. To this order the 'Prelude' unmistakenly belongs. If of all the writings of Olive Schreiner, this alone had been given to the world, it would have been sufficient to establish her as a great artist.

'The Prelude' was the story of one day of the life of a five-year-old child. On that day girl twins were born, one of whom died. The other was taken to the heart of the five year old 'with a passionate life-long love'. The child, left to herself:

> Goes through a variety of experiences, some external, some wholly of the inner life, and all of them felt with the intensity which is the normal temperature, so to speak, of some natures, as it was that of Olive Schreiner herself. And, indeed, objective as the writer is, the child of 'The Prelude' is Olive as a child and round the woman she built up a circle and a story in her imagination, but the soul of child and girl and woman was hers, too.

Expanding the point Ruth wrote that anyone who knew Olive would recognise the connection. Those who had not 'had the great privilege' might 'catch their glimpses of her here, in the story of the child Rebekah, without any painful sense of spiritual privacies invaded'. But only the characterisation of Rebekah is alive, 'almost overwhelmingly alive', and the younger sister, Bertie, 'is well observed and sufficiently convincing'; all the other characters are 'shadowy to the reader'. Yet the description of Bertie, 'in her slow, pitiful degeneration in her London imprisonment ... [although superbly written] is rather described than created'. Indeed 'one feels that there might quite easily be things about Bertie that Olive Schreiner does not know, but she knows Rebekah as she knows herself.' In many passages, superb as they are, reflecting on her life, or

> writing to her husband of what love between man and woman might be ... making a parable for her children of the relations between the black and white races, talks as many people have not yet forgotten hearing Olive Schreiner talk, writes as Olive Schreiner wrote ...

In the fervour with which these accounts are told the story 'sinks into a secondary place'. There are two purposes in the novel and 'up to the time when the unfinished book was laid aside, the artistic issue had not been fought out between them.' One was to tell the story of the lives of two sisters, the other was the need to explain to men and women how women felt about love. Olive herself had called it 'the most womanly book that ever was written'. Thus it was that Ruth could conclude her review by saying:

> There are sentences in this book which must shake the heart of the strongest – aye, and the happiest – of women to the bitterest of inward weeping, till raging sorrow for what is, and aching longing for what might be, in the relations of men and women, are merged in some likeness of that love for other women, 'not because they are myself, but because they are not myself' which was the woof of almost every book she ever wrote, and of almost every personal relation of her whole life.

Undine

'Olive Schreiner's Lost Novel' was the headline over Ruth's review of *Undine* in the *Cape Times* on 30 March 1929. *Undine* was, in fact, Olive's first novel, but had only been published for the first time that year. The review began with a discussion of the strange fate of the manuscript which had been given to Havelock Ellis in 1884, but without the last chapter. Although Olive had subsequently asked for it to be returned so that it could be destroyed, Ellis had ignored her request. When no more was said about the book Ellis assumed that Olive had mistakenly thought that she had had it, and had destroyed it. The last, incomplete, chapter was kept by Olive because, she noted, 'the biographical element in it made me soft to it'. After her death Ellis gave the manuscript to Cronwright who had not known of the novel's existence. He found the last chapter among her papers.

The fact that *Undine* provided readers with some account of Olive's childhood was not Ruth's concern. Instead, she was intrigued by the change of style between this first immature novel and *The Story of an African Farm*, into which incidents from *Undine* were freely transferred. By publishing side by side the opening paragraphs, which were identical in material, Ruth could show that in the second novel:

> Naïveté had become impossible, while the fitful rhythms of the first had given way to sentences of a balance and melody, a cadenced singing rose, which was to become the characteristic style of her books. It as a style which lends itself rather to impassioned feeling and lofty thought than to analysis or subtle description, the style of a writer who was rather a great teacher, a great moralist, with a strong infusion of the poet, than a great novelist.

Concluding the review, the last she wrote before her talk on Olive in Cape Town, she offered a new explanation for Olive's failure to write a second novel equal or superior to *The Story of an African Farm*. 'It was only in part her failing health and the circumstances of her private life.':

> The reason in chief is that she was first the great woman, the great lover of her fellow-beings, and then the great artist. She had said to herself, as she makes her Rebekah say in *From Man to Man*: 'because of my art, my love and my relations to my fellow men shall never suffer; there shall not be a loaf of bread less baked. No sick left untended, no present human creature's need of me left unsatisfied because of it' ... if for her work's sake she had turned away from the sorriest human who needed her, she would have outraged the profoundest law of her own being. Moreover, her loaves of bread and her sick were often unpopular causes, wrongs to be righted. Against any public injustice or cruelty the whole dynamic force of her personality arrayed itself a final, reckless, spendthrift generosity; the sufferings of oppressed peoples or nations or groups were more real and more intolerable to her than are our those of our nearest and dearest to us. And when she wrote or spoke of such sufferings she became of more than mortal stature, even in her latter days, half crippled with mortal illness.

The Talk

Ruth's talk on Olive, delivered under the auspices of the English Association on 9 August 1929 before a large and excited audience, and reprinted in an enlarged version in the *Cape Times* in 1930, concentrated on Olive as a person: an intensely human person, a lover of humanity, a neighbourly and kindly person, and a person whose good-fellowship extended to all races, all minorities, and even to the menagerie of domestic animals that filled her home.

Ruth had already offered her appraisal of Olive's writings in her articles and did not repeat them here. What she said about the personality, the humanity, and the generosity of her subject – almost exaggerated in its homage – was also a public rebuttal of Cronwright's crass characterisation. Some of the points made by Ruth have been alluded to above. What does not emerge to the reader, unaware of Cronwright's snide comments, was the demolition of the published biography – although his positive contributions were acknowledged. In the talk Ruth took into account Olive's eccentric behaviour when she was ill, but condemned her husband for not recognising her more usual kindness and consideration. In a faithful summary, probably copied from Ruth's manuscript, was her own insightful appraisal:

> As she came to know her personally, she became more and more keenly aware, first, that the Olive Schreiner of her books, and the Olive Schreiner who championed in their most unpopular days the cause of Women's Suffrage, and that of the Jews, who were being massacred in Russian pogroms; of the Boers, in the years of the Boer War; of the Indians in South Africa; and of the natives; and the Olive Schreiner of private life, were all one person in essence. And second, that her personality was of an amazing and perhaps unique quality.

Saying that she wished to record something of that personality 'because she believed that to future generations it would assume a significance and possess a beauty and a splendour, which it did not assume for the generation of today': Then, in a passage that was passionate and filled with an optimism that was never borne out, Ruth maintained:

> It was natural that the present generation should take for granted the liberty of action and of mind and of spirit for every particle of which the contemporaries of Olive Schreiner had battled with stern and unremitting effort. The generation to come, more conscious of the distances they have gone along the road, would understand what they owed to their forebears of the 19th century. And among those forebears they would regard with love and almost with awe that one little woman who, in an age when the women of Europe were still so constricted in body and mind that they were useless, refused to conform.

Although Ruth was convinced that later generations would be aware of their debt, she also said that Olive never bore herself as a teacher. The salient fact, she stressed, was Olive's love of humanity 'with a love as strong as it was tender, as unsentimental as it was self-forgetful'. The world she longed for was, as it seemed to her, in no way to be attained save through love'.

Ruth examined Olive's exploration of her theories of love in her works – the fullest exposition of them being in *From Man to Man*. Olive's rejection of religion emerged as much from her heart as from her intellect, said Ruth. As a very small child she had rejected the religious explanations of life and death. She had also rejected with horror the belief of eternal damnation. It was a horror so great 'that it almost sent her out of her mind'. Ruth continued:

> Let no one dare to imagine that the religion of love and service and truth that were hers was an easy one. It had no week-days. It had no compromises. Its claims were merciless and at the most merciless were honoured in full, though the price was a mortal wound.

The significance of Olive Schreiner in South Africa was recognised only by a small circle of admirers. Ruth's importance lay in her tireless furthering of the reputation of the country's greatest writer. Solomon Schechter could not have foreseen when he had suggested that Ruth might meet Olive that his daughter would become her most impassioned champion.

5
THE FAIREST CAPE?

Ruth left sparse accounts of her first sight of Cape Town; no exclamations of delight as the town was explored; and no descriptions of the houses rented or owned by the Alexanders in the seaside suburbs of Muizenberg or St James. The many articles she wrote and submitted to the *Cape Times* were curiously devoid of descriptions of the city. Many years later, when she had taken a critical stance in favour of the dispossessed coloureds, Indians and Africans, she wrote about one aspect of the city in newspapers and journals and in two unpublished works: *The Exiles,* and the first pages of what she hoped to enlarge into a history of the coloured people.

It might have seemed inappropriate to a woman as sensitive as Ruth to have written about the 'fair Cape' after she had sampled life among the coloured people. Her omission is the reader's loss.

Among the few accounts of Cape Town by writers who were also critical of South Africa's repressive racial laws was one short impression penned by Lancelot Hogben, then professor of Zoology at the University of Cape Town, who, in his autobiography, was more concerned with the beauty of the rock pools, 'almost unbelievably rich in marine animals'[1]. However, he did say of his arrival at the Cape in 1929 that:

> Table Bay, surmounted by cloud-capped Table Mountain and fringed with densely wooded slopes, is one of the most beautiful harbours on the four continents I have visited.[2]

A fuller impression appears in Vera Brittain's book *Testament of Friendship* which includes extracts from letters written in 1926 by her friend, Winifred Holtby, the novelist, who spent four months in South Africa lecturing on behalf of the League of Nations. Holtby, a supporter of the British Labour Party, sympathised with the aims of the Industrial and Commercial Workers Union of Africa (the ICU), and, helped by liberal whites in South Africa, set up a support body in Britain when she returned home. Her visit received widespread publicity, and it seems probable that this led to Ruth's support of the ICU.

When Holtby arrived in South Africa in the summer of 1926 she was thrilled by what she saw. Vera Brittain writes of her wonderment:

> Not in England, not in Central Europe, not even in Italy, had Winifred ever seen a city which filled her with the same ecstasy as Cape Town. She could hardly land for the excitement of trying to take in, all at once, the dazzling white sands and the purple-blue backgrounds of mountains; the green forests of fir and pine crowned with peaked and jagged rocks; the long white town straggling with its suburbs for fifteen miles along the indented coast ... she felt drunk and dazed with the shouting chorus of colour – the vivid turquoise water, the deep cobalt shadows, the purple, grey and rose-pink of the rocky hills.[3]

The gardens, said Holtby, were filled with 'the riotous extravagance of summer flowers'. And as she was driven to one of the seaside suburbs 'every street seemed to have purple mountains behind it and the turquoise ocean in front'. There is not much more. Holtby was touring the country, observing, meeting people, and lecturing. Her letters conveyed her impressions as she crossed this vast subcontinent and she was distressed by the social conditions she observed, the poverty amidst plenty, and the rigid stratification of the people. From Cape Town she went inland and soon discovered the reality of segregation. In Durban she attended a meeting called by the Indian Congress to protest against the Asiatic Bill, an occasion she described as 'seven thousand heathens praying that a Christian government may see light'. She also related:

> My most conspicuous importance, I enjoyed not from any merit of my own, oh dear no! But by the very simple action of walking through Durban with an Indian. It is true that

> he was a highly cultured and respected Indian. It is true that he had been appointed to conduct me, as an interested and neutral spectator, to the Town Hall Indian Congress. It is true that I was a lecturer for the League of Nations, and therefore debarred from any barrier of race and colour. Yet as I went, I think that everyone in the street turned round and stared, stopping their conversations.[4]

After visiting many of the bigger towns Holtby went to Johannesburg where she saw the country's racial policy in its ugliest form. In that town, she said, she had seen four different worlds. First, that of the intellectuals: 'It was small and exquisite; a world of witty, agreeable, intelligent, and generous people'. The second world was that of the women, leisured and wealthy, with their armies of African servants. They were not 'happy, significant or secure and their values were vulgar'. The third world was that of the businessmen, who supported and enriched the second world. That was all she saw of the whites, but perhaps it was enough, despite the existence of the poorer whites who did not live a life of luxury but were still privileged by virtue of their skin colour. There was however another 'world' which she saw and found appalling:

> Not only here, but in every town that she visited, Winifred became keenly aware of a Fourth World half hidden, menacingly aloof. At dawn its citizens poured from the locations into the mines and workshops; they polished the parquet flooring in the Parktown bungalows; they emptied the ash-bins and cleaned the streets; they drove the carts drawn by limpid-eyed, softly treading donkeys. The roses and hibiscus and moon-flowers of the suburban gardens concealed little hovels from which, in the early morning, crept black 'boys' and 'girls' who might be married men and women with families, to prepare the tea and sweep the houses and cook the breakfasts of their imperial employers. Right under the noses of the white men and women, they led their own dark, mysterious life.

Although there is no mention of their meeting it was inevitable that Ruth would have attended one or more of Winifred's many lectures (it is said that she addressed forty meetings in Cape Town) and, perhaps, extended her activities into the 'Fourth World' in Cape Town where Ruth spent so much of her time.

Ruth's writings about the slums of Cape Town, even if was only one of many such cesspools, tells the story of those who were sacrificed in the pursuit of profits, as justified in notions of 'racial purity', or of 'national exclusiveness' all under the umbrella-terms of 'Christian Trusteeship' or what was later to be dubbed 'segregation' and, ultimately, 'apartheid'.

District Six

Biographies cannot be readily reconstructed from novels which, rich as they are in providing atmosphere and details, are not sources from which facts or dates should be extracted. As a consequence it is not certain when Ruth first came to know the inhabitants of District Six sufficiently well to write about them with intimacy. But know them she did, probably just before the war. By 1925/26, when the war was becoming a memory, but when South Africa was still in the grips of a recession, she must have felt confident enough to start writing about them.

They appear in her novel, *The Exiles*,[5] and in the document on the 'Coloured People',[6] written in the 1930s. Her description of them was based, as she said, on a quarter of a century's contact in which she 'lived in or near Cape Town and was in touch with the Coloured people, had friends among them and was engaged in work in connection with them'. Although romanticised, her account was written with a knowledge of their disabilities in a racist society, and of their struggle to survive in 'the inherent crazy rottenness of the social structure of the society'. Through the contact, Ruth wrote:

> I saw much of the misery and of the inarticulate despair and apathy mentioned in the [Government] Report. I saw the exploitation by the respectable prosperous whites of the Coloured population, that is of the proletariat. It was

> an exploitation not more culpable, but more shameless, than that in towns where employer and employed were of the same colour. It was made possible by a public opinion based on the conviction that the dark-skinned people ... were of a different order of human beings, a conviction that underlies ... every piece of repressive legislation ... and the whole body of social discrimination exercised against them ... I saw further the unbelievable goodness to each other which, as with the submerged and forgotten everywhere, exists and recreates itself without external stimulus or example. I saw intelligence, beauty, responsiveness, charm, initiative, flowering out of bitter poverty, often out of squalor ... Here was a proletariat and a tiny emergent middle class, in numbers equal roughly to the white population which lives upon its labour, outlawed by them ... from all share of the amenities, and from all but a fraction of the educational, cultural, social facilities of the place.[7]

It took time for Ruth to acquire this knowledge but her empathy with the coloured people was transparent. In her history she writes:

> The stranger who lands in Capetown, once he has recovered from the awe-inspiring first sight of Table Mountain ... is unlikely to be further impressed until he has passed the Dock Gates ... the coloured people will be of a variety of dress, complexion, and general appearance that will be a new spectacle for him ... It is not the white folk that will awaken his interest ... they will seem on the whole better dressed, healthier-looking, taller than the white people he might see in the streets of any English market town. But they will be of the same types ... Nor, when he turns into Adderley Street, the main street of Capetown, will the principal shops, the principal cafés, the railway-station and the post-office, long engage his interest.

It was the coloured people who were interesting, she continued: the women with 'tight fitting bodices and wide gathered skirts touching the ground', some with bare feet unless it was very cold, and with head dresses of bright silk or of kerchiefs twisted round their hair:

> their skins all the shades from the olive ivory that would be white in a Latin town to the blue-black-black that seems to have a bloom on it like a black grape ... and covering all the grades of appearance from dandified to ragged.

The faces might be that of 'a lad with a fez on his head, and with a pale brown skin but negroid lips'; or two little girls 'one nearly white, and one many shades darker'; two dainty young women with 'dark brown skins and Chinese slanted almond eyes'. These faces were not to be seen in teashops or restaurants, in the bars or the cinemas in the theatre or in the concert hall. 'Nor were white and brown seen to be talking together, or if they do it is a rare thing. And if there were such persons they would attract anger or contempt from those with white faces'. 'The criminal element, that group that gets into police records, also lives in District Six,' she noted:

> In that congested area, where poverty and ignorance continually create and foster the *lumpenproletariat* of the community, the idle and the diseased and the beaten ... live cheek by jowl with the proletariat which is none of these things, that is, self-respecting and courageous, not to say heroic.

In *The Exiles* Emanuel Braun, the newly arrived lecturer from England still on board ship, and Miriam, his new-found friend, see the 'towering rectangular mountain and the unsightly buildings along the water-front'. They also see a group of Indians:

> In the bright newness of their best clothes, come down to welcome an Indian notability ... a turbaned-snake-charmer drawing his little crowd of dark-skinned idlers ... the curio-

> sellers, ragged, impudent, waiting to sell their ostrich-eggs, feathers, branches of gleaming silver-leaves.

The couple are soon separated, Miriam carried off by her relatives while Emanuel is met by the head of his department. Out in the street Emanuel sees men and women standing or sitting 'behind baskets piled high with flowers the heaped colours of which were almost painful in the strong light ... The long bank of massed colour, set off by the browns and blacks of the flower-sellers.'

These were a people apart, separated from the whites by skin colour, by occupation and by residence. The man who sold the newspapers, the maid in the hotel, the flower girl, the taxi-drivers, the dark-skinned and the poor lived in District Six, segregated by convention in their houses, schools, places of refreshment and amusement, at the workplace and even in the churches. Of the total population of Cape Town in 1921, 113 200 were classified as white and 94 000 were mainly coloured – the overwhelming number of whom, except for domestic servants and gardeners, lived in District Six.

The characters in the novel were imaginary, but the events, said Ruth, were taken from incidents that were true. She describes a scene in which Emanuel encounters the drabness and the horror of District Six on a working day. Walking up a 'street less crowded than on Sunday and busier', he saw that:

> The shops were all open, and at the doors of many of them stood the owners, exhorting, cajoling the passers-by, to step in and look for themselves. The smells of new cotton stuffs, of cheese and soap and meat and fruit, of spices and curry, of a tannery and a jam-factory, both near at hand, competed with each other ... He saw a procession of three little ragged black children, a lanky girl and two chubbier smaller boys, moving along slowly and carefully, carrying on their heads, each of them, a tin of bread fresh from some baker's oven ... The street was given over to the out-of-works, the children too young for school or crowded out of school, and the women doing their shopping ... The

> children were less gay than on that warmer day. Their Sunday clothes were laid aside, and in the colder air their thin arms and legs, their insufficient clothing, were more piteous to see ...Then, with a spasm of physical sickness, he saw a baby of two, dressed in a scrap of sacking, sitting on the curb ... [its face] smeared with blood from cheek to chin ... sucking, quite happily, at a bit of butcher's offal dropped by a man carrying his load from the reeking cart outside to the reeking shop within. He plucked the loathsome morsel from the child's lips, whereat it set up a wail, and [he] fled round a corner. There he leaned up against the dubious wall, scrubbing frantically at his hand, and fighting down his nausea.

'Scenes from District Six' written by Ruth, some important, others of passing interest, were published in the *Cape Argus* in the last few years of her stay in the country. The best were no different in style and content from her earlier work, but there were several items that were merely 'pot-boilers'. The account of a man and a woman fighting in the street, in the rain, for a bag of cheap sweets, headlined 'The Desperados', appeared on the leader page, portraying a life in which the smallest of luxuries was coveted. It ended when the bag was torn and each of the contestants laughingly sucked the portion he or she had retrieved. A story, 'The Girl who was Malay Tricked', *Cape Argus*, 14 May 1932, described a farcical search on a beach which produced a rag doll pierced with pins which had seemingly been buried on purpose to persuade a lover to forego an elaborate marriage feast.

Pride of place in the magazine section was given to Ruth's lament that Plein Street, previously busy from eight to eleven on a Saturday night with thronging crowds, mostly of coloureds, was now empty because the Provincial Council had decided to close all businesses at midday on Saturdays. Written with gusto as only she could write, and with descriptions that she could have used in a novel, this was surely a piece that used an energy that seemed inexhaustible. More seriously there was a short article by Ruth deprecating the 'donors' of charity for needy if not starving families who sent putrescent food, rotten produce and children's toys that were broken or had missing parts, and old clothes that could not even serve as cleaning rags. Such donors were sick and Ruth wrote about them in fury.

District Six was the focus of an article in the *Cape Argus* of 18 March 1933 entitled 'The Intruders'.This was a poignant piece, made all the grimmer by being written so close to Ruth's departure from South Africa, leaving no obvious successor to continue the work of her playgroup. Once a week fifty children – twenty-five boys and twenty-five girls – were chosen from an assembled crowd to visit the play centre to receive milk, biscuits and some fruit. It was Ruth's onerous task to choose from those who were the most needy 'the saddest, the sulkiest, the most neglected in appearance, the most resigned'. On the occasion of which she wrote there were two new girls, neither more piteous nor more ragged than the others. They were silent, only their eyes speaking, and on an impulse, as the queue shortened, she chose them. There was a storm of protest from those who remained. 'They were new children. Never seen before,' came the protests and then, dispirited, the children could shout no more. Wryly Ruth wrote that 'only a lunatic would try this drop-in the-bucket business', and, adding the comment that the two new ones were taken into the company by the other forty-eight, she closed the article with the terse comment: 'Which things are a parable. But not a cheerful one. I would recommend it, however, to students of social science, whatever that is.'

On 18 July 1932, in an article in the *Cape Times* on 'The Penny Bank: A Little Known Side of District Six' Ruth wrote that in the consciousness of the people of the Cape, District Six was 'the region where lurid things happen, things that one reads about at breakfast. Somewhere about its unknown streets lurks the "underworld", where anything is possible'.

> How should it be otherwise? The area contains the greater part of the slums and the greater part of the very poor people of Cape Town. It contains a more heterogeneous mixture of colours and races, a greater degree of overcrowding and a larger number of out-of-works than any other in the Peninsula.

> District Six may be comparatively well-off or wretchedly poor, but that in either case is hard-working, thrifty, self-respecting, kind, decent. It abounds in men and women unselfishly devoted to the welfare of their people, of good citizens in the fullest sense.

She described in the article the main street on a Saturday afternoon, families sitting relaxed; a drunk, waving a bottle of sherry weaving his way across the road; and a ragged, unkempt woman lying supine on the pavement, ignored by the children because this was a sight that 'was so little remarkable'. She wrote about narrow passages with their swarms of children, and all the smells of cooking and 'that other unforgettable smell ... that is like bottled essence of poverty'.

This was the backdrop to the 'more significant and in a sense more hopeful' scene. In a narrow street, to a little house reached by a flight of a dozen steps, came 'children of all ages and all shades of colour, and a few grown-ups' to pay their money (and that of their siblings and their parents) into a Penny Bank, run entirely by volunteers. Launched in 1925 it had a subscription list in 1932 of 900 depositors:

> The children, who come in dozens bringing their pennies, their threepences, and in a few cases even their half-crowns, hand in their little green books with an unchildlike knowledge of their importance. They are dreaming no dreams, as children in other districts do, of this or that longed -for object that may be theirs in the course of time; they know that these silver or copper coins, put aside at the cost of a sacrifice every tiniest detail of which they have shared in, are so many bricks in the slow raising wall that shall protect them in some sort against the sea of misfortune always threatening to overwhelm them.

The money paid for schoolbooks, for rent, for the price of a ticket to the convalescent home, the cough mixture, the extra food the doctor ordered, the pair of new boots, or perchance a funeral, always of lavish splendour.

The 'bank' was also a place of refuge for the young mother; for 'the little weary down-at-heels woman ... showing clearly that she never has a minute to look at herself and has lost the habit of doing so'; or for 'the white man, not very old but already crippled with rheumatism, who takes so long to get up the steep steps that the children, with the cruelty of children, show their impatience, that they have to be called to order'.

The Penny Bank was a valuable institution but it barely touched the inhabitants of District Six. On 25 July 1929, the tenth anniversary of the infamous influenza epidemic of 1919, Ruth voiced her concern in the correspondence column of the *Cape Times*, writing that at a time of common terror and common pity the well-to-do had expressed their horror at human beings lying ill and dying in such holes. As a consequence there had been pledges in speeches and in the press to clean up the slums. Not one thing had been done.

> The prevalence of disease, the proportion of crime, the bands of untaught, untrained children whose only playground, school and encyclopaedia is the street – all these factors have certainly not decreased, nor has there been anything but vague attempts to deal with them on the part of the community.

The apathy towards the slums, for which everyone was responsible, was aggravated 'by the barrier of colour'. The whites told themselves that the slums existed because of the shortcomings of the people who lived there. Were they are not aware that the whites in France, and in Britain, said the same about their slums? 'In those countries the "poor" are thought of as being thriftless – while here it is the dark-skinned people who are thought of in the same way.' Ruth then wrote of 'the irrefutable fact' that slum property was the most lucrative of all property. Each room was let at a rental which made the whole house worth more than a house in the most prosperous suburb. Each cellar was let for a room; stoves, sinks and baths were not provided, 'and there is no question of any single room in the slums remaining vacant, even for a night'.

Enforced social segregation had not yet come to Cape Town and Ruth also described the world of some of the Jewish immigrants who had made their homes in District Six and set themselves up as retailers:

> Rows of shabby and unclean shops whose walls and cupboards are sprinkled with Yiddish characters, sloping streets crowded with Coloured people, Indians, Russians, Poles, narrow lanes ... I recalled ... the group of men that stand around the counter and jewellers holding debates in Yiddish.[8]

These Jews were given money by their richer co-religionists to set up their hawking rounds but were otherwise excluded from, or were uncomfortable at, the functions of the older, more socially integrated, settlers. This led Morris to organise a new synagogue at which the immigrants could feel wanted and at home.[9]

Ruth did not devote much time or space to the affluent whites in the wealthier suburbs of Cape Town – the first three 'worlds' described by Winifred Holtby. Her comments about them in her novel were generally caustic. She condemned those academics who, even when they appeared to be friendly, were racist and anti-Semitic; and she despised the moneyed middle-class Jews. Miriam (Ruth's alter ego) expressed Ruth's sentiments when she said:

> My aunt Rose feels that the one thing she can do for my father is to marry me off as soon as possible. And she says that men don't like 'clever women', and that she hasn't allowed Sally, my cousin, to go to college, because it would spoil her chances ...
>
> And the meals! We had morning tea with scones and two kinds of cakes, and a large lunch, and afternoon tea was more elaborate than the morning one, and dinner larger than lunch. We seemed to be eating all the time.
>
> Visitors came and went ... and they all sat around ... and ate and ate, and when they weren't looking at me they were all talking about their children and their servants and

> Jewish 'affairs', concerts or bazaars or dances for the benefit of something, that they were getting up to.

When she stepped outside the world of the novel the picture was more complex. Ruth had an expanding group of friends in Cape Town who did not resemble the stereotyped middle-class inhabitants described in her novel.The 'Aunt Roses' were real enough, but there were others who were more sensitive to the wider society. Yet, despite the qualities they displayed, which made them agreeable, and even stimulating company they seldom ventured into District Six, and did not establish friendships across the colour line. There were exceptions – but they were never more than a tiny minority.

At Home in Cape Town

Despite her contention that it was not whites who would awaken the newcomer's interest, Ruth's first articles, published during the war years in the South African *Lady's Pictorial,* were directed at the middle-class whites who took the journal. In December 1915, she wrote:

> After more than a year – a year which has left its indelible mark on almost every (sic) woman in the land – the war goes on. Those who have achieved some understanding of what such a war means to a nation, and, more specially to the women and children of that nation, thank our gods for the press of special work that fills our hours, and get through the days, weeks and months as best we may.

She called for improvements to existing schools, the introduction of compulsory free education (for whites?), and the provision in every large city of a crèche, a free library, playgrounds and playrooms for wet weather. She wrote of the 'white-faced girls exhausted after the day's drudgery, that kills the mind and warps the body', who had to be saved because they were the mothers of tomorrow.

It is not necessary to question Ruth's views of the society in which she moved. She had grown up in a home that was intellectually stimulating but conservative and now lived in a society where few whites moved across the colour line. Although she was impressed by Gandhi and his friends, she had little opportunity to mix socially with people outside the society to which she had been brought. Moving initially in the circle of conservative parliamentarians, Zionist groups, members of the Jewish Board of Deputies and of the synagogue, Ruth still had much to learn.

The South African English language publications for which she wrote were almost all under the financial control of the Chamber of Mines and were conservative in policy and proponents of the prevailing philosophy of ethnic segregation. This was a constraint which Ruth only overcame as she became more radical in outlook. Then, when she chose to write about political issues, she submitted articles to the New York *Nation*.

Some of her first pieces, influenced by Olive's *Woman and Labour*, addressed problems facing young women in general, and more particularly the miserable wages paid to waitresses. On 19 November 1915, she wrote in *The Cape* in a style that was to become the hallmark of her articles:

> It was Ruskin – was it not – who said the needless misery of the world around him got on his nerves, and prevented his painting, or reading, or sleeping, until he had done what in him lay, to lessen it. Some such spirit, not of altruism, but of pure dislike for discomfort, has made it difficult for us to enjoy our afternoon tea or after-theatre coffee in the cafés of Cape Town with any decent degree of self-complacency.

She wrote of miserable working conditions and the low wages paid by the larger restaurants: on average, 17s 6d a week, from which waitresses paid at least 20 shillings a month for rent, 10 shillings for train fare, 5 shillings for washing and 8 shillings for food for four Sundays a month. That left 27 shillings for clothes, shoes, doctor, recreation, cigarettes and all other expenses. They also had to pay for all broken crockery and for shortages of money handed in at the end of the day.

The article concluded with the account, taken from police records, of a white girl of nineteen arrested on a charge of soliciting. The girl had said:

> I've nobody to look to but myself. I've no experience or qualifications for any sort of work. I was a waitress for a year, and I earned three pounds a month, and got varicose veins badly. Now I am about forty. And then with a snarl 'What do you propose to do about it?'

Ruth asked: 'Ladies and gentlemen of this fair city of ours, what do you propose to do about it?'

In January 1916, under the title 'A Living Wage', Ruth wrote again in the *Lady's Pictorial:*

> There is a fine, bracing, early-in-the-morning-with-the-cold- tap-running flavour about the phrase 'the struggle for existence'. But ... there is nothing either fine or bracing about the struggle. Exhilaration excitement, even joy, there may be in fighting, in overcoming, in battling onwards., provided always and only that at the end of this fighting there is something, an objective, an ideal, either attained, or as yet unattained, but still desired, and still possible. To struggle to live – and that, through the most supreme difficulty and suffering may be infinitely worthwhile., to struggle to exist, that is, just not to die, can assuredly not be worth the effort...
>
> Workers needed not merely an existence, but a living ... adequately paid, not of too great a duration, not too mechanical ... to blunt all sense of anything besides; a good sound education for that work, and the possibility ... of the full and free development of any gifts or potentialities ... and beyond these, an occasional opportunity for cakes and ale, or, if you prefer a more high sounding name, romance... that sudden enchanting sense of adventure, of splendour ... is a passion as

> fundamental, as instructive, as hunger or thirst – and far more vital.
>
> Those without training, eagerness and without hope, toil cheerlessly, in a discontent that is evil, in a patience that is worse, through the long stretches of grey days … Realise with your minds, as you do already in your heart of hearts, that it is for the right to *live,* not bread, not existence, that men and women have really fought throughout the ages, and are still battling today.

Decrying those who did nothing to correct the situation Ruth called for the passage of a Minimum Wage Bill. Consequently Patrick Duncan, a Cabinet Minister, wrote to her asking about the wages paid to shop assistants in Cape Town – details which she said she could not collect, particularly as she had not been well and was taking a month's holiday in Durban. She suggested that a fair minimum wage for Cape Town would be £6 a month with food, and £8 without food.

There is a gap in the writings attributable to Ruth after the war. If she wrote for local newspapers or journals her contributions were mostly printed anonymously. The first pieces I have found were pasted into a scrapbook. Writings that were undoubtedly hers between October 1922 and December 1924, included reviews of books, several short accounts of events about town and 'snapshots' of New York – all in the *Cape Times.* As previously they were obviously written for a white readership.

On 22 September 1923, there was 'On Wet Week-ends', a pot-boiler on the problems faced by everyone from schoolchildren to statesmen when the weather altered weekend schedules. On 17 October an article on 'Morning Tea, A South African Custom' noted the disappearance of men from the civil service, the law, or the top strata of commerce who slipped away an hour before noon with the announcement that they would be away 'for ten minutes: a well worn formula which fools nobody when they depart for a half-hour or more. And simultaneously, the ladies of the house sit down to the morning repast, alone, or with friends who have dropped in to compare anything from recipes to their babies' new teeth.' It was, Ruth wrote, a peculiarly

South African institution which she hoped to see retained, as it provided in the hour before noon 'relief from the drabness of the town's centre'.

On 3 November, in a short essay on the umbrella, it was observed that class was shown by the different handles or coverings, but to no consequence – when the rains descended they were all alike. There was something essentially humorous about the umbrella, wrote Ruth. It was an object that one had 'to rescue from the eye of sonic fellow creature at a crossing ... or hang onto as it suddenly develops into a quite good working parachute'. With all its difficulties it was a saviour 'when the rain threatened to wet hair or face or the floods overwhelmed us'.

Ruth had found a medium which the *Cape Times* found congenial and she wrote on 'Familiar Things', on 17 November 1923; 'On Coughs' on 8 December; 'On Holidays', on 25 December; and 'On Getting Up', on 5 January. These were followed by essays on being photographed, on dogs, on a return to school, on examinations and so on.

In about April 1924 Ruth visited New York. The exact date is uncertain but the evidence appears in her writings in the *Cape Times*. The first intimation that she had gone abroad was the appearance, undated, of an article entitled 'A Sea Voyage'. It carried no names of persons or places, no dates, and no stated destination and the voyage was unexceptional. Ruth wrote:

> The days come and are gone quickly enough, and yet each somehow holds more hours and a more intensive personal life than do the days on shore. A friendship, nay, a love affair shall come into being and blossom to maturity within forty-eight hours. An implacable enmity takes even less time for development. And the ship has become our world, safe, known, taken for granted.

This piece was followed by six numbered articles headed 'Snapshots of New York'. Numbers two and three were anonymous (as were most of the items pasted into the scrapbook). 'The Russian Inn', the first of the cameos, appeared on 10 June 1924. The Inn stood outside the 'dazzle and glitter' of theatreland, but it was noisy and colourful, filled with the blue haze of tobacco smoke. The tables were all filled and the air hummed

Courtesy of The Library of the Jewish Theological Seminary

Solomon Schechter

Courtesy of The Library of the Jewish Theological Seminary

Solomon Schechter engrossed in the examination of the Genizah Fragments, Cambridge c 1898

Ruth in repose

Ruth and Morris Alexander

Ruth at home in Cape Town

Solly, Esther and Muriel

Morris Alexander and Solly engaged in one of Morris's favourite leisuretime pursuits

Mother and children

(Photographed by G. & E. Lavis, Eastbourne)
Courtesy of the National English Literary Museum

Olive Schreiner shortly after her arrival in England in 1881

Courtesy of The National Library of South Africa

Olive Schreiner in later life

Ben Farrington

Ben Farrington on Table Mountain

COURTESY OF THE NATIONAL GANDHI MUSEUM, NEW DELHI

Mohandas K Gandhi during his Johannesburg days, with his secretary Sonja Schlesin and Hermann Kallenbach

(Photographed by his son Adrian Hogben)

Lancelot Hogben

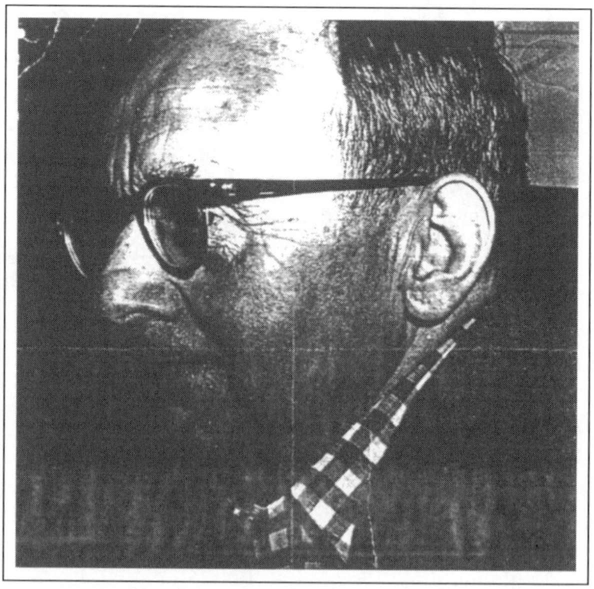

(From Ruth Schechter's file of family photographs)

Frederick Bodmer in the early 1950s

with as much Russian as American, some Yiddish and a little French and German The menu offered the usual food, but there were also all the favourite Russian foods and dishes. The small band – a piano and four violins – played Russian music, 'wildly exciting, sweetly mournful'. When the fiddler played the song of the Volga boatman, first one voice, then another joined in until the whole place was alive with the melody. Ruth left the Russian Inn at one thirty, the music not yet over and the tables still filling.

The second snapshot appeared on 16 June, and was the story of 'Fifi' the eight-year-old son of the janitor (or more grandly, the superintendent) of the building alongside the River Hudson where she stayed. First she told the story of the Greek janitor – on whom tenants depended for repairs to the apartment doors and windows, for the plumbing and the electricity. Those in his good books had their woes attended to; others had to endure the inclemency of the weather, or the failure of the amenities. Fifi, whose name graced the title, was a chubby boy of eight. He had seen Ruth four years before and, now grown, had come to tell her that his mother was going to take him to Lyons where he would train for the priesthood. It was not a very illuminating snapshot, nor was the item that followed it. Headed 'Afternoon Tea', it described the differences in custom on this repast. Morning tea, served regularly in South Africa, was ignored in New York but afternoon tea was regularly taken, with thick slices of cake.

The fourth snapshot was of 'Jenny' and told the story of a fashionably dressed and bejewelled young woman who had risen to take charge of the French language section of a large and well known bookstore. Of uncertain age, heavily made up, with conversation that varied between the childish and the mature, Jenny was a portent of the move by women into managerial sections of commerce, earning a salary that many a man might envy

'Bus Number 5' described the omnibus of the elite which travelled down Riverside Drive, alongside the River Hudson, riding across smooth streets. No standing was allowed in this exclusive coach that passed through the upper-class residential area then turned east toward Fifth Avenue with its 'alluring and expensive shops where the treasures of both east and west' could be found. It was a bus that allowed the traveller to overlook the finest areas of New York 'in stately comfort'. From Fifth Avenue the bus travelled into less glamorous regions of the town – to the warehouses and office blocks – but by then most of its passengers had already left it to window shop. 'If we cannot buy,' wrote Ruth, 'and who are we that we should shop where Sir Alfred Mond felt poor? – We can at least flatten our noses against the shop windows. It is worth while.'

The last snapshot appeared on 23 July 1924 when for the first time Ruth allowed herself some comments on life in the United States. In a few sentences she mentioned prohibition and race riots. Until that point I had wondered at the superficiality of the accounts of the first city in the Western world, even though they offered some glimpses of what the visitor might see.

This essay – entitled '"Saint Joan" and Others' – visited Broadway, the centre of New York's theatreland where the emporiums of entertainment were lavish, with scenery built on a colossal scale, and usherettes draped to embellish the stage setting. However, wrote Ruth, the acting was uneven. Apart from one or two of the principals, those who graced the stage were mediocre. Furthermore there was no speech discrimination: English tongues clashed with American drawls, spoiling the effects of the play. The audiences, she wrote, were mixed, many having chosen the play more because the theatre was close to their hotel or subway than because of intrinsic interest, and this was reflected in the audible comments. During the intervals the impact of prohibition was evident in the absence of the queues that had always been a feature of theatre life, and the audience sipped from cups of iced water. In concluding her article, rich in its evocations of theatre settings, heterogeneous audiences and their reactions, Ruth wrote:

> 'Saint Joan', by the way, that play of power and wit, ends with a characteristic and splendid Shavian audacity, which affords a magnificent curtain. Joan, come back to earth to hear of her canonization, and warned by her ex-inquisitor that if she returned in the flesh she would be burned again, as promptly and with even greater cruelty, stands alone in the centre of the stage. With arms outstretched, she says:

> 'Oh God, when will this world of Thine be, safe for Thy saints? How long O Lord, how long? ... And like an horrid answer comes a newsboy's shriek from the lobby: 'Race riot in Chicago. Two killed ... Ku Klux Klan says Smith must go... Baptist heretic denounced.

At long last Ruth had discarded her baby camera and provided a snapshot that bore some resemblance to the United States of 1924 – to racism, prohibition and crime, and the maladies that afflicted the country.

Once she was in New York it was a logical step to contact the offices of the *Nation* and suggest that she write for it. The first of the articles published in that paper was a review of *The Letters of Olive Schreiner, 1876-1920,* on 14 October 1925.

Social Life

Ruth's social life, with or without Morris, is opaque. She had been introduced to Morris's family and colleagues, his friends and his co-workers in the Jewish community. It was a fairly wide circle but she only had close links with a few members of it. One of these was Hermann Kallenbach. It was therefore not simply on a whim that Ruth wrote to him on 22 December 1914 when she heard that he had been interned because he was an Austrian citizen. She expressed her regret and indignation. 'Alec feels just as hotly as I do about it , and I nearly wept outright (and did I fear, as soon as 1 could get away).' The only comfort she felt was her belief that he would 'be able to help' his fellow-prisoners. She was sure that he was 'finding comfort and occupation in that direction'.

> Of the war one cannot trust oneself to write. The horror of it lives with one, by day and by night. My sympathies are with England, still more with Belgium. But even the dubious consolation of hatred of the enemy is denied me. I think perhaps you will like me better now.

While Olive was in South Africa Ruth was drawn into her circle of friends. Her acquaintances also grew to include many of Cape Town's painters and sculptors and people she met at her lectures. Her reviews in the local press showed that she regularly attended orchestral concerts, saw the plays that were staged in Cape Town and read widely. In her search for more intellectual discussion she visited the South African College (after 1916, the University of Cape Town), but whether she registered as a student or only met members of staff is not known. She was friendly with several lecturers, and it seems that at least one of the men was in love with her. Although the feeling was not reciprocated, it must have provided proof to Ruth that she was an equal among equals in the corridors of academe.

The Family

Ruth was not looking for any new liaison: she was still in love with her husband. Writing to Kallenbach in October 1915 she said: 'He really is the straightest soul I've met in young mankind, I love him and respect him more now than when we were first married, and that is saying a great deal.' Her three children also absorbed much of her time and energies. The two girls were the cause of great anxiety. The elder, Esther, entered a mental home when still young and remained under care throughout her life; Muriel, or 'Bobbet', was also unstable and spent many years under psychiatric treatment. Solly, the youngest, presented few difficulties. He went on to read science (under Hogben) at the University of Cape Town and medicine in Britain. He married in Cape Town, divorced in London, remarried and emigrated to Australia where he had three sons and appears to have severed relations with his parents. He died at a relatively early age and there is little information to flesh out the lives either of him or of his sisters.

An Election Campaign

Morris's parliamentary career faced a crisis shortly after a general election in 1920 in which he retained the Castle seat for the Unionist Party. General Smuts (then Prime Minister) invited the Unionists to join with his South African Party (SAP) to provide a stable government before the impending financial post-war slump and to stop the National Party's move to secede from the Commonwealth. Morris was suspicious of Smuts's motives and his suspicions were reinforced by a letter (dated 27 May 1917) written to Ruth by John X Merriman, a leading Cape parliamentarian who, at one stage, had been a candidate for the South African premiership. Merriman spoke of his 'despair' at Smuts's speech five days previously at the Savoy Hotel in London delivered, he wrote:

> to persuade the gullible British public that legislation whose effect – I will not say whose intention – is to reduce the native to the status of a barbarian serf, is founded on the 'Bed rock of Xtian' [Christian] principles, is indeed an evil omen.
>
> Smuts is a man of whom I am very fond – but his very intellectual facility makes him danger, perhaps the greatest we have. As an apostle of 'liberty'. Whether for black or white, he is grotesque.

When the two parties agreed to unite Morris refused to enter the new United Party. In this he had the full support of Ruth, who had adopted ever more radical views. When Smuts called a further general election Morris's name was proposed for Castle as an Independent candidate and he was returned unopposed. Leaving Ruth in charge of constituency affairs Morris made a rapid visit to London to see his brother Louis who was seriously ill.

Ruth, who took over the work in the election room, with the assistance of Olive, kept Morris informed. On 4 December 1920 she wrote:

> The band has begun to play. You've an excited leader in the *Argus*, an embittered reference in the leader in the *Cape Times*, this morning ... and an amusing letter entirely to your address in the same lofty chronicle.
>
> Moreover, this morning ... the telephone bell rang and Sir David Graaff [the future Prime Minister] wished to speak to you. I said to the underling that you had [?] yesterday for England, whereupon he said 'Hold on a

> minute', and came back and said goodbye. What was it to be, think you? Bribery or threat?
>
> Olive was here nearly all day; she is very pleased with your attitude and with your speech, and thinks you have assured your future in this country, not ruined it.

After mentioning people who had said they supported Morris, and adding news about the family, Ruth wrote:

> So I send this letter off with a happy heart. We have each other, and our love, and our dear children, and work to do for those who need us; we are singularly blessed in a world full of unhappy things.
>
> *Auf Wiedersehen*! I miss you badly.

Her letter on 14 January 1921 was even more enthusiastic. Morris's committee had 'worked as only your committee ever can and does'. Those who had helped her, or carried out tasks, should get special thanks. The names Ruth mentioned included men who were to enter parliament at a later date, like Douglas Buchanan, and others whose position cannot be identified, like O'B, Frank Heamans, De Sax ('given me every afternoon, Sundays, holidays, gone with me to the committee meetings, run my errands – it's been like having a younger brother at one's beck and call'), and the clerk in the Post Office 'who came over from his counter to grasp my hand and tell me how glad he was'.

Quite unselfconsciously Ruth also wrote about Farrington 'who has been the sweetest of all':

> He's given me endless time, running his paper and association in between, and he's cheered me up and helped me when 1 was tired, and sworn vehemently and relievingly when anyone attacked you. He has saved me effort, particularly this week, when I was so often tired and in great pain, so that I am amazed when I think of it.

The letter continues on an up-beat note:

> My dear, you have scored a tremendous moral victory; your position is very strong, far stronger then it has ever been. Directly you land, or before, you will be inundated with requests to help 'indirectly' this candidate or that. Make up your mind before you get off the boat, before the people come to you.
>
> My dear, my dear, my big man, you stand at the parting of the ways. Within the next few weeks you must become either in very truth the leader of a new party 'with malice towards none, with charity towards all, with courage ever to fight for right as God gives us to see the right' – or you sink to an unrecognized appendage of this group or that. Little fear enough for you of that. But if it is to be the other way for you, the way that I swear is yours if you choose to tread its lofty, difficult path, my darling, it is you who may yet bring peace to this torn country. Then you must be very careful, very certain in these first steps along the road.

Morris would have recognised the encoded message parodying Abraham Lincoln's second inaugural address as President of the United States on 4 March 1865. With the end of the American Civil War in sight he had said: 'With malice toward none; with charity for all; with firmness in the right, let us strive on to finish the work we are in; to bind up the nation's wounds; to care for him who shall have borne the battle, and for his widow and his orphan – to do all which may achieve and cherish a just and lasting peace among ourselves and with all nations.'

Ruth had cast her husband as the leader of a new party that would offer a lead to the country and act as liberator of the 'slaves' of South Africa. It was quite unrealistic, in the light of the country as it was in 1920, or of Morris's capacities to suppose that he, or anyone else, could restructure the country.

Morris sat alone in the House until 1929 when he lost his seat. It was not for want of trying to build support for his ideas in Parliament. Men were recruited to his short-lived Constitutional Democratic Party but failed in their attempt to secure seats in local councils or in parliament.

In the course of his duties Morris opposed discrimination on grounds of race, creed or colour, but was more inclined to petition some authority before whom he could state his case. Although he was never in the forefront of those who took such a stand, he was one of the few in Parliament who opposed the removal of the Cape African vote in 1935-1936. He also supported the cause of women's suffrage although he did not extend this, as did Ruth, to the demand that all women, irrespective of race, be enfranchised. In 1937, after Ruth had left him, he renewed his fight to have Yiddish recognised as a European language for immigrants to South Africa. Morris's fight against discrimination was recognised in a short study included in *Some South African Politicians,* by LE Neame, a prominent journalist. The entry, based on a profile written by Morris, read:

> The foundation of his politics is the principle of no discrimination on the ground of race, religion or colour. The test he applies relentlessly on all occasions. Upon this ground he fights for the south-eastern European, the Coloured man, the Native and the Indian ... He has the moral courage to back the unpopular cause.
>
> He is the acknowledged leader of Lost Causes. He will stand up for aggrieved public servants against the State, for faith-healers against doctors, for dental mechanics against dentists, for conscientious objectors against vaccinationists. No matter how forlorn the hope, he leads it with all the energy and the determination and the painstaking preparation that could be given to the most promising cause. Nothing rouses him to anger more that privileges, ring fences, colour bars, race prejudices and all obstacles to freedom of action and thought.[10]

Despite her earlier hopes for Morris's future as a political leader, or perhaps because of those hopes, disillusionment began to grow. It is not known when and over what issues the break came, but taking into account new friendships and new ideas that were forming, it is possible that Ruth was alienated by Morris's speech in Parliament in April 1923, after the brutal suppression of the general strike on the Rand, in which he declared that 'Judaism was the very antithesis of Bolshevism'. Whatever her opinion about the strike, which had distinct racial overtones, this was a position she could not support, particularly after Olive Schreiner's passionate defence of the Bolshevik government in 1919.

Yet it was not only the political differences that led to her dissatisfaction with her position at home. New friendships which provided stimuli that she had missed since she left her parents' home, and new views of world events, all played a part in her development. Once the differences became apparent the possibility of a collapse of the marriage loomed. The final break was still some years ahead and, inevitable as it became, it should not detract from the honourable position that Morris Alexander held in South African political events.

After 1926 Ruth wrote with caustic pen on the nature of colour discrimination in South Africa. Acting as South African correspondent for the *Nation* in 1926 she condemned the pitiable plight of the Indians and widened her canvas to discuss the inequalities that confronted Africans. She also attacked the Native Bills laid before parliament in 1928 for their plans to remove the native vote and for their harsh segregatory provisions. Ruth went beyond other critics in saying that parallel legislation, intended to leave the position of the coloureds in the Cape unaltered and give them one Parliamentary representative in the rest of the country, could only be intended to increase the differences between the coloured and African communities.

6

ENTER BEN FARRINGTON

In March 1920 Benjamin Farrington arrived from Ireland, with an impressive reputation as a student of English literature, Greek and Latin, to join the University of Cape Town staff. In the previous four years he had been an assistant lecturer, teaching classics at Queen's University, Belfast. In 1922 he became a senior lecturer and then professor of Latin.

One of Ruth's first friends on the campus, the historian J S Marais, then in the classics department[1], introduced Ruth to Gerard Paul Lestrade who had just completed a Masters degree in classics, before studying ethnology abroad[2], and shortly after Farrington's arrival in Cape Town he, in turn, was introduced by Lestrade to Ruth. In a letter written to Farrington in 1932 Ruth confessed that Lestrade had been more than a little in love with her.

Farrington became a constant visitor to the Alexander home and followed Ruth's lead in taking a fresh look at the social issues in South Africa. The marriage of minds between the two started shortly after they met. It can be assumed that the physical attraction followed some time thereafter. Letters to the twenty-nine-year-old Ben from members of his family in Ireland in 1920 indicate that he had written about Ruth often and warmly. On several occasions he was asked how his 'Jewess' was. In one letter, in August 1920, from a widow about to marry his brother Stephen, he was asked whether his relationship was platonic (which the good lady did not hold with), or whether he went further. Ben undoubtedly ignored the question. Whatever occurred, or did not occur, was not a subject that he would have discussed.

Ruth had much to contribute and it is obvious that Ben was engulfed in her enthusiasms. She had a deep feel for the people of South Africa, a knowledge of the problems faced by black communities inside a repressive society, and a passionate love of freedom and justice.

In response to my request for information, Laurens van der Post broke his customary silence to write that 'the cultural life of South Africa, when Cape Town mattered far more than it does today, would be sadly incomplete if that period did not include the presence and influence of Ruth and Ben'. Every writer of note, he wrote – not strictly accurately – who arrived in Cape Town in that era when travel was mainly by ship, had a letter of introduction to Ruth. Whether it was Olive Schreiner before her death, the Rev C F Andrews, or indeed any other lecturer or writer of note, they were bound to meet Ruth and, just as inevitably, Farrington. Some years after receiving this letter I found an extract from an article Van der Post had written for a *Cape Times* Centenary Supplement, of 27 March 1976. In this he said of Ruth:

> My principal weekly book reviewer ... the daughter of a distinguished Cambridge Jewish Professor and wife of an eccentric and liberal Member of Parliament. She had been a close friend of Olive Schreiner in her last years, had literary connections all over the world – E M Forster in the voyage which produced *A Passage to India* had stayed in her home – and she had supported us over *Voorslag* [*Whiplash*] with courage and intelligence.[3]

De Burger[4]

When Ben arrived in Cape Town he was deeply concerned about events in Ireland. During his time in Belfast he had been witness to the repression of the Irish uprising. Though he did not come from the Catholic community he had joined Sinn Fein (Irish for ourselves). The letters he received in Cape Town from friends and relatives through 1920 were filled with stories of the British troops – including the notorious Black and Tans – of shootings, imprisonments, and political turmoil.[5] He met people of like thought and gathered the nucleus of an organisation which was to be called the Irish Republican Association of South Africa IRA(SA). He also prepared for the publication of a fortnightly paper to be named *The Republic*.

A radical in Irish affairs, he knew little about South Africa. After visiting Johannesburg during the summer vacation of 1920 he wrote home justifying segregation, the pass laws, separate trams, and so on: what is not known is whether he was already in contact with members of any political party and had accepted their propaganda.[6]

While he worked towards the publication of *The Republic*, he found another outlet for his views. In August or September 1920 he wrote articles for *De Burger*, a Nationalist, Afrikaans-language newspaper. It seemed an obvious step to take: the English-language papers in South Africa gave no publicity to the Irish nationalist cause, while a bond between the nationalists in Southern Africa and Ireland had been established at the time of the South African War. The Nationalist press opened its columns to members of the IRA(SA), and members of the National Party were welcomed at Irish meetings. In September 1920 Ben was introduced in an editorial headed 'Sinn Fein'.

> Elsewhere in our columns readers will find the first of a series of articles written by Mr Farrington, a lecturer at the University of Cape Town. It is certainly unnecessary to draw attention to the article. The Irish question has drawn the attention of the world and the British government has systematically set about blackening the Irish, just as they always defamed us during and before the Boer War, so that it is necessary to persuade someone who knows about the Irish at first hand, to write about it. Every small people fighting for its national life, has our sympathy. We, who had the same experience in the last century and must still struggle today to remove the grip of Imperialism from our throat, can understand the position of the Irish.[7]

Readers today will find an obvious irony in the coupling of the Irish struggle with that of the Boer Republics but Ben was so imbued with nationalist rhetoric and so politically new to South Africa that he wrote without any qualms. The introductory article headed 'The Irish Republic' started rather stiffly with Ben recording his birthplace; his attendance as student and as lecturer at the three universities in Ireland (Dublin,

Belfast and Cork); and his contact with many of the leaders of the Irish Republic, ministers of state and their staff, and officers of the Republic's educational corps. He then provided an overview of the Irish struggle against British oppression, much of it being the standard history, complete with the then prevailing philosophy of nationalism that could be found in the writings of peoples across Europe who had campaigned for, or aspired to achieve, their independence. He began:

> I understand the origin of the Sinn Fein movement and the aims that it pursues and which it has partially attained. It is just six months that I left Ireland so that my information is not only first-hand but also comparatively fresh.
>
> The Irish had never acquiesced to the conquest of their land by England. This regime is not only morally indefensible, it is the most flagrantly corrupt government in modern Europe. In the last 70 years the population of Ireland was reduced from eight and a quarter million to four and a quarter million. In the seventeenth century Cromwell put men, women and children to the sword and sold thousands as slaves. Today Lord French declares 'I will trample the wild animals under my feet'. If the British administration wishes to extirpate the Irish, they have succeeded with great success. Naturally the Irish people opposed this strenuously. British law forbids them carrying weapons but there are always weapon available: whether it be agricultural implements or small arms.

In their struggle, wrote Ben, the Irish had hoped for assistance from the French in 1798 and the Italians in 1848. In 1867 the Fenians had taken up arms and the last rebellion had been in 1916 when there was hope that weapons would arrive from Germany. At this point the Irish strength had been two to three thousand men with 'guns and some maxims'. That is, they were in the minority.

There were two requirements if the Irish rebellion were to succeed. The first was that every opportunity for a successful uprising should be seized, the second that it should only be pursued if people were ready to fight for national freedom. The writings of Irish leaders who had fought and died mirrored the whole history of modern Europe. Although previous rebellions had failed in Ireland they provided a rich heritage of ideas about government and social justice, changing the nature of the movement for national freedom.

When earlier risings were suppressed there had been nothing left but to wait for the next opportunity to rebel. But in the past thirty years two new movements had appeared. The first was the Gaelic League, founded in 1891, which declared that the land was Gaelic. This determined the history, grammar, music and customs of Ireland which had been suppressed by foreign control, thereby robbing children of an ancient language and an ancient culture, replacing them with an unsuitable language which did not suit their soul, nor their 'speech organs'. In place of this language and culture a civilisation had been substituted which had only recently been 'woven together by a nation of shopkeepers'.

The second factor was Sinn Fein, formulated by Arthur Griffiths in 1905. Its policy was extensive and intensive, rejecting Westminster (as a means to achieving anything). England had destroyed the industrial and commercial life of Ireland – now the Irish had to take real power in their own hands by investing money in Irish industry, buying Irish goods, acquiring a ship and in this way regaining something of their former trade. There were unknown sources of wealth in the land which needed to be investigated and exploited.

Ben rejected this policy as impractical, maintaining that it had made no impact on the people. 'It appeared unbelievable that we would win freedom simply by buying Irish goods.' For many years Sinn Fein had languished. It had had little or nothing to do with the uprising of 1916 which was the work of the Irish Volunteers which had started in 1912 as an answer to Carson's Ulster Volunteer Force, and the Citizen Army which had emerged from the Labour movement after a large strike in 1913 to defend the citizens against the police who behaved brutally. Because of the new philosophies (and the ideas of the Gaelic League in particular), the failure of the rising in 1916 had actually promoted the spread of republican and national ideas. The Irish republic had been created and was only waiting for international recognition.

Ben's second article was on: 'Racial Division and Religion'. In this he wrote that any movement that believed that religious and racial differences should be settled by the sword did not deserve to survive. The two founding principles of republicanism and nationalism were toleration in religion and the subordination of racial difference to national unity. A century before Presbyterians had been leaders in the Irish national struggle, now many of them were revered by Irish Catholics.

'The belief that a victory for Irish nationalism would mean the persecution of Irish Protestants is, in my experience, one of the biggest obstacles preventing the Afrikaner from sympathising with Ireland. When I remember that the Huguenots were thrown out of France by Catholic intolerance and became an important element in the population of this country, then I am not surprised,' he wrote.

In the third article, 'The Religion of the British Rulers of Ireland', Ben provided a résumé of the religious split: the English followed the protestantism of Elizabeth while the Irish remained Papist. War was fought on Irish soil to be followed by the treaty of Limerick which allowed the Irish Army to fight in France. The army had scarcely left Ireland when the treaty was annulled because Irish Catholics were deemed to have no rights. Punitive laws were imposed. The British confiscated the property of church and state; Catholics were not allowed to own a horse worth more than £5; could not acquire fixed property; could not act as guardians of their own or anyone else's children; could not educate their children at home or abroad. None could occupy any civil or military position, and every priest was instructed to clear the land. Prelates were not allowed to practise their religion. Irish priests who refused to be registered were at first branded on the cheek and threatened with castration, but this was stopped by the British ministry. The punishment reverted to branding until it was revoked by the Irish upper house.

The fourth article, on 'Religion and Republicanism in Ireland', claimed that religious restrictions were used to rob the people of their birthright. Irish Catholics, ninety per cent of the population, were reduced by the Penal Code to poverty and remained uneducated. 'Through religious sectarianism our conquerors humiliated us and consequently the movement for Irish freedom had a religious appearance. Every little town had a Protestant Episcopal church and every one,

Protestant, Presbyterian or Catholic, had to pay a tithe for the church's maintenance. The appointed clerics stayed in England – proper absentee landlords – sustained by the large rents that had to be paid.'

In 1861 this system had prevailed in nearly two hundred towns. In most of these there were ten or fewer Protestants while there were thousands of Catholics. The tithe was often taken at the point of the bayonet in the presence of the Protestant cleric.

Gustav de Beaumont, a Catholic priest in Ireland, (described by Ben as a French historian), had, Ben wrote, said in 1837 that he had seen Indians starving and negro slaves in chains but believed that the Irish, deprived of all possessions and of their freedom, outdid the others in their suffering. Two years after these words were written and seven years into the long struggle known to the Irish as the 'tithes war', there was a change. Instead of the tithe being collected directly from the agricultural population it was collected from the people and paid directly by the large landowner to the church.

Famine had followed for four generations (an exaggerated statement) even though Ireland was England's bread basket. In about 1847 the famine had killed two million people although Ireland exported enough grain to support twice that number. Those who kept back grain for themselves and their family were found guilty of treason and banished. During this time the church had offered bread to the starving if they accepted Protestantism. Most chose to starve. This practice was only stopped as the direct result of the Fenian movement's action. 'Today there is one Irish priest for every 891 parishioners, one minister for every 554 Presbyterians, one cleric for every 363 Episcopalians, and yet the enemies of Catholicism say there are too many Catholic priests in Ireland,' wrote Ben. No more of his articles were published in *De Burger*. On 12 October 1920 a letter from R I C Scott Hayward, of the IRA(SA) Cape Town branch, informed readers that the university authorities had put pressure on Farrington, as a lecturer, to stop writing for the press.

The Irish Republican Association of South Africa

Ben edited *The Republic* from 20 November 1920 until 3 June 1922. In his first editorial he wrote:

> *The Republic* is the official organ of the Irish Republican Association of South Africa. The objectives of the Association are to labour for the international recognition of the Sovereign Independence of the Irish Republic, and to assist the people of Ireland in their struggle for the cause and to unite the energies of men and women of the Irish race in South Africa for the purpose of preserving national traditions.

The editorial also promised that *The Republic* would provide reliable news about Ireland and explain the significance of Irish republicanism and what was happening in Ireland. Thereafter Ben made a passionate plea for Irish nationalism whose tradition had 'remoulded Europe' in the nineteenth century. His editorials were erudite, drawing on his extensive knowledge of the ancient classics and his knowledge of Irish history. But although their appeal was often similar to the writings of nationalists everywhere his demands for Ireland were different in one respect: he claimed that the Irish demand for national independence preceded those of any other European states.

> The Irish nation ... is older than the discovery of America. It is older than the British Empire, in whose name it is now being strangled; and older than 'Merry England' in the happy days before the English lost their soul in their endeavour to gain the whole world.The Irish are a Christian people, but the Irish nation is older than Christianity... We would be false indeed to our trust if we neglected the ancient wisdom of our people.

Explaining the motives that had led to the origin of Irish nationalism he said, with some equivocation:

> We have no quarrel with Englishmen for overflowing the confines of their country (*sic*), though we have some quarrel with the method of establishing themselves in their adopted lands. But the Irish people have in no sense 'overflowed'

> the confines of Ireland. Upwards of five millions of the Irish race have been scattered to the four corners of the world in the last seventy years while the population of their mother-country has wasted away. They did not go because there was no room for them in Ireland, but because they were driven from their native soil by a foreign government ... They went because it was the settled policy of the foreign government that they should go and they had no means of resistance.

By the time the third issue appeared, on 18 December 1920, Ben could announce that 'our success has been instantaneous'. Branches had been formed everywhere and the journal was being read by thousands

> We feel that the lying propaganda of the English press is the chief obstacle in the way of our enjoying the sympathy of honest people everywhere. Our endeavour must be to spread the truth about Ireland and to create in South Africa an informed and sympathetic public opinion.

In the same editorial he wrote of the destruction wrought by British troops in Cork, the third town in Ireland, and 'the richest'. The burning of the municipal buildings, the city hall, the public library and the frontage of a quarter mile in the main street had caused damage estimated at seven million pounds. The burning of Cork, he wrote, 'was comparable to some great natural catastrophe in which a city is engulfed by an earthquake or overwhelmed by a volcanic eruption'. In a flow of patriotic rhetoric Ben (if these were his words) described Cork as 'a city not built by hands, the incorruptible City whose builder and maker is God'. Then he turned on the British member of Parliament who, he maintained, had lied when he had said that the Irish had burnt down their own town to bring odium on the British:

> How impudent the speaker. And how base the audience, of such words as these! We shall believe him when we have proof that the Indians shot themselves at Amritsar, that

> the natives of Tasmania exterminated themselves, that Central Europe and Russia blockaded themselves, and that twenty-seven thousand women and children in the Transvaal and the Orange Free State burned their own homesteads and committed suicide in the Concentration Camps.

As editor of the paper Ben was responsible for its contents as well as for the editorials, but aspects of the latter are not always congruent with his other writings. In quoting from them I am not always certain whether Ben's contributions were not themselves edited by members of the Central Council of the Association – but it is a question that cannot easily be answered.

The warmth with which the National Party welcomed members of the Irish community, and the IRA(SA) in particular, led to questions inside the Association about the extent of political collaboration with the Afrikaner-orientated National Party. With a general election pending there was a heated debate in Johannesburg on 1 December 1920 on whether the IRA(SA) should publicly support the National Party or only express thanks to them for sympathising with the Sinn Fein cause. The senior men in the IRA(SA) opted for the latter course and, after acrimonious argument, a resolution to that effect was passed.

The Republic declared that the Association would not support any party. Those who wished to vote Nationalist should do so in the same spirit as that shown at the many National Party gatherings at which the Irish cause was supported. But no bargain existed. Those who favoured General Smuts or Colonel Creswell [leader of the Labour Party] should vote for the party of their choice. The Association existed for one single reason – 'to secure international recognition for the Irish Republic'.

In the eighth issue of *The Republic* on 26 February 1921 Ben claimed that Ireland 'had never been so near success as at the present moment'. Tracing the battles in Ireland since the first years of the seventeenth century, he could only record a series of defeats. There had been men who had had the determination, and even the vision, but the conditions for success had not been present. For generations all the efforts of the nationalist had failed. Now victory had been achieved and 'they are fighting, not to establish but to defend the national institutions of Ireland'.

Writing of 'mis-leaders' like John Redmond, Ben was fiercely critical of those who cheered when Irish blood was spilt in fighting England's wars while they prevented Irishmen from getting arms to fight for Irish freedom. On the subject of the importance of the formation of the Irish Volunteers and the establishment of the Irish Republican Army, Ben wrote:

> It was an insane Ireland that continually cried out against English tyranny in Ireland and pathetically enrolled itself in the English armies which forced English tyranny in Egypt, India and South Africa. It was a sane Ireland that created the Irish Republican Army. *We are not among those who believe that Ireland can achieve her end by force of arms nor in the least inclined to glorify military valour above all other sorts of valour.* Those who understand … Arthur Griffith's plan know that … when the armed men have been overwhelmed the fight is only beginning, the fight of the whole people is to ignore all English institutions and be loyal only to their own. [My emphasis]

Although things were serious, 'Ireland is going to win' … 'Ireland in centuries has not been so consciously a nation as she is today'. Ben still had to learn quite a lot about historical processes, and where there was a shortage of understanding he could find no answers. The editorial continued and included a tribute to those who had fought in the battle for freedom:

> When we try to estimate the causes of this astonishing change we are at a loss; for the deeper causes lie utterly outside the scope of the historian's investigation. A nation apparently dead springs to life. We have to account for a resurrection from the dead. One cannot net such a miracle in the finest meshes of cause and effect. We see and worship. And the old music wakes again in the heart and beats in

> the brain, and the pulses keep time to the march of noble words remembered: no words and no music nobler and deeper than that grandest of popular songs: 'When laws can stop the blades of grass' ... But we are no nearer the reason why. Why Pearce should wish to die for us: why Terry MacSwinney should give himself for us; why unknown Irishman in every corner of Ireland gave themselves utterly, enduring prison, torture, starvation, death and indignities worse than death – these things we cannot know. We only know that without them nothing of what has been accomplished could have been won.

In Vol 1 No 11, 9 April 1921, Ben started writing a series of articles on the northern province of Belfast. In reciting the history of the region from pre-Christian times he had few peers. He had a vast repository of facts and could record the scholarly fame of Bangor and Armagh in the sixth century – long before the awakening of neighbouring countries. Ulster was also the centre of resistance to the British army of Elizabeth's generals, the centre of the greatest rebellion in the seventeenth and eighteenth centuries. Coming to more modern events, Ben wrote that the Ulster question was a deliberate creation of English politicians:

> For centuries England held Ireland through the landlord class who were originally Englishmen planted in Ireland. When ... feudalism was in danger of being banished from Ireland, the remnant of the Irish landlords and the English Tories ... [was transformed into] the alliance between the Irish capitalists and the English Imperialists. And this new grip on Ireland was found in Belfast.

Originally there had been an alliance with the feudal lords in which the peasantry had been kept oppressed in return for the lords acting 'as the English garrison' now:

> It will pay you to prevent your labourers organising to demand the just reward of their labour, and it will pay us

> if you do that by turning them against the national aspirations and the religious beliefs of their fellow-countrymen. Keep them quarrelling about the Pope while you and I divide the spoil.

In Vol 1, No 14, On 21 May 1921, Ben turned on Britain in general and Lloyd George in particular for their duplicity over their policy in Ireland. He declared that England had had the choice of recognising its role in repressing the Irish, and had avoided it, 'but for Ireland there is no choice. He is a renegade who does not resist English rule in Ireland to the utmost'. There was neither shame nor contrition in England which extolled those who rejected slavery – from the Greeks at Marathon to the bravery of William Tell – but 'hangs the patriots of Ireland'. 'She welcomes the Young Italians, extols the Belgians, but banishes Young Irelanders to her penal settlements.' He indignantly accused Lloyd George of lying about the responsibility for the violence on the Irish mainland.

The editorial of 19 November 1921, Vol 2, No 27, was devoted to the condemnation of partition which divided the six northern counties from the rest of Ireland. Ben had received reports of delegations from Tyrone and Fermanagh, from South and East Down, the city of Derry, from the county of Armagh, and most impressively from Belfast nationalists, protesting against their exclusion from the rest of Ireland.

On 3 December 1921, Vol 2, No 28, Ben discussed the role of nationalism in the 19th century. He quoted, with approbation, from Mrs Alice Greene's epilogue to her late husband's *History of the English People*:

> A new ideal had in its turn caught the hearts of the peoples – the doctrine of nationality – and had fired men with an exalted resolve that, delivered from the abasement of servitude, the nations should be free to carry on the spiritual tradition of their fathers, in religion, in literature, in the shaping of their social life, even in the conduct of their trade for the advantage and uplifting of their own lands. The most democratic call yet heard, it summoned men of every class and degree to give their service to the

> land and people of their birth, and as it bound the whole community in one purpose of large emancipation, it opened to them wider issues than an industrial struggle to win material advantage for a single class. By reverent memory of ancient human conflicts, by the sense of obligations to an unknown future, imagination was lifted beyond the bonds of the present.

The volume closed with quotations from her husband's letters which reinforced her own views:

> The sympathies of people with peoples, the sense of a common humanity between nations, the aspiration of nationalities after freedom and independence are real political forces ... [and again] The great force which has transformed Europe, which has been the secret of its history ever since 1815, is a political 'sentiment' – that of nationality.

From this standpoint Ben could declare that England was fighting a losing battle and that 'Imperialism as she sought to maintain it in Ireland, is out of date, and cannot find a supporter in any outside country'. Surveying the future, in which England's commercial empire would be robbed of its supremacy by the growth of the American and Japanese navies he foresaw, following Dean Inge, a dwindling of the British population and a reversion to a rural society which would cultivate the soil. Meanwhile Ireland's population would grow and the problem would be to remove the artificial restrictions to her prosperity. It was the 'end of an epoch,' Ben declared, 'and it is essential to understand what was possible and desirable in the future so that we may control events before the crystallisation of a new epoch begins'.

The first convention of the IRA(SA) was held in Bloemfontein in February 1921. Resolutions were passed about the recall of British troops from Ireland; the recognition of the Irish republic; the promotion of Irish goods worldwide; the establishment of a 'centre and rallying point' for expatriate Irish; and the establishment of a permanent secretariat to promote these resolutions. One of the outcomes was to be the calling of an Irish World Race Convention in Paris in January 1922, a meeting credited by de Valera as a South African-Irish initiative. Farrington was elected to represent the IRA(SA) and, in Paris, was elected secretary of the Convention. At the last session a Central Executive Council of the Irish International (Fine Ghaedheal) was elected.

From its inception there were overtones of conflict at the Paris conference. Ben had to withdraw his proposal for the creation of a memorial to commemorate 'the goodwill of the Irish abroad'. He had suggested that this be a practical memorial 'such as a technical institution, a library or museum for every Irish university, or a fund to purchase Irish manuscripts ... and the erection in Ireland of a building to house them'. He also supported a resolution calling on the Irish abroad to owe political allegiance only to the government of the country in which they were permanently resident. This resolution was also rejected. He was later to write in *The Republic* of 22 May 1922:

> Your delegate saw the scheme for an Irish International being handed over to men who were incapable of understanding any other type of organisation than an Irish-controlled league of hyphenated Irishmen, the very ideal of that mischievous system of politics which it was his ambition to destroy.[8]

But the Executive Council did not function. The Conference was wrecked by differences over the Anglo-Irish treaty. There was a demand for a second, pro-treaty, secretary for the new council of Fine Ghaedheal, supported among others by Ben. The proposal was rejected.

Back in South Africa the dispute over the treaty rumbled on. Ben continued to support it and published a long article by Arthur Griffiths in favour of it. This was in conflict with a resolution of the Central Executive that the journal preserve a neutral attitude towards the rival policies of De Valera on the one side and Griffiths and Collins on the other. In Vol 2, No 38, on 6 May 1922 Ben wrote:

> The Editor departed from this agreement on the receipt of the news that civil war had broken out in Ireland. Marking

> time was in any event difficult for him. Events refused to mark time. He felt that a new situation had arisen on which he must exercise his own judgment ...
>
> Members have no claim on him to compel him to write against his views: and he has no right to use the columns of the official organ to express opinions not generally held. Under these circumstances, with mutual goodwill, the relationship should cease.

There was a rumble of discontent in the IRA(SA) and it collapsed as a result. Two more additions of the paper were printed, with Ben remaining as editor but restrained from writing any editorials. It then ceased publication and the Association went out of existence.

After the collapse of the Republican Association Ben's views developed along fresh lines. This is apparent in his review of *The Irish Revolution and how it Came About*, by William O'Brien, in the *Cape Times* of 9 August, 1923 and found in the scrapbook. The book was the second volume of personal reminiscences by an Irish Member of Parliament, a judge and a Catholic. The author had very little to say about the Gaelic League, Sinn Fein 'in the original sense, or the revolutionary Labour movement with its Volunteers ... His concern is merely to show us how the field was left clear for the operation of these forces by the collapse of the Irish Parliamentary Party'. Ben believed the book was important because it provided 'first hand evidence of this veteran leader of the small All-for-Ireland Party in Westminster, of the descent of the Nationalist Party [when they accepted a salary from the British treasury in 1911] from one base level to another of corruption and compliance; of the fumbling and evasive conduct of the Home Rule Bill by the Liberals; and of the efforts that were made at various stages, after the outbreak of hostilities, by leaders, both on the English and the Irish side to arrange an accommodation'.

More fatal still, Ben believed, was the dominance of Irish politics by the secret Catholic society known as the Board of Erin Branch of the Ancient Order of Hibernians, revealed for the first time by William O'Brien. This sectarian body had fought the Orange Order by 'imitating its basest tactics and pitting one inflamed bigotry against another'.

Spreading through Ireland it had secretly dominated the United Irish League until it became 'the dispenser of all the power and patronage in Ireland'. It had reigned supreme from 1906 to 1916. In one respect the rising of 1916 had been an effort by disinterested men to 'dispel the fog of obscure intrigue which secrecy and sectarianism had cast over the politics of the nation'. He described the sweeping victory of Sinn Fein in the election of 1918 as 'the triumph of a cleanly idealism' and believed that the platform on which O'Brien had stood, and wanted the Nationalist Party to stand, 'deserved to be quoted':

> (a) That a solution of the Irish difficulty must first be sought among Irishmen in Ireland, and (b) that its legislative enactment must be the work, not of one particular English party, Liberal or Unionist, but of all British and Irish parties in common.

The effect of such a policy could be foreseen (as O'Brien noted with justifiable pride) in the Wyndham Act of 1903 for the abolition of landlordism; and its neglect produced the 'one greatest plot of 1921' in the partition of Ireland. 'Mr O'Brien's unfailing advocacy of these principles is deserving of all praise.'

Ben followed this article on 24 July 1926 in the *Cape Times* with an equally favourable review of Sir James O'Connor's *History of Ireland, 1798-1924*:

> What is rare in him is that he should have coupled with his close observation of affairs, the passion for honest thought, and the public spirit that has gone to the making of the two large volumes before us – a piece of writing which sends through the unwholesome atmosphere of Irish thought a breath like a cleaning wind.

The main thesis, he wrote, was that for more than a century Ireland had suffered from a war mentality in its most aggravated form. O'Connor, in discussing this, had expressed an 'unvarnished view upon every topic that is usually avoided in Ireland' because:

> It means pulling hundreds of men off their pedestals. It means taking a dispassionate review of all the chief politicians, agitators, revolutionaries, patriots and martyrs, their policies, propaganda and methods. It means discussing the attitude of the Catholic Church from the bishops to the curates on the main political and social questions that have agitated Ireland. It means looking at the Catholic versus Protestant and the North versus South problems in all their nakedness. It means exposing the crudities and the insincerities that have gone together with some better qualities, to the making of the various elements of the Irish-Ireland movement.

O'Connor, Ben continued, 'has a finely independent judgment, a wide knowledge of men and affairs and a genius for frankness. He set down a list of the many myths of Irish history which he takes to be false – including many that are still taken as proven – and has severely down-graded the importance of many of the movements and the flash-in-the-pan rebellions, restoring the history of the country to its right proportions.' In doing so, though, he had been unjust to some individuals, and had 'done less than justice to the character of some of the leaders'.

Ben reviewed a few other books on Ireland, but none of the reviews was as significant as those of the O'Brien and O'Connor books. Without ever surrendering his support of Sinn Fein he seems to have refined his ideas on Irish events and turned to the works that were to emerge from the reading he had undertaken for his courses of lectures. Other works came from his pen and had their own intrinsic interest.

The 'Making' of Ben Farrington

To write about Farrington in Cape Town without mentioning Ruth is almost impossible. He was not only part of her circle, he complemented her in bringing it to life. Ben was a remarkable man who towered over his contemporaries as thinker and author, and as a personality. Yet, except for his articles on Ireland, little is known about his life in South Africa outside the activities of Ruth and her circle – and even that is circumscribed by an absence of information about his contact with Ruth, with whom he was deeply in love.

He had written to members of his family about Ruth soon after they met and he was to say in a letter to Julius Lewin, years after her death, that Ruth had 'made him'. Quite how she had done so was not explained and possibly defies a simple assessment. Their friendship, and their love, covered two decades in Cape Town and Swansea. From her letter to Gandhi in 1926 it can be surmised that Ruth brought with her the experience of a family's warmth; an outlook enriched by Olive; a humanism deepened by contact with the people of District Six and the radical leaders of the coloured community. But even this does not add up to the inspiration that would have been transmitted by a woman who was herself developing through the years in which they were in close contact and gave so freely of her affections.

As for the impact of Ben on Ruth, there can be no doubt about that. Ben inspired all who heard him with his enthusiasm for the Greek and Latin classics and English literature, and the two could read the classics (in their original languages). He brought intellectual stimulation, intelligent conversation and a love that Ruth had not previously experienced.

During his years in Cape Town Ben published *Primum Gaius Homo*, a text book for his courses in Latin, in 1927, and *Samuel Butler and the Odyssey* in 1929. This was an enlargement of his review of Butler's account in the *Cape Times* on 18 April 1924 in which he argued, in agreement with Butler, that the *Odyssey* and the *Iliad* were written by two authors, the second of whom was a woman with little knowledge of military matters. His articles included a review in the *Cape Times* in June 1923 of the revised translation of *The Eclogues of Virgil* by TF Royds; *The Choephoros of Aeschylus*, translated by Gilbert Murray, on 29 October 1923; 'Nicander Nucius' (1925); 'Shelley's Translations from the Greek' (1928); 'The Life and Work of Vesalius, (1930); 'The Last Chapter of De Fabrica of Vesalius' (1931); Chapman's Homer' (1934); and 'Vesalius on China-Rost' (1935).[9]

He also collaborated with Professor I Schapera who edited a volume for the Van Riebeeck Society in 1933 entitled *The Early Cape Hottentots*, consisting of one account written in Dutch and translated by himself and two accounts written in Latin and translated by Ben. In his introduction Schapera states that the three texts, all written within two decades of the arrival of Van Riebeeck, contained the first accounts of the life and customs of the native people. In his appraisal of the works he wrote:

> We cannot be sufficiently thankful to the old writers for recording their impressions and observations of Hottentot culture while it still flourished in all its traditional manifestations. We may lament their many omissions, criticise their statements of so-called fact, ridicule their opinions and smile at their eager credulity; but with all their deficiencies they have left us a mass of accurate information which can no longer be obtained.

Ben's first translation was of 'A Short Account of the Cape of Good Hope' by William Ten Rhyne, who, travelling to the east, stayed for four weeks in October-November 1673. Although Ten Rhyne's interests were primarily botanical he had also inquired about the natural resources of the country and the manners of the native people. Farrington was to write:

> When stripped of its verbiage and classical allusions, his account of the Hottentots can by no means be regarded as detailed. Nevertheless his remarks on their mode of life, warfare, cattle trade and medical practices are particularly valuable additions to the scanty information previously published on these topics, and he also has some useful observations on their physical peculiarities and bodily mutilations. His list of tribes, too, is of considerable importance. It shows how within twenty years from the foundation of the settlement the groups in its immediate vicinity had degenerated into mere hangers-on and followers of the Dutch, how tribal distinctions were being lost and individual leaders coming into prominence, and how only the more remote tribes still retained their original character.

J G Grevenbroek, who arrived in the Cape in 1684, wrote a letter in 1695 which filled a small quarto volume of 120 pages. It was called 'An Elegant and Accurate Account of The African Race Living Round the Cape of Good Hope, Commonly Called Hottentots'. Ben described it as 'well written in a large hand' and filled with tags from Virgil, Horace and other Latin writers. Although the author expressed 'his own unmerited and unspecified grievances, he attracts by his honest indignation at the abuses of the time, and by his charming, if absurdly expressed, enthusiasm for the Cape and its native inhabitants.' Thereafter the work consisted of translating the texts, altering the punctuation, and 'providing good readable English'.

Before working on the translations Ben wrote several reviews which covered a large range of works. The early cuttings in the joint scrap book kept by Ben and Ruth are too mutilated to be of much use and it is not possible to determine which might have been written by Ben. Did he review the mutilated and therefore unreadable *Prose and Verse Written [for?] the Irish Theatre* in April 1923, or *The Minoans* in June? One review which was almost certainly written by Ben is that of *Marcel Proust: An English Tribute*, edited by C K Scott Montcrieff. The reviewer says of most of the twenty-one contributions that the word 'tribute' is not always appropriate. Proust is taken to account for his slowness, his long sentences, and so on. After discussing some of the contributions – some 'reasonable', others 'insufferable', the review closes on a caustic note:

> To the irreverent lay mind, which has merely enjoyed whole-heartedly so much of Proust's work as it could get hold of, the least interesting, and most irritating of the articles in the volume are those which discuss the message of the Master. That a genius sought and found expression for these gentry is beside the mark. Indeed, 'had it been only for the sake of the satisfaction of literary creation', says, as one may expect, Mr Middleton Murry, 'he probably would not have written at all'. Why, why, must they make their literary gods, too, in the images of their own Freud-ridden selves?

After that Olympian bolt it was a relief to find Ben's review of W H Moreland's *From Akbar to Aurangzeb*, (no date), in which he praises the increased emphasis on writing history from the economic standpoint. This seems dated today, for how else could Moreland have summed up his enquiries in his concluding passage? There he is quoted as saying, in lines that are parallel to Ben's description of Ireland:

> Weavers, naked themselves, toiled to clothe others. Peasants, themselves hungry, toiled to feed the towns and cities. India taken as a unit, parted with useful commodities in exchange for gold and silver, or in other words gave bread for stones. Men and women, living from season to season on the verge of hunger, could be contented so long as the supply of food held out: when it failed, as it so often did, their hope of salvation was the slave-trader, and the alternative was cannibalism.

Ben also presented papers to the English Association. His first, as reported on 1 September 1925, in the *Cape Times*, was on Philemon Holland, the Tudor translator, who had been called 'the Translator-General of his age'. He had been a fellow at Cambridge, studied at Oxford and taught as an usher at the Free School in Coventry, where at seventy-five he was appointed Headmaster and where he also practised medicine. After ten months he asked to be relieved of the office of Headmaster and died at the age of 85. Holland knew French and Italian, Greek and Latin, and his translations, into immaculate Elizabethan English, were always highly accurate and have not been surpassed.[10]

His next paper, in May 1928, was on 'Trelawny, Friend of Byron and Shelley'. Ben gave an account of Trelawny's strange life-history: at the age of eleven he had worked in the merchant service; two years later he had moved to the navy, deserted at seventeen and, ever the adventurer, served four years with a pirate. In 1882 he joined Byron and Shelley at Pisa, and after Shelley's death, served with the Greek chief, Odysseus, in the Greek War of Independence. Trelawny had had difficulty trying to write a life of Shelley and, instead, had written an autobiography: *The Adventures of a Younger Son*. In 1858 he wrote *Recollections of the last days of Byron and Shelley*. Ben said of him:

> The amazing freshness and actuality of this book written long after the death of the poets, and of its statements was borne out by all available evidence as a phenomena to be pondered. The essential truth of the conversations recorded was doubted by none and they were proof of a very high order of intelligence in the apprehension of character and the ability to convey it to others. . .
>
> Trelawny knew that Shelley was unique, and that his spirit was dying within him, proud as he was, for lack of recognition and encouragement. Had the sea not claimed the poet, Trelawny would have done for the man himself what he himself could only do for his memory.

Behind the seriousness of Ben's papers there was a sense of humour. There were also few inhibitions in some of the articles he wrote for the popular journals. However he was not superficial. In a review of a Herodotean account of the Indian mutiny, as presented by L J D Richardson, (*TA INÄIKA*, *Cape Times*, 16 July 1927), Ben gave an account of the author's imitation of the Greek historian's account of the battle of Plessy in 1757 that led to the Indian mutiny. Herodotus's art consisted of 'quoting oracles that seem to foreshadow the tragic events to which his history moves'. By taking a striking modern event, the main outlines of which are familiar, writes Ben, and recasting it in the manner of the Father of History, he has 'provided an illuminating demonstration of the method of the historiographer and put us all in his debt'.

The reader is no less in debt to Ben for his article 'Sunium's Marbled Step' which appeared in *The South African Nation* on 29 October 1927. It was witty and erudite, Ben taking pleasure in introducing his readers to sayings taken from the Greek writers in a way which was not usually found in the columns of the daily press.

> The proper way to get to Sunium, if only it would work, is Byron's way, that is to address a command to the universe

> at large to 'place' one there. The next best way, if you can afford it, is a switch-back journey by taxi over primitive roads. For the present writer there was only one way, the light railway from Athens to Laurion and a six mile walk from there to the Temple of Poseidon, or the Columns, as the local inhabitants call it. These six miles might well take 'a nimble young man', as Pausanius puts it, two hours to accomplish. And since there is an interval of just four hours between the arrival and the departure of the train, the nimble young man must not loiter if he is to see the Columns at all and get back to Athens that night.
>
> Moreover the train from Athens to Laurion is a tragedy. One can assert this on the authority of Aristotle, who says that 'a tragedy endeavours to complete its circuit within one revolution of the sun, or to fall but little outside that limit'. This is just what the train does. It is due to leave Athens at eight a m, to reach Laurion at noon, to start back at four p m, and to be in Athens again at eight. But the traveller should remember that these are only its tragic aspirations.
>
> It is well, however to get the cook to call one before six o'clock, and to arrange with her nephew, who is sure to drive a taxi, to be in attendance to take one to the station ... Such an arrangement worked excellently – except in one small particular ... He lodged at a solitary building in a large park with gates half a mile apart opening on the roads that ran to the north and the south. Of course, no sooner was he outside the gate on the south side, with the spring lock snapped behind him, than the taxi ... became audible hooting despairfully at the north gate.

Then, as in ancient tragedy, there was a 'recognition scene'. Without 'a family heirloom, a distinctive birthmark, or a scar from a boar's tusk' the recognition was not as easy to effect as it was in early times. However it was effected, and the story was 'cast in the ancient tragic manner'. In poetic mode, Ben described the interchange between the taximan and himself: with a chorus of interested bystanders greeting the decision by the driver to take his client to the train. Of course the train was an hour late and only the appearance of a Russian exile, driving a car, got him to the ruins.

> The icy wind that on that January day ... made it impossible for one who had been already half-frozen for some six or seven hours to spend more than a minute or two on the spot. But the glistening pillars on that bold foreland, the Land's End of northern Greece ... do not need more than a few seconds to make their indelible impression on the memory. One of the things often said about the literature of the ancient Greeks is that it shows little feel for nature. It is, as a matter of fact, not true. But if their literature did not prove it, then the exquisite harmony between their architecture and their landscape would itself suffice to show that the most beauty-loving people were not blind to nature's beauty ... And in this what remains of their architecture bears out the lesson of their literary monuments. Greek landscape, except for the limpid air that bathes it, is not more lovely, more bold, more varied than many another land supplies. But though there are hills everywhere to match the Acropolis, there is only one Parthenon; and of the many lofty forelands thrust out into the world's seas where is there one so nobly crowned as Sunium?
>
> Deathless is the word that is usually applied to such beauty; but how can one say that in Greece of all lands, where what survives is but the merest fragment of the beauty that is dead? ... The best thing that archaeology has taught us is that in Greece ... epoch has succeeded to epoch of noble art. Some such reflections as these will be found very necessary to keep the traveller from going mad on the return journey ... The train was, in fact, two-and-a-half hours late. But Aristotle has also said that 'a tragedy should be embellished with appropriate language in its

> several parts', and it was a relief to render this service to the train.

Ben's reviews and articles took many shapes. His versatility was apparent in his review of *The Sciences and Philosophy*, by J S Haldane, in the *Cape Times* on 22 June 1929. In this publication of the Gifford Lectures of 1928 Haldane had confronted the problems in biology of mechanism versus vitalism and, rejecting these theories, found a solution in Hegelian philosophy, indeed, arguing that 'only the spiritual is real'. Haldane had said that:

> Since philosophy is our ultimate interpretation of reality, every philosophy must claim to be realistic ... reality is not to be found in mathematical, physical, or biological interpretations of reality, since these interpretations deal only with abstractions from the psychological interpreted world of interest and values, which is thus prior to them, or more elementary. So-called materialism, or philosophy which bases itself on the physical interpretation of experience, is thus out of experience.

Ben had unravelled Haldane's thinking, and that was all that was required in a review. It is doubtful whether he ever accepted this thesis fully, even when he joined the Communist Party in Britain and edited one of its journals. He was, perhaps, on more familiar ground when, in the *Cape Times* of 15 June 1931, he reviewed *The Letters of John Keats*, edited by Maurice Buxton Forman. This was an enlarged version of previous volumes – now including all the known letters and fragments of letters, the sources given together with biographical memoranda of the correspondents. There was not much that had not appeared before but it was important to have the material brought together in its entirety, with corruptions in earlier texts removed and the dates of many letters printed with greater certainty.

Ben was lyrical about Keats who 'displays to perfection the art of putting the whole of himself into a letter. He unpacks his heart alike of the most whimsical feelings and the most serious meditations.'

> To rise from the reading of the four great Odes, with the sense of their perfection strong upon one, is perhaps to feel that he had after all managed to say the highest that was in him before death silenced him. But to follow letter by letter his ever-deepening sense of the consecration of the poet's calling: his appreciation and analysis at once humble and bold, of such mighty exemplars as Milton and Wordsworth: his day in day out study of Chaucer, Shakespeare, Spencer; his acquisition of French ... Italian ... His gradual moulding of his everyday living to the requirements of his ripening genius.

To read this review -as alive today as it was over sixty years ago – is to add a new dimension to the reading of one of Britain's greatest poets. It also elevates Ben above many others who write their reviews with such little understanding or diligence.

A Time of Reflection – And a Time for Change

Available records have little to say about Ben's activities after the collapse of the IRA(SA). He did not seek publicity and was content to keep a low profile. On the other hand Ruth's activities were bound to affect the course of his life. Ruth's radicalism evolved slowly, but it did not do so in a vacuum. Two major events made her review her previous interests: one was her work with the people of District Six which provided examples of absolute deprivation, the other the jingoism coming from the National Party which threatened to uproot the Indian people and to place ever new restrictions on the African people.

Ruth's work in District Six was done initially with a minimum of publicity. Her response to General Hertzog's plans to extend segregation, however, was quite the opposite. From 1926 she wrote critical articles on Hertzog's attack on the rights of Indians and on the 'Native' vote. The first of her many articles on the subject appeared in June 1926 in the New York *Nation*.

Ben undoubtedly knew of her writings and was empathetic to what she was doing. It must also have been a defining moment in his development, because D F Malan, who was in charge of the legislation against the Indian people, had been the editor of *De Burger* when it published his Irish articles.

There is no information about Ben's continued association with the Irish movement, nor is it known whether he ever associated himself with the Irish Brigade that participated in the revolt that marked the end of the General Strike in 1922. There is also no information about his support for Ruth's work in the black communities but it is inconceivable that he did not sympathise with her work in District Six.

While there can be no doubt about Ruth's impact on Ben, it was not a one-way process. When she first met him, she still maintained her religion, her Zionism and her closeness to the Jewish community. If she had any doubts about her beliefs they were not allowed to break through a life-time of observance. Then came Ben's accounts of persecution, torture and death in Ireland that were the equal of anything that had happened to the Jews in Eastern Europe and were probably just as fiendish. This must have had an impact on the belief that the misery of the Jewish people was unique.

As Ben and Ruth became ever closer – and became lovers – they must have discussed the miseries they knew so intimately, and there were some indications that they heard some of these matters discussed by members of the Communist Party with whom they were in contact. One unpublished document that I was able to read in Uppsala – an attempt at a biography of Ray Alexander (Mrs R E Simons) – states that after Ray Alexander heard Ruth speak on Olive Schreiner, she had found and read everything that was available by that writer[3] . Whether this led to closer contact between her and Ruth was not recorded.

Ruth's Letters to Ben

For a brief period between March and April 1932, when Ben was abroad, Ruth wrote daily accounts of her activities. They were undated, recording only the day of the week. Collected together, they were posted every Friday to catch the outgoing mail. Every page was illuminated by Ruth's love for Ben, and her wish that he was back home. They gave a daily account of visitors to and events in her home. They detailed her arrangements with the *Cape Argus* to print some of her articles. Ruth told of the extraction of all her teeth and wrote of the need to postpone a song recital because she could not possibly appear before an audience until new teeth had been fitted. And there was news about her children: Esther – confined to an institution – who played the piano and received her mother's letters but never commented. Ruth wrote of her intention to send her songs. Muriel had been staying in New York under the watchful eye of Frank, writing some (unspecified) mid-term examinations until, in exasperation over her irresponsible behaviour, her uncle could tolerate her no further and was sending her home. Ruth wrote in some despair of what she might expect when Muriel arrived but hoped that with Ben's assistance she would cope. Morris, who she described as depressed, partly because of his mother's death, but also because he was getting no briefs and could barely pay his office expenses, was not mentioned as a source of help with their most difficult of daughters. All that she could say was:

> I'll do what I can with her with love and patience and all the strength I've got; but I'm not going to let her needs, real or imaginary, swamp me, or us. And in both campaigns you will keep me. I still dare not think of your being really at hand to turn to.

Ruth told of the books she was reading, both for her talks and for reviewing. One was Romain Rolland's book on Goethe and Beethoven which dealt with their meeting and parting because they did not get on. 'He analyses the two with great skill and no sort of sentimentality, admiring both, but seeing both.' The reviews were needed urgently because Ruth needed the money for Muriel's psychiatric or psychoanalytical treatment. Ruth mentioned Clare Goodlatte as someone who could be consulted to give advice about Muriel. It was this reference that alerted me to the possibility that contact at the English Association, or at the *Cape Times,* had led to a friendship between the two women.

The letters are punctuated with references to the people who came to visit or, on occasion, whom Ruth went to see. Some of the names are familiar, others are unknown to me. A name that caught my attention was that of Sewell who had invited Ruth and Solly (her younger son, who was her joy) to dinner. Sewell held a lectureship in the English department and was, I am informed, a 'Marxist'. He had sent a first novel to Gollancz, the publishers, but it had been promptly returned. He was at work on a second novel, to be called *Goodbye, Cape Town!* He had also offered to read philosophy with Solly. In 1935 he accepted a Chair in New Zealand. However, like most of the references in these letters, there is no indication of other contacts by Sewell with Ben and Ruth.

In a later letter Ruth returned to the problems generated by family difficulties:

> Darling I wouldn't feel so bad about Esther if I were sure she didn't suffer. But I fear she does ... Behind that mute obstinate brooding must be pain, if only partly conscious pain.
>
> As to now going away, as I write it seems unlikely. Alec [a shortening of the surname used for Morris] looks old and worn and depressed, and until Bobbet [Muriel] is no longer a pressing problem and things look better for him I can't leave him. It may have to be the old terms for many a long day yet; and as to Solly, I think he should stay here until the end of 1933, his MA [actually MSc] year.

Turning to her relationship with Ben and getting to the core of their long-standing love, she wrote:

> I wouldn't blame you if you felt the old footing wasn't good enough. I suffer under it as you know, too. Yet what riches it has; how as I write, my half-true bravery dare not even look at the mental picture of it. To see you, to hear you, to touch you, to have done with loneliness, not to need to bear up and be hard and cool from hour to hour and day to day. To read with you, walk with you, get a meal ready with you – ah well, it's not so far off now.
>
> Goodnight, precious Ben.

In mid-March she wrote that visitors would be coming to condole with Morris on the death of his mother and to attend the evening prayers which would be held at their home. 'they will call, and condole and do prayers with Alec, and look at wicked me – oh damn!!'

Ruth's letters provide a picture of her activities and attachment. They also capture the flavour of her environment.

> I am writing on the stoep [verandah]. It is one of those exquisite warm-cool days we have now, and it is all so lovely that it seems impossible there should be so much trouble in the world. My flowers are lovely; I've two great vases of dahlias, one orange, crimson, salmon, gold, one three shades of purple, and a show of delphiniums, a vase of lovely airy cosmos, a jar of zinnias and one of a quite lovely orange flower, daisy-like, from Mexico. And the spinach, carrots, tomatoes growing in the garden, and peas just coming up. Joseph [the gardener] is a peach.
>
> I have just received [Collette's newest in English], *Morning Glory* or *Jour de Naissance*. I think it a beauty; it's a more or less frankly autobiographical account of her last love-affair, and her deliberate withdrawal from it and others after it, her farewell to that side of life. You may imagine how perfectly it is done. There is also by the way a marvellous portrait of her mother. I'd send it you for the boat only that I'm afraid you'd be identifying her with me, and yourself with the young lover.

Most intimately, in a later letter, Ruth wrote that Ben had told her more than once what he loved in her. Now she wanted to reciprocate:

> Oh Ben dearest, I love your hands and your laugh and your body and the way you sit and read. I love your wit and your good-tempered daily living and your courting and your heavenly good manners of the heart. But most I love something in you at once strong and delicate, not easy to put into words, a sort of patience and disciplined

> harmony of the intellect, a steady determined tempering of your mind and spirit, a persistence yet spontaneous continuous education of yourself, that lies deep and fixed beneath any superficial uncertainties or frights, and that links you to all the great humanists, dead or alive or to come. It's exquisite to watch – and it's the essence of you.

In one of the last of her letters, Ruth wrote:

> It's lovely that you've been getting on so well with the Plato. It does sound a queer mixture. I do look forward to your letters on him. Couldn't they be the nucleus of a book? The choruses of boys and men sound rather like the system Aldous Huxley describes in his *Brave New World*, an amusing and ludicrous peep into the future, in which by a process called 'hypnopaedia' the agonies of living, the elements of morality as it exists in that future are inculcated by an unceasing voice saying the same thing over and over again on the pillows of the children and youngsters as they sleep.

The intimate sketches of the relationsip between Ruth and Ben stop with these letters and, as has been the case throughout this account, only one side is presented. From Ruth's account, Ben's letters were supportive and loving, and it is unlikely that she would have destroyed them. Even the details of what he was reading and writing are missing, and my letters to the University of Swansea, and conversations with his relatives, have not revealed anything further. It is just conceivable that Ben himself, or his second wife, removed this most intimate of correspondence.

7
RUTH AND FRIENDS

Ruth as Lecturer

Though Ruth was in demand as a speaker in Cape Town to women's groups, to Zionist societies, to university clubs and to many other organisations, there are few accounts available of the contents of her talks. She was said to have been a delightful speaker: her voice was pleasing, she was calm and self-assured, and she was able to keep her audiences enthralled. In May 1913 when she spoke on 'Woman Suffrage' in Newark, *The Oheb Shalom Review* reported that:

> Mrs Alexander charmed her audience with her pleasing voice and manners, and with the simplicity and directness of her address. The interest that her arguments had aroused was shown by the numerous questions that were asked of the speaker.[1]

Sixteen years later, the *Cape Argus* report on her talk on Olive Schreiner, was just as enthusiastic:

> Mrs Ruth Alexander read a brilliant paper on Olive Schreiner before the English Association last night. She drew such a large crowd that I was able to find a seat only with difficulty.
>
> Mrs Alexander has a very pleasant manner. Her voice is quiet and musical.
>
> She has a habit of smiling, too, every time she lifts her eyes from her manuscript, which helps in 'getting over' her meaning.

The confidence that Ruth showed in her talks can be traced back to her life in Cambridge: in her declaration to Morris Alexander at the age of twelve, her organisation of the farewell party for her father when he left Cambridge, or in her letters to Israel Zangwill. Later, the compliments paid to her in Olive's letter must have boosted her ego and helped her confront many an audience.

It therefore comes as a surprise to read in a letter written to Ben in April 1932 that she was ill at ease throughout much of her stay in South Africa:

> I feel as if in some ways I'd grown up so late ... I've only just now, practically, got rid of my self-consciousness; even those last desperately bad months have somehow given me a new ease with people – and even with you, my darling.
>
> I feel now as if I couldn't now mind in the old way if you didn't like something I'd written, and so couldn't make you hurt me in the same way, by making you self-conscious. I've been so sad, and life has shown me such tragedy that I feel as if little things had to stay little things for keeps.
>
> Wouldn't it be funny if I turned into a successful writer in my forties? I'd be earlier [younger?] than Trollope. Sometimes I feel as though it might happen.

The comments are so cryptic that some of Ruth's meaning is lost. Why had Ruth, so seemingly successful in all she had done, been sad? What tragedies had life shown her? And what were the little things that 'had to stay little things for keeps'? It is impossible to guess: a collapsed marriage; two children who brought sorrow; or was it Ruth's contact with the people of District Six? The answer might lie in any of these, or might conceal other issues of which there remain no record.

Whatever lies hidden, the biographer can do no more than quote Ruth's words and wonder at the events that can turn an outwardly even life into one which holds inner hurts that are withheld even from her contemporaries.

The English Association of South Africa

Ruth's membership of the English Association of South Africa[2] brought her into contact with new personalities and provided an additional platform from which her views could be aired. The Association appears to have had two main objectives – to arrange for periodic public lectures and to suggest lists of set works for the matriculation examinations. The lists that were drawn up were traditional and not altogether relevant to the needs of young South Africans, a point that Ruth was to make in one of her early articles in the *Cape Times* – possibly before she joined the Association.

The minutes of the English Association are sparse but the secretary kept copies of press reports on public meetings until 1927. Besides members of the Association who delivered papers – some interesting, others dry and academic – visiting authors from Britain were invited to speak and this kept members in touch with currents of thought abroad.

In August 1929 Ruth gave her address on Olive. The account, based on Ruth's memories, demonstrated the falsity of Cronwright's claim that he alone was able to speak authoritatively about Olive. She set out to restore the image of this great writer and, using her talents as a critical reviewer, and remaining faithful to Olive as an intimate friend, she treated the posthumous publications of the author's work with forensic sharpness. Cronwright, as editor, must have been aware of the criticisms levelled against him and would not allow Ruth to quote from Olive's letters in her talk. In fact Ruth was only given permission to quote Olive's words if Cronwright read the text before the address was given; if what was said at the talk and in subsequent publications did not depart from the text; and if the address was prefaced by his disclaimer of any responsibility for what was said.[3] Morris believed that Cronwright had overstepped the mark but Ruth did not have the time to dispute the matter because the date of the lecture was scheduled and the paper she delivered was unchanged from the version Cronwright had seen.

In her will, Olive had stated that she did not want any of her letters reproduced and that, on Cronwright's death, they were to be given to her niece who would have instructions about what to do with them. The fact that no such instructions were found did not give Cronwright the right to select from, destroy, or publish his collections.

Ruth had promised that she would write a book covering Olive's life and works and, although the Cape Town talk and her reviews would have provided a base for such a publication, the project was taken no further. Instead she wrote about Olive, and elaborated on what she had already said on several occasions, in her reviews of other books and in commemoration of Olive's life.

Clare Goodlatte

The only available list of members of the English Association is dated 1933. Ruth's name appears, as do those of Ben Farrington and Clare Goodlatte, whose story is as little known as Ruth's. Only references to her in some of Ruth's letters to Ben indicate a familiarity that I might otherwise have missed.

Born in December 1866 in Ireland, Clare was educated in London and then at St Andrews in Scotland, where she took the LLA (the Associate – but not Bachelor – of Laws) and her teacher's certificate at Cambridge University in 1886. She had advanced as far as possible in an era in which women had few opportunities in higher education, and when most Bachelor degrees were not open to them in Britain. Goodlatte's first teaching post was in Port Elizabeth from which she transferred to St Peter's school in Grahamstown where she was persuaded by a Mother Cecile to join the Community of the Resurrection. Together they organised the Grahamstown Training College for women, with Mother Cecile as principal and Goodlatte as an assistant. There she remained, except for a visit to Scotland in 1898-1900, when she took a Froebel course in primary education. She returned as vice-principal and in March 1905 succeeded Mother Cecile as principal, thereafter directing the development of the College.

In 1920, having reached the retirement age of fifty-four, Clare left the college. Before she went she was given a farewell gift of £280 which she immediately returned with a request that the college buy three school shields and six South African paintings. She then resigned from the Order, took off her habit, turned her back on religion and took up residence in Woodstock, which was next to District Six. Henceforth she wore trousers and a Stetson hat and was known in Cape Town as the 'Red Nun'.

Further information about Goodlatte's activities in Cape Town is to be found in her letters to John Chapman, a farmer and former pupil.[4] The letters covered events, small and large. In one she described an intruder in her house who fled when she confronted him, and a (white) woman who was begging in the street. She mentioned books she had read, reviews she had written, theatres she had attended; she wrote about the severe drought affecting South Africa; about her first air trip, which she found thrilling; the visit of the royal family seems to have left her all agog and, although her early letters steered clear of social and political issues, there was one letter in which she wrote disparagingly about Jewish intellectuals whom she found 'too critical for happiness, too "superior" to be comfy, and too fond of frowsting indoors, in floods of talk, to be quite wholesome'!

Goodlatte found a social niche when she was elected secretary of the Woodstock and Salt River Ratepayers Association. Under its auspices she called for an end to the local smoke menace. After having some book reviews accepted she also became an assistant editor of the *Cape Times* for which she wrote leaders, reviews and articles of general interest. On 25 January 1926 she wrote to Chapman about the Indians, also in disparaging terms:

> I am really puzzled about the Indians. They are certainly not good citizens from a health point of view, and their little shops are a nuisance, and they are unreceptive mentally. But we *did* get them out – the lowest class – for our own convenience. We are reaping what we (or our fathers) have sown and we find it a noxious crop. But it is hard to find the right course. Smuts has preserved an unbroken silence; but I suppose we shall shortly have a big speech from him.

There were signs of a change in attitude in March when Goodlatte said that she had written a 5 000 word article critical of the government's

'Native Policy' and the Colour Bar Bill. She sought a publication in the United Kingdom because she was certain that no South African paper would publish it. It was, in fact, also rejected by both the *Manchester Guardian* and the *19th Century*.

There was no great change in basic attitude in the letters which followed Goodlatte's earlier writings, even though she was now writing about the prevailing white racism and 'a growing bulk of repressive legislation'. The first indication of real change came when she joined the liberal Joint Council of Europeans and Natives 'as a token of sympathy and goodwill'. At the same time she met white trade unionists. As a result of these changed views, she wrote in the *Cape Times*, on 16 December 1929, about the plight of the piece-work labourers who were paid by the day and received nothing on public holidays. Whites received an average weekly wage of 48 shillings and coloured families subsisted on 28-35 shillings a week.

On 6 May 1931, Clare was appointed Assistant Secretary of the Joint Council and, on 19 May, Secretary. In a letter dated 6 May 1931 she wrote of her revulsion at coloureds 'being made to feel outcasts in their own city'.

It was the granting of the women's franchise that hastened her political change. Unlike Ruth, she had welcomed the enfranchisement of women for the opportunity it provided of actively entering the political arena. She explained, after an interval, in a letter to Chapman:

> I have joined an Independent Labour Party at the time of the May elections – it is the Socialist wing, a daughter of the English party of the same name and policy. Here the movement is only three years old; I had not known of it, but joined up directly the election campaign brought it to my knowledge. I am a socialist by nature, and now in old age I have the joy of being in the thick of socialists – the intellectual crowd of University education and sound theoretical knowledge and also (much nearer and dearer to me, though I like them all) the manual workers, skilled and unskilled, European, Coloured and Native. I have been made General Secretary of the Party, which is very tiny,

> but growing as a result of the election fight and, I suppose, of the attractive force of socialism ... I cannot imagine any country *further* from Socialism than our South Africa, but it is good to be at constructive work again and my heart is in it.

She now wrote increasingly of her interest in socialism. She dropped her incipient anti-Semitism, expressed distress at the deportation of Jews from Germany, and recommended that Chapman read John Strachey's book *The Menace of Fascism*. But Chapman would have no truck with socialism and, although the letters continued for a time, they were written at greater intervals and then stopped. Goodlatte had found a home in which to expand her interests.

The Independent Labour Party split and a section, including Clare, became the nucleus of the Lenin Club. A section of that club in turn formed the (Trotskyist) Workers Party of South Africa in 1935. Clare was not only with them, but was the secretary of the new party and editor of its journal, *Spark*. Many of the leading members were Jews – the people she had once denigrated. But that was all in the past: there had been a sea change in her likes and dislikes, and past prejudices were swept away.

Clare Goodlatte died after a long illness in 1942. An obituary in the journal *Education* by Helen Olendorf recorded:

> On April 23rd there died in Woodstock the woman known to thousands of past students at the Grahamstown Training College as Sister Clare, or more commonly, more affectionately, as Clarie. To her neighbours, to the Woodstock Ratepayer's Association, she was Miss Goodlatte; to her Communist friends of later years, she was Comrade Goodlatte.
>
> It is not known who Goodlatte thought of as her personal friends and it is not known when she met Ruth, nor when she joined the English Association. In her political affiliation, after 1931, Goodlatte went beyond Ruth and although Farrington presented a paper at the

Lenin Club, he did not join the group. Ruth and Goodlatte met, found common interests, and Ruth felt that she could consult her when her daughter Muriel was experiencing difficulties. But their paths diverged and it is doubtful whether they kept contact.

Ruth's 'Salon'

At some stage Ruth invited friends to periodic meetings at her home which were generally referred to as her 'salon'. It might be more correct to say that it was Ruth and Ben's salon because they became inseparable and did so much together. Hogben remarks, without further elucidation, that: 'before our arrival, she had the only salon which attracted the Cape Town intelligentsia'.[5] Unfortunately, as in so many other cases, there is little documentation relating to the salon. One of the few references to it, found in the diary kept by the leading right-wing and anti-Semitic cartoonist, DC Boonzaier, is a mention of 'musical evenings', but gives little information on the gatherings though he makes no secret of his dislike of Ruth and her social activities.

According to Paul Koston, owner of Cape Town's left bookshop and a visitor at the salon, gatherings included on occasion Moses Kottler, the sculptor; Rose Movsovis; Ben, Kallenbach (when he was in town); Sybil Honikman, who moved to the far-left and also joined the Lenin Club; Julius Lewin; David Schrere, lawyer and businessman; and Jean van der Poel. Morris always chose to go fishing when the salon met, although, in this sphere too he was the 'Leader of Lost Causes' – he rarely caught a fish.

One of the personalities drawn into Ruth's circle was Pieter Wenning, a talented artist who had emigrated to South Africa from the Netherlands. Resident initially in Pretoria he was a member of the Theosophical Lodge in that town, and was undoubtedly known to Kallenbach. This could explain his contact with Ruth and might also account for the attention she gave him during his illness.

A reference to Wenning's presence at the salon is contained in Boonzaier's diary. He expresses irritation at Ruth's attention to Wenning, who had been formally sponsored by Boonzaier to allow him to leave his job in Johannesburg to settle in more congenial quarters in Cape Town. From June 1916 to December 1920 Wenning devoted all his time to his painting while Boonzaier looked after him financially and socially and promoted his work as an artist. But there were early signs of friction. On 20 July 1917 Boonzaier noted that:

> There are signs that Wenning is not giving his uninterrupted attention to painting as at the beginning. Musical evenings at Mrs M Alexander are constantly referred to. Also the concerts of the Municipal Orchestra.[6]

In July 1920 Wenning took ill and was admitted to hospital. Boonzaier, who said he never visited anybody in hospital, stayed away and this led to a permanent rift. During November Wenning was taken to the Alexander home and once again Boonzaier did not visit him, noting in his diary on 30 November 'I never hear from him, and as I am not on friendly terms with Mrs A I have not been to see him'. In early December Boonzaier received a short note asking for Wenning's box, easel, and other effects, left with Boonzaier when Wenning entered hospital.[7]

Wenning left Cape Town on 21 December 1920. He was seen, wrote Boonzaier, at Wynberg station by Kottler, 'looking very ill and weak, he was walking on the platform leaning on Mrs Alexander's arm'. Wenning was then, according to Boonzaier,'carried off' to see the art collection of Michaelis:

> Mrs Alexander planned this visit and they must have passed my house on their way there. As it is clear now that he has assumed a more or less hostile attitude to me purely and simply because I did not dance attendance on him like the few female busybodies who have surrounded him in recent times, but who never exerted themselves much on his behalf before ... I feel perfectly sure that this Alexander woman influenced him in his behaviour (he can be influenced by anyone) and that he could have acted very differently had he been left to himself.

Boonzaier speculated at some length about the causes of Wenning's 'suspicions' that he (Boonzaier) had become antagonistic to him. He remarked that, though the Alexanders had known Wenning for several years prior to his recent illness they had never bought any of his pictures.

> Mrs A is in short a 'celebrity hunter' and as Wenning became known as one of our foremost artists she made a dead set at him ... W on his side thought her many pressing invitations a nuisance, especially as he knew that she was not interested in his painting. He used to mimic her habit of greeting him each time they met with the words: 'When are you coming to see us again?' And made every effort to escape these visits. But the lady was not to be shaken off – as I know from personal experience – and no matter how you tried to talk of other things she always returned to her 'When are you coming to see us?' And when you did find yourself at her house she had nothing particular to say! Then came Wenning's present illness and now finding the poor fellow helpless she took complete possession of him, installing herself at the hospital and carrying him off to her house in the end. What affinity there was between them I cannot tell, though it could certainly not have been a mutual devotion to art.

Wenning died in 1921 and there are no further references to Ruth in the diary. Boonzaier's anti-Semitic cartoons appeared in *The South African Nation*, which also carried some of Ruth's reviews. As Boonzaier had commented, they had nothing to say to one another.

Lancelot and Enid Hogben

Hogben, zoologist and Socialist-humanist, arrived in Cape Town with his wife, Enid, in 1927. He was to become more widely known as the writer of his popularisations *Science for the Citizen* and *Maths for the Millions*, but his academic work and his scathing criticism of eugenics were far more significant. Besides his scientific work, Hogben also found time to read extensively and wrote on page 103 of his autobiography:

> While I was in Cape Town, my reading became increasingly restricted to historical and philosophical themes. I became interested in colonialism, in the contribution of Eastern civilisations to Western science and mathematics, in the new brand of Marxism that was emerging in the Soviet Union, in the psychopathology of race prejudice, in the rational credentials of theories of race superiority and in the population problem then coming to the fore. In an isolated community such as the English-speaking minority of Cape Town, intellectuals can, and then did, experience a constant terror of losing touch with contemporary thought in the distant centres of civilisation. Like most of my circle of this period, I was eager to sample any new book about which people were talking in Britain.

Hogben considered most of his professorial colleagues (apart from Eric Walker, the historian) intellectually unstimulating and found the junior academic staff more companionable. Among them were Farrington – 'who awakened my interest in Greek Science and the early Greek Anatomists to make me read everything about them' – and Frederick Bodmer, who whetted Hogben's appetite for the French encyclopaedists.

Hogben's four years at the university from 1927 to 1930 had a galvanising effect on the radical members of the university staff. He also transformed his own department by using local fauna for demonstration and experimentation. One of his outstanding discoveries was the 'Hogben pregnancy diagnosis test' using the Cape clawed toad *Xenopus laevis* whose change of colour indicated pregnancy.

The Hogbens were visitors at Ruth's salon and, following their practice in Britain, kept open house on Saturday nights. Senior students, junior staff members and 'many of the Cape Town intelligentsia outside the University' were invited. The conversation, when political, was openly anti-segregationist. Edward Roux, a leading member of the Communist Party, said of their 'open house' and the new friends he met:

> The most exciting of these was Lancelot Hogben ... at the height of his intellectual powers and in his most iconoclastic phase ... happily shocking the local philistines as well as some quite nice people in Cape Town. He had become the centre of a group of intelligent and charming people.
>
> Hogben combined his leftist position in politics with strong opposition to religions, nationalist and all such. He disliked flags and national anthems and did not care at all whom or how he annoyed by his gestures of iconoclasm.
>
> Parties at Xenopus [the Hogben home] were rarely formal, almost never by invitation. What happened was that people dropped in, especially at week-ends and then the most stimulating conversations would follow. As the hour grew later Hogben waxed more brilliant and outrageous. At such casual gatherings I met most of the Hogben set.
>
> Of these Frederick Bodmer was probably the one from whom I learnt the most. He was a Swiss, at that time lecturer in German at the university, also a serious student of politics. An eccentricity for which he was famous was his liking for some tumble-down house, of which there were a number in the suburbs of Cape Town, and there camping in one or two of the rooms. By nature indifferent to luxury and unwilling to burden himself with possessions beyond bare necessities which included a bed and a frying pan, he led a life stripped of all trimmings, a life that was simple and even austere ... Bodmer was the ideal host, casual in his erudition, throwing off carelessly brilliant aphorisms in his oddly accented English.[8]

In a brief account (in his autobiography) of political developments in South Africa, Hogben's thoughts ran parallel to those of Ruth. Whether these were his own independent reactions to events in parliament and reports in the press, or reflected talk in the University corridors, is uncertain but not very important. Hogben writes that together with the sculptor, Herbert Mayerowitz (a close friend who he had found at Ruth's salon), he sat in the visitor's gallery in parliament when the Native Bills were debated. He said he had been horrified by what he heard from all sides of the House. Indeed he was disenchanted with much that he observed in the country. In one account he expressed his concern at the practice, then common, of meting out disproportionately differential sentences to blacks and whites for the same crime.

Hogben was deeply distressed by talk then circulating that the government could insist that university lecturers would have to use Afrikaans if the majority of students attending a course so desired. It was also rumoured that the Minister of Education would be given powers to dismiss professors who expressed atheistic views when students were present. He saw this as a personal threat because he was President of the Students' Rationalist Society. Despite his fears Hogben always attacked racism head on. One incident of blatant racism, displayed at a dance at the university, was so important that Ruth was to make it the cathartic centre of her novel.

In *The Exiles* Emanuel Braun, the hero, having just learnt that he is coloured, visits the home of his new-found family in District Six intent on reclaiming his coloured identity. There he experiences all the tension and the awkwardness that come with ignorance, class difference and life style. Defiantly, Emanuel invites two relatives, who were among the earliest coloured students admitted to the university, to a dance on the campus. Inevitably Emanuel's racial origin is disclosed at the dance and this leads to a fight. The event does not go unobserved and Emanuel's lectures are subsequently boycotted and his bed apple-pied. The story in the novel revolves around, and is resolved by Emanuel's forced resignation as a lecturer. His friend Miriam is also disowned by her guardians and this completes her escape from the Jewish community.

The incident was real although different in detail from that recounted in Ruth's book. According to Hogben, Alexander Zoond, a young Canadian lecturer in his department, fell in love with a well known coloured woman and invited her and her cousin to the University's annual dance. Informed of this intended contravention of campus custom, and aware of the possible reactions, Hogben and his wife took the group to the dance under their wing. According to Hogben the two women were doctors, both Glasgow graduates, but it is more likely that they were

Dr Aswardah Abdurhaman and Cissie Gool (much renowned for her beauty), daughters of the prominent political figure Dr Abdurhaman.

Hogben and his students saw to it that nothing happened at the dance but could not avert a meeting on the campus summoned to protest against this 'outrage'. One rabble-rousing student accused Hogben of having brought an African prostitute to the dance in a state of intoxication. Hogben consulted 'the husband of Ruth Alexander' (as he put it) and, on Morris's advice, threatened an action for slander against the Students Representative Council. The students capitulated and, at a specially convened meeting, made a public apology which had been written for them by Hogben who, as he said with obvious relish, had laid stress on the need for racial coexistence.[9]

Contact between Ruth and Ben and the Hogbens seems to have remained casual, even though they shared a dislike of racial discrimination and delighted in informed discussion. Hogben's views on racism were summed up in his introduction to Cedric Dover's book *Half Caste*, published in 1937. Entitled 'Preface on Prejudices' it was written in his usual sardonic (if exaggerated) style:

> The form of sport to which I am most addicted is consequential conversation. I was deprived of it during four years' sojourn among the *Pigmentocracy* of South Africa by repeated attempts to communicate through the medium of dialogue conducted like this;
>
> *Any South African Graduate:* If you had lived in this country as long as I have you would know that a native can't be taught to read or write.
>
> *Myself:* Have you ever visited Fort Hare Missionary College?
>
> *South African Graduate:* Don't talk to me about missionaries.
>
> *Myself:* Well I have. I have seen a class of pure blood Bantu students from the Cis-Kei [Eastern Cape] working out differential equations.
>
> *South African Graduate:* What would you do if a black man raped your sister?

Knowing the Hogben's opinions on racial issues, Eddie Roux appealed to them to rescue two African leaders in hiding from a lynch gang in Worcester. Enid, together with Roux and Johnny Gomaz, both members of the Communist Party of South Africa, brought the pair back to Cape Town.[10]

This type of intervention was rare in left-wing politics in South Africa at the time, probably because of the turmoil within the Communist Party subsequent to the Communist International's insistence that the Party change its policy of class unity and adopt the call for a 'Black Republic'. This call split the party; members resigned or were expelled; the membership was drastically reduced and, for a time, activities were severely curtailed. Only the arrival in the country of Communists from Eastern Europe made it possible to revive some party branches.

The political scene in Cape Town was made more complex by the appearance of the Lenin Club, organised by followers of Leon Trotsky, one-time Commissar for Foreign Affairs, founder of the Red Army and leader of the opposition to Josef Stalin in the USSR. Although several of Ruth's associates joined the Club, she stood aloof and did not openly associate herself with either of the two left groups.

Whatever her political sympathies, and however radical she became, Ruth was discreet. There is no indication in her articles that she had any political affiliation. Occasionally, as in her review of the Sacco and Vanzetti letters (see Chapter 8), or her discussion of Rabindranath Tagore, her sympathies became apparent, but she maintained a distance from the Communist Party and its front organisations.

Bodmer, who seems to have been closer to Hogben than to Ruth's circle, was for a short period chairman of the Trotskyist-orientated Spartacus Club, the successor to the Lenin Club, but most academics in these circles stayed away from formal political groups. Bodmer applied for the Chair of German at the University of Cape Town but, when it was given to a right-winger, or 'truculent Nazi' (to quote Hogben), he left the country and, under Hogben's editorship, wrote *Loom of Language*. He joined the staff of the Massachussetts Institute of Technology where he taught German but, probably because of the anti-red feeling in the USA, stayed aloof from political parties.

The Hogbens, who did not join any political group, became convinced that the country was growing increasingly oppressive and left South Africa. Hogben took a Chair at the London School of Economics. Among his more prominent contributions was his sustained attack on eugenics.

An Educationist Speaks Out

One of the people who was strongly influenced by Ruth was Jean van der Poel. Destined to become a prominent historian at the University of Cape Town, she was said to have been a visitor at Ruth's salon. In 1937 she translated the *Communist Manifesto* into Afrikaans (with the assistance of Jacques Malan, editor of *Trek*). The book was published by the Workers Party to commemorate its ninetieth anniversary, and Trotsky was invited to write an introduction. Jean van der Poel is not known to have joined any of the left-wing groups, and it is possible that she became less radical as she settled into an academic career.

She did, however, write one pamphlet – *Education and the Native*, a 'Paper read at the Conference of the South African Teacher's Association at Cape Town on June 28th, 1934'. It was a condemnation of the financial starvation of the schools provided for Africans and of the pitiful extent to which African children were educated in the country. The statistics she presented were of a people, the majority of whom received no education whatsoever, with those who secured entry to primary school seldom advancing as far as the third year. As a consequence the overwhelming majority were illiterate, with only a tiny minority reaching the eighth standard – whereupon some could train as teachers for the few secondary schools that existed. This, said Van der Poel, met the requirements of the mining houses and the farmers, who wanted unskilled labourers who would work for starvation wages.

This information was not new and Van der Poel was certainly no champion of the missionaries who, at the time, provided the bulk of the school buildings, the financing and the staff. Nonetheless there were few who would have spoken out on this subject at the time – and Van der Poel could speak as an educationist of some authority. After pointing out that the more highly-paid African teachers earned a mere £60 a year and that there had been no increment since April 1928 she wrote:

> The truth is that white South Africa does not want to see an educated black South Africa, that a reactionary public opinion, nurtured on a traditional colour prejudice, continues to fear and to hate Native advancement.
>
> If South Africa is not prepared to regard education, if not as the right of everyone born into the modern world, at least as an investment which will show returns in later years, then the native will never be educated.

Van der Poel concluded from her analysis that:

> The position is so hopeless that one is forced to ask oneself whether there can ever be a radical improvement in Native Education short of a fundamental change in the economic structure of society in South Africa.[11]

New Directions

With Ruth and Hogben departed the salon seems to have been replaced with new, more politically orientated circles of which there are few details available. Some followers of the Trotskyist movement gathered at the house of Y Burlak and listened to music on seventy-eight discs, and there was also a gathering at the house of Dr Abdul Hamin Gool, Cissie's general practitioner husband. One story is told by Bernhard Herzberg, who left Germany for South Africa soon after the Nazis took power. In 1934 his companion, Eva, who was present at a musical concert in the Cape Town City Hall, saw a lone figure in the segregated area set aside for coloureds and joined him. Dr Gool, who loved music, invited her to visit his house on the following Saturday evening. Herzberg, who accompanied Eva, provides an account:

> I shall never forget our walk through the non-White District Six, to save money. We were both received with open arms

> not only by the doctor but also by all the diverse company. Every Saturday, Dr Gool and his wife Cissie held open house. It was the only dwelling in this racially divided city where folks from all walks of life, and any kind of origin, met, in defiance of ingrained custom. Assembled there was a veritable League of Nations. We met ... Frederick Bodmer. Next to him sat Sam Kahn, a leading Stalinist Communist. Painters were there too: Gregoire Boonzaier, the son of a *Die Burger* cartoonist ... ; and Frieda Locke, a painter of note ... Cissie presided over this gathering with her husband. She was sitting next to her father ... busy berating him, calling him an Uncle Tom, for his lack of radical opposition to the prevailing political and social system in South Africa.
>
> I spotted an African intellectual, [I B] Tabata, a prominent member of the Trotskyite Spartacus Club, in earnest conversation with Dr Eddie Roux ... In another corner of the room I observed Hans Friedrich, a rabid Stalinist and refugee from Nazi Germany. He sat there smugly propounding the view that the advent of Nazidom did not constitute a defeat of the German working class.

Politics was high on the agenda and Herzberg took up the argument, appalled at the complacency of a man who would not recognise that the Nazis had destroyed the Socialist and Communist movements and that the trade unions had ceased to exist in Germany. In another corner of the room there were arguments over the Comintern's recent demand that the Communist Party of South Africa adopt the 'Black Republic' slogan and an equally heated argument over whether there should be a 'one-stage' or a 'two-stage' revolution when the country underwent change.

The focus of the gathering had altered, the faces were different and the numbers involved had shrunk. The most significant change was the presence of black faces which reflected the changing nature of South African 'liberation' politics, and the divergences in the ranks of the left.

8
AMY AND THE COMMUNISTS

Reviewing Sacco and Vanzetti and American Justice

It was unusual for the *Cape Times* to print as radical a review as that submitted by Ruth on 28 June 1929. Yet there it appeared, an account of two books with a searing condemnation of the judicial system in the USA: *Boston* by Upton Sinclair and *The Letters of Sacco and Vanzetti*, edited by Marion Frankfurter and Gardner Jackson. The review was preceded by an editorial comment stating that the paper had never felt called upon, or competent, to judge the United States judiciary, but that the review was being printed because such judgement was implicit in the two books and in the opinion of the reviewer. The statement was probably only part of the story. Although the *Cape Times* was marginally more liberal than the rival *Cape Argus*, it still presented a conservative view of both local and international news.

It might have been a coincidence that the reviews were written after Amy, Ruth's sister, had been arrested in Gastonia, North Carolina, and charged with first degree murder together with other Communists. Whether coincidence or not, the events of Gastonia would have sharpened Ruth's perception of police harassment and terror. On the other hand Ruth had already taken a radical stance over Hertzog's 'Native Bills' and had few illusions about claims made on behalf of the state, the executive, or the judiciary.

Ruth began her review by sketching the background to the arrest in May 1920 of Bartholomeo Vanzetti and Nicolo Sacco, accused of having shot and killed a paymaster and a guard delivering a pay roll to a shoe factory. Found guilty, despite having unshakeable alibis, they were imprisoned until their eventual execution by electrocution in 1927. These two Italians of humble origin who belonged to a small anarchist group, were draft-dodgers and were unknown to anyone except their families and friends, their fellow anarchists, and the police who were watching their group, achieved world-wide prominence.

The trial was a travesty of justice with the district attorney and the judge appealing to the prejudices of a biased jury. The injustice of the charge and the sentence, the irregular nature of the review of the trial, and stories of the rampant bias of the jury foreman and the judge were universally condemned. The two men received the support of intellectuals and others – the volume of their letters was sponsored by an international support committee composed of Benedetto Croce, John Dewey, Theodore Dreiser, Maxim Gorki, Horace Kallen, Sinclair Lewis, Romain Rolland, Bertrand Russell, H G Wells, and Stefan Zweig. On the night of their execution, wrote Ruth, protest meetings and demonstrationswere held all over America, and when news of their execution was known abroad there were strikes and demonstrations in almost every big city of the world. The review concluded with the words of Vanzetti after sentence was passed:

> If it had not been for these things, I might have lived out my life talking at street corners to scorning men. I might have died, unmarked, unknown, a failure. Now we are not a failure. This is our career and our triumph. Never in our full life could we hope to do such work for tolerance, for justice, for man's understanding of man as now we do by accident. Our words – our lives – our pains – nothing! The taking of our lives – lives of a good shoe-maker and a poor fish-peddler – all! That last moment belongs to us – that agony belongs to us!

These words were widely quoted when the fate of Sacco and Vanzetti – the names were always mentioned together – was discussed, in print or at protest meetings. It was chance that the books appeared when Ruth had cause to be concerned about the trial of her sister Amy but, whatever the timing, the hysterical anti-red sentiment and the ever-prevalent racism that had America in its grip, would have roused Ruth if she had read any of the radical books then coming out of the US.

Brother and Sister

Ruth's appears to have had a close relationship with her brother and sister but the absence, by and large, of letters or other documents conceals the extent of their contact. The lacuna however, was dramatically filled in 1929 when Amy, four years younger than Ruth, was involved in a strike in a cotton mill in Gastonia and charged with first degree murder after a police chief was killed.

The strike and the trial that followed made headline news and, besides their implications for workers everywhere, were the cause of pain and anxiety to Ruth. It is not known whether the news came unexpectedly, or whether Amy had been in contact with her siblings before this development. The mere fact of the arrest and the indictment would have been heard soon enough and led to an exchange of sympathetic letters. Frank would most certainly have written to inform Ruth of what had happened, but over and above these suppositions there are no letters available to inform us of the impact of the news.

I have found little material on Frank Schechter, except for the bare outline of his career, with only one ray of illumination when he spoke to Raphael Levy about his role in the trial of his sister Amy. He had fought in the US army in the First World War and was badly affected during a German gas raid which probably accounted for his early death in 1937. He was known to be a highly successful patent lawyer and had received a Doctorate of Jurisprudence from Columbia University in 1925. When Amy's appeal against her sentecne was heard, Frank acted as advisor to the appeal team. The case against Amy was not sustainable and she was released.

Amy's career, as detailed in a Party newspaper, indicated that she had worked for the Labour Research Bureau in London during 1920-21 as a proof reader, translator and labour journalist. She joined the British Communist Party in 1920 and, returning to the US in 1921, joined the American Communist Party (CPUSA). Amy, described officially as a labour journalist, was an activist and was moved by her party to areas of industrial action across the country. She was an organiser for the Save-the-Union Committee in central Pennsylvania during the mine strike of 1927-28 and, later in the same strike, joined the Miners' Relief

Committee in Pittsburgh. During the New Bedford and Fall River textile strike of 1928 she was the publicity agent for the National Textile Workers' Union (NTWU) that had been organised by the CPUSA.

In 1928 it was decided to organise the cotton mill workers in North Carolina. The workers in the mills were underpaid and subjected to an oppressive system known as the stretch-out system which required them to attend to many more machines than had formerly been the case.

> Wages at Loray averaged between $9 and $12 a week; work shifts between eleven and twelve hours a day. Simply to survive, whole families, including grandparents and children, had to sweat in the mills. The village was overcrowded, the houses were rickety and unsanitary. Wages and work conditions had been deteriorating for the past several years; only a year earlier the stretch-out system and a wage cut had been introduced. If ever there was a situation that conformed to the classical Marxist vision of an exploited and suffering proletariat in opposition to heartless capitalists, this was it.[1]

The second factor that influenced the American Communists was the thesis emanating from the Moscow based Communist International in 1928 that revolutionary struggles were about to break out universally in what was called the 'Third Period'. In South Africa this had led to the demand that the Communists call for the 'Black Republic'; in the US the CPUSA was directed to agitate for an independent black state, and to form independent 'revolutionary' trade unions – distinct and separate from 'reformist' unions. Following this directive the Loray Mill, the largest in the area, was chosen for unionisation. Fred Beal, a New Bedford strike leader and member of the CPUSA, was sent to establish contact with the workers. He spent three months in a neighbouring town doing so.[2]

Beal won the workers to the cause of unionisation, but in March 1929, the Loray Company precipitated a strike by firing twenty of the workers who had joined the union. It was not the best time to strike but there was little alternative. On 1 April both shifts walked out, demanding a $20 minimum weekly wages, a forty-hour week, abolition of the stretch-out system and recognition of the union. The Central Committee of the CPUSA was divided on strategy. One section wished to confine the strike to the worker's demands, but as the strike continued trade union issues were dropped and political slogans came to the fore. Many communist functionaries appeared – from the Young Communist League and the International Labour Defence – and Amy was sent by the Workers' International Relief to assist the 3 500 strikers.[3] The *Daily Worker*, the party's paper, was passed around, startling and inaccurate statements were distributed, and the workers were assured that revolution was 'around the corner'. [4]

The strikers were reviled and accused of anti-Americanism. The Gastonia daily paper published a picture of the American flag with a snake coiled at its base, and the inscription: 'Communism in the South. Kill it'. Advertisements appeared under such headlines as: 'Red Russianism Lifts its Gory Hands Right Here in Gastonia'. Handbills were distributed saying: 'Bust up Your Russian Union and Let's Go Back to Work' or 'Would you belong to a union which opposes white supremacy?'. Gastonia was ripening for violence. Opponents of the strike, led by the mill owners, organised a vigilante gang calling itself the 'Committee of One Hundred' to fight the union. The local press urged the destruction of the strike and the 'red Russianism' that inspired the strikers. Police terrorised picket lines – composed mainly of women and children – and mill owners evicted strikers from company houses. On 18 April one hundred masked men slipped past the National Guard and demolished the frame building used by the NTWU as its headquarters, destroying the store of relief groceries. Although fourteen people were arrested and a hundred witnesses testified, the county Grand Jury refused to indict anyone.

The strikers were told that conciliation could be achieved only when they had rejected their Communist leaders. Defiantly, they erected new union headquarters and a relief store, and set up a tent colony to accommodate the two hundred families evicted from company houses.[5] The strike spread to textile mills in neighbouring towns, in all but four of which the workers' demands were granted and the strikes called off[6] but no settlement could be reached in Gastonia.

The CPUSA, in speeches and pamphlets, refused to see that the strike had been broken. Resorting to provocative rhetoric they claimed:

> The struggle in Gastonia has reached a far higher stage – that of armed struggle ... This furnishes irrefutable proof of the process by which the inner contradictions of capitalism in the imperialist period bring on economic struggles which speedily take on a political character ... The strikers stood with arms in their hands and exchanged shot for shot with the police.[7]

There was no exchange 'shot for shot'. Instead in a raid on a strikers' camp on the night of 7 June, there was an exchange of gunfire and among the dead was the chief of police. This was the signal to the police to arrest sixteen Communists, three of them women, among them Amy, and charge them with first degree murder. The strike was over. Working hours were slightly shortened, night work for women and children was reduced, but there no other concessions were made.

In major cities throughout the West there were demonstrations and organised petitions in favour of the accused, seven of whom were found guilty of second degree murder. Pending appeal the CPUSA demanded that they break bail and flee to the USSR. Farce had been added to tragedy – four of the men remained confined in the USSR but Beal, having kept his passport, returned covertly to the USA where he published *Proletarian Journey*. He included the story of the strike and a damning indictment of what he had witnessed in the factories and villages in the USSR.

Amy's trial, and the subsequent appeal were of concern to the Schechter family who could do little but wait for the outcome. Only Frank, with a law degree could intervene. Raphael Levy, a cousin of Ruth, was to write:

> The trial soon attracted national press attention. More important, Frank left New York for Gastonia, and behind the scenes successfully directed a defence in that heavily charged anti-communist, anti-New York Jew, anti-negro atmosphere, that cleared Amy and her group.

> [In 1932, when Levy spent a weekend with Frank and his wife]. Frank spoke of the red-hot hostility that was directed at him and his colleagues of the defence by the towns-people of Gastonia, then a superb example of a Southern company-town still steeped in the hatreds, passions and bitter memories of the American Civil War, when the North defeated the South and Lincoln freed the slaves...
>
> And in the centre of this, in a sense, was Frank, a brilliant attorney, trying to make sure that Amy and her associates did not become either self-appointed martyrs, or the targets of a Southern lynch mob.[8]

Ruth followed the course of events closely, while Morris, who was trying to effect a reconciliation with Smuts, could only have been embarrassed by the publicity in the press. The relationship between Ruth and Amy was known, as was Ruth's growing radicalisation. There is unfortunately nothing in the above that might provide an inkling to Amy's character, and nothing to show what events led her to the Communist Party. Did she hear from Ruth after the meeting in Cape Town with Olive in which Olive spoke to Ruth so enthusiastically about the Russian Revolution? Or did Ruth follow Amy's move to the left in some belated fashion? With a dearth of documentary evidence there are no other clues to indicate what connections the two had before 1929.

It was four years before the sisters met again in the US. When Ruth left South Africa in 1933, breaking her ties with Morris, she went first to New York, where she stayed for more than a year. During that time she worked on her novel and met Amy on several occasions. She also wrote for *The Nation* a review of a third rate Soviet novel, *Driving Axle* by Ilyenkov, which showed firstly that she was becoming more sympathetic to the Communists and secondly, that in embracing that cause she had surrendered some of her critical faculties. She wrote of the 'self-forgetting devotion to an impersonal idea which is the basis of Communist life. The formidable drive of that devotion, which is swiftly becoming one of the main factors in contemporary history', and said that those who read the book would understand this better and would ponder its significance.

A letter dated 5 April, written by John S Schechter to Elsie Alexander, widow of Solly Alexander, in Australia, states that Amy's married name was Kweit and that she died in 1962 – facts not confirmed and not known to other members of the extended Schechter family. Besides stating that she was a labour organiser and a writer on political matters, the writer said that Amy had lived in the Soviet Union before the Second World War and had written articles on education there.[9] It is a sparse note, but it is all that is available to me.

The contact between the sisters – brief but warm – did not last beyond Ruth's visit to New York. After her departure from the US Ruth did not hear from her sister again. The three children of Solomon and Mathilda Schechter had chosen paths that drew them further and further apart.

9
RUTH AS WRITER

The Growth of a Radical

There is no diary to inform the reader of Ruth's political development. Olive's influence was obvious, but it cannot be assumed that Ruth always followed her mentor directly or automatically. There is no doubt, though, that Olive's radical insights left their imprint. The changes can be clearly read in the articles and reviews that appeared under Ruth's name, both in South Africa and the United States.

As Ruth developed and acquired new friends, she developed her own ways of answering the problems of the day. When she opposed the enfranchisement of white women she found allies in District Six, some of whom belonged to radical groups and carried the agitation into coloured organisations.[1]

Other influences on Ruth's growth to radicalism came from Kallenbach, who informed both her and Morris about the steps taken to counter the Government's anti-Indian legislation, and from Gandhi's explanation of his philosophy of *ahimsa*.

Ruth's visit to the ICU headquarters in Johannesburg was another important step on her political path and one which was mentioned in a journal article. But there is little or no information about her responses to other major events. How, for instance, did she react to the General Strike on the Witwatersrand in 1922? And what did she do when the British seamen went on strike in Cape Town and Durban in 1925 with the support of local Communists and some trade unionists? During this period mail and journals, newspapers and books, failed to arrive. Is that why there is a gap in her list of reviews during the period? And did she sympathise with the agitation in the Indian community when they heard that the shipping company intended recruiting Lascars in India as scabs?[2]

The 'Native Question' and the Vote

> The colour problem in South Africa has been made more acute by the policy of the present Government, which frankly favours repression of both the natives and the Indian inhabitants.The government aims to diminish, ultimately to eliminate the Indian population; it has proposed a measure restricting the areas in which Indians may live, thus establishing virtual ghettoes; taking away the right to buy or lease land except in narrowly limited districts in Natal; and creating other limitations on the rights of people already living under heavy restrictions.

This was the introduction to Ruth's article on 'The Colour Question in South Africa' in *The Nation* on 23 June 1926. It was the first of her reports on the growing repression in South Africa. The question of the future of the Indian community hung in the balance and people with a liberal or radical outlook were perturbed.

Dr D F Malan had announced in Parliament on 23 April that the governments of South Africa and India had agreed to hold a round-table conference to discuss the 'Asiatic problem' in South Africa, pending which the Asiatic Bill would be postponed. The South African government in making this offer had claimed that public opinion would not view with favour any settlement which did not safeguard the maintenance of 'Western' standards. These standards were never defined but allowed local authorities to place Indians in 'bazaars' (that is ghettos) on the grounds of incompatibility. The delegation, whose names had been released, could, through their knowledge, their tact and their unfailing courtesy, have an important effect on the outcome, wrote Ruth.

Whether the words of Dr Malan would exorcise the fears and prejudices of the whites remained to be seen: meanwhile the prospective conference had 'lifted the whole question on to a higher plane, but the trend of the present government in speech and legislation was in the direction of a harsher declaration of white supremacy, and there was little in the press or in the talk of the public that would indicate that it was unwelcome.' Continuing, she wrote that the position of the Indian community 'in the Transvaal and Natal remains pitiable enough. The restrictions and the uncertainty of their future rests heavily on them.'

> A few of them [the local Indians] have attained comfort, if not wealth, but most of them are poor and without facilities for education and self-improvement. They live among people who almost universally dislike and distrust them, even while making use of them, and who will do nothing to help them to improve their conditions. They lack leadership, and have rather deteriorated than otherwise since Mr Gandhi left them. On the other hand, for the bulk of them, repatriation would take them away from home rather than return them to their own place. Many of them are South African born of the second or third generation; and even those who are only domiciled here have for the most part been overlong away from the self-contained and caste-ridden atmosphere from which they came. Pariahs in this country, they are likely to be outcasts in their motherland. To this pass have the joint exertions of India, South Africa, and England herself brought them that commerce might be served.

The condition of the Africans, she wrote, was more pitiable than that of the Indians 'and more ominous, a menace to himself and to South Africa as a whole'. Following the Prime Minister's statement that whites were outnumbered three to one by Africans, white fears bordered on panic and the Secretary for Native Affairs and the Police Commissioner pleaded before a parliamentary select committee for a new draconian Prevention of Disorder Bill. 'It is not even pretended that the object of the Bill is other than to permit the effectual terrorizing and silencing of certain native agitators.' Yet 'only a handful of Africans have sufficient education either to become liable to these drastic penalties or to lament the franchise which is denied them'.

She continued:

> The concern of these people is to no other business than of keeping alive. Yet Parliament, in its last session, imposed a

> high protective duty on the cheapest native blankets, pleading that these could be manufactured locally. This was a truly cruel tax placed on a people who earn as little as fifteen, ten, or even six shillings a month. And this year it is proposed to add a tax of ten shillings per year to a 'native development fund', over and above the uniform hut tax of twenty shillings. Despite the obvious poverty of the people the government is introducing a Colour Bar Bill to implement its 'civilized labour' policy [which reserved many occupations for whites].

Concluding pessimistically, Ruth observed that the proposed policies would be well received by whites. There were no real differences between the political parties, even if sectional economic differences led to a temporary difference of attitude to the Colour Bar Bill. The South African Party, identified largely with the Chamber of Mines, opposed the Bill because it would deprive the mines of a certain amount of cheap labour. 'The outlook for the next generation of South Africans is gloomy indeed.' It was a well researched article, unfortunately marred by the racial overtones in her summing up:

> Led by crudely educated men of their own race, men embittered, ill-balanced and often extremely egoistic, barred from avenues of employment long open to them, and from all hope, whatever their ability, of rising any higher in the scale of industrial work, it is like enough, as General Hertzog said at Malmesbury, that the frankly rebellious speeches of Kadalie and Professor Thaele are 'going to be an incentive toward the beginning of a movement among the natives in general to get into their possession the most widely extended powers for having a say in the control of the country'.

Ruth still had to acquire a broader perspective on African leadership and move away from the prejudices that informed government ministers: In her early period in the Cape she did not see the position clearly. The

Western Province did not have a large African population – 'In the Cape Province the Cape Coloured population provided a continuous gradation of labour between the white man at the one extreme and the native at the other'[3] so Ruth set her sights on the plight of the coloureds. However, by the time she wrote her article on the ICU a year later, she had altered her viewpoint.

Three years after this, General Hertzog, planning to settle the country's 'Native Question' for all time presented four 'Native Bills' to parliament. The African vote, already restricted, would be curtailed even further; a Native Council established; the extent of land that Africans would be allowed to settle would be enlarged to a maximum of thirteen per cent of the country's surface area; and the position of coloured voters would be slightly improved by the provisions of the Coloured Persons' Rights Bill. The first two 'Native Bills' were finally combined and in 1937 a Bill was passed to restrict the further entry of Africans into the white controlled towns. The terms of the proposed legislation were draconian and several liberal voices were raised in opposition, but they were in a minority. The Bills were rejected at a joint sitting of the Senate and Parliament because a two-thirds majority was required before the franchise, which was entrenched in the constitution, could be altered. The opposing vote was more political than principled, and only in 1936, after the National Party and the South African Party fused, did the Bills receive the required majority.

Ruth's article in *The Nation*, 'The Colour Line in South Africa', on 19 November 1928, was incisive. Parliament was waiting for the evidence still to be taken by the committee appointed to report on the Bill but, she wrote, a reading of the drafts were 'sufficiently depressing to those who do not think of the population of South Africa solely in terms of the million and a half whites who at present control and exploit the five and a half million Indians, Natives and Coloured people ... A policy at its best aggressively paternal, at its worst severely repressive is outlined in the measure dealing specifically with the native peoples.'

Her political understanding had taken a big leap forward. Her evaluation of the clauses dealing with the vote was excellent, but the land issue, which was of prime concern to the Africans, and had been a point of resentment since the Land Act of 1913, was only mentioned *en passant*. On the question of the vote Ruth had gathered the available information and had found the hidden purpose behind the proposed 'improvement' of coloured conditions.

Representative government was introduced in the Cape shortly after the abolition of slavery in 1830, based on a non-racial franchise for adult males who could write their name, address and occupation, and who occupied premises worth £75 a year, or earned at least £50 annually. When responsible government was granted to the Cape in 1872 the franchise was extended to allow all males to vote, but did not allow those who were not white to stand for the Legislature. The same qualifications were still in force and only a minority of Africans and coloureds could satisfy them. Under the new provisions the restricted vote for Africans was to be withdrawn. Instead there would be Native Councils of seven members under the supervision of the Native Affairs Department. The coloureds under the new dispensation were to have their status 'raised'. Their vote in the Cape would be left untouched and the coloured population outside the Cape – which numbered over 31 000 would be given one representative in Parliament. 'It needs only be pointed out ... that the average constituency of the country is about three thousand,' wrote Ruth. 'But even to be placed on the register the Coloured man will have to prove to a special board that he is a Coloured and not a native.'

The purpose of the legislation was clear, Ruth wrote – it was to alienate the coloureds from the Africans: 'Is it impossible that some idea of this sort has occurred to the gentlemen responsible for the framing of the Coloured Persons' Rights Bill?' Ultimately the Africans were disfranchised and the status quo retained for the coloureds, ensuring the political separation of the two peoples.

The government went further in reshaping the electoral system. In her article 'A New South Africa' in *The Nation* of 27 May 1931, Ruth explained that the granting of votes to women in 1930 had opened the way for radical changes in the pattern of voting in the country. Initially the legislation only extended the vote to all white women in South Africa. This diluted the effectiveness of those African and coloured men who had fulfilled the requirements for exercising the vote. A second Bill removed the conditions for the vote for white males over the age of twenty-one in the Cape. This diluted the value of the black vote even further. The last step would follow. The removal of the Cape African voters from the voters' roll waited only for a select committee report.

Other repressive legislation was pending. Ruth wrote of one piece in particular, then in the committee stage – the Native Service Contract Bill – which applied especially to African labourers on farm lands. Previous legislation was extended to allow African guardians (male or female) to bind minor African males under eighteen years to labour tenancy by verbal or written agreement. The regulations governing such contracts were severe, and included punishment by whipping not exceeding five strokes for contravention of any regulation governing labour tenancy. The contract remained binding on the individual if the ownership passed to new hands. Although the contract could be terminated within three months there was no obligation on the old or new owner to inform the labourer of the change.

Ruth also listed conditions in the Cape in which, she wrote, the social 'temper' had worsened. There was increased disease with no available medical attention – she quoted 'a well-known missionary' who said more was being spent on cattle diseases than on those of Africans; the depression, which had led to an increase in pensions for whites had no parallel for Africans, none of whom received pensions, and the coloureds who did benefit received a minuscule increase. The article concluded with a list of instances in which the courts had passed different sentences for identical crimes depending on the skin colour of the defendant.

One further article, entitled 'In the Twilight of Liberty' and published in the *Cape Argus* on 26 November 1932, dealt with new and projected legislation and pulled no punches:

> Out of Africa always something – unexpected. Ever since 1914, when the Riotous Assemblies Act made it possible for any magistrate to prohibit any meeting anywhere by which he considers that 'the public peace' would be endangered, South Africa has presented to the world the curious spectacle of a young country, more or less democratic in constitution, in which the two governing

> races are busily competing and co-operating to rid themselves of those liberties usually considered the basis of a democracy. Freedom in South Africa, so far from broadening slowly down from precedent to precedent, is narrowing in with gathering momentum from precedent to precedent.

There was not much left to remove, wrote Ruth. A government representing scarcely more than a majority of the whites, had been handed powers that 'a Mussolini would have applauded'. Cassandra-like, she continued, in terms very similar to those used by Hogben in his autobiography:

> We may not hold meetings where we like or on what questions we like. We may not say what we like or do what we like in public, regarding relations between natives and Europeans ... Our Colleges and universities are well muzzled; [referring to the rumours of the time] they may in future decide only in so far as the Minister chooses what they shall teach, how and in what language they shall teach it, and what appointments they shall make.
>
> Political and religious liberty in South Africa, even for the European section of the population, is moribund. The fact, it is true, does not seem greatly to trouble white South Africa; but while the sun shines and the movies move very few things trouble white South Africa for long.

Noting other new laws that were being discussed, Ruth asked: 'What next?' And she mentioned the 'comic but terrifying' request made in all seriousness by a Nationalist woman's branch 'that it be punishable in future to libel the nation as it is now to libel an individual'. The portents were poor and Ruth closed on an extremely pessimistic note, writing that generations unused to freedom of speech or of thought 'will have ceased to concern themselves with unprofitable matters'. But she was thinking only of the whites; the revolt of the blacks was not yet so obvious.

This seems to have been the last article she wrote on the legislation being prepared to control the African people. When the Bill to disfranchise them was passed in 1936, she had already left the country. In Parliament hardly any representatives opposed the measure. Morris Alexander, to his credit, was one of them.

Before Ruth stopped writing on political developments in South Africa she took up an issue that has now almost been forgotten. Writing in the editorial column of the *Cape Argus*, on 29 October 1932, she questioned the attitude of the Dutch Reformed Church to the position of Jews who converted to the Reformed Church. She began with the proposition that:

> To comprehend the essence of a religion is always difficult for those who do not belong to it. To grasp its dogmas is possible for anyone with some degree of education; but the spirit of a religion is a subtler matter.

Recent discussions within the DRC had centred on whether Jews who had converted were to join the ordinary congregations, 'or were they to form themselves into a separate church?' Even worse, it was suggested that Jews who converted – and there would not be very many – should do so in secret, because they 'were liable to incur the enmity of their fellow-Jews and be deprived of their possessions. This was 'sheer nonsense. It is worse; it is dangerous nonsense ... it is the stuff of which blood-accusations are made'. It was the superstition 'that believes in the existence of a Jewish world-conspiracy'.

Ruth was writing on the eve of Hitler's rise to power in Germany, and this superstition was to become part of the Third Reich's propaganda against the Jews. In South Africa the Reformed Church provided the philosophy around which racism and segregation was built.

Ruth's articles retain a freshness that outshines the work of other commentators of the time. Her radical inclinations and her increasing concern about events in Europe, besides their intrinsic value in capturing the spirit of the criticism in South Africa, adds to an understanding of her move towards the Communist movement.

Articles on War and Peace

Ruth spoke warmly about writers who opposed war as a solution to national conflicts. She was not a pacifist but her viewpoint was essentially anti-war. It was therefore not surprising that she began her review of the work of H W Nevinson, the war correspondent, *Cape Times*, 4 January 1929, with a passage from Olive's *From Man to Man*. Towards the end of that book Rebekah said to her sons:

> It's a finer thing to be a 'man' than either of you can know now. But it's not being able to lift a great weight or strike a great blow, or crush things beneath you that can ever make you that ... But when that day comes, as it must come to you at last, when your bodies lie still and dead, whether it be in a palace or a poor man's hut, on a solitary Karoo plain or in a crowded city, whether you have been rich and famous or poor and unknown ... then if one should stand besides you and look down at you, knowing all the story of your life, they should be able to say: 'This strong man's hand was always stretched out to cover those feebler; this great man's body never sought good or pleasure for itself or at the price of something weaker' ... Then, though no eye could see it, you would lie there, crowned ... the noblest thing on earth, the body of a dead man who had lived the life of a 'man'.

This, wrote Ruth, was a fitting epitaph for Nevinson, whose book *Last Changes, Last Chances* covered his life up to his seventy-fourth birthday. He had begun his career as a war correspondent during the Greco-Turkish war and had worked through the First World War and the turmoil that followed. As a correspondent he wrote as he saw events, refusing to use 'sob-stuff' or to lie. When driving in the country around Amiens in 1918, 'near what had been Meanil' he had written:

> We made our way down through the bare sticks of what was once a wood, but was now strewn with appalling

> fragments of man, and Montague [his fellow observer] looked at me sideways to see if I had noticed them. I did notice them, but there was nothing left to say.

'All Barbusse could scarcely give to the non-combatant a more vivid realisation of what war is really like than this sentence ... ' wrote Ruth, in praise of a man who epitomised 'chivalry, humour, courage, and the liberal spirit'. Nevinson perpetuated his philosophy in his personal life too. When Roger Casement, who championed the Irish cause, was reviled, tried as a traitor and then condemned to death for his support of the Germans in the First World War, and subjected to hideous scandal that destroyed the chance of a reprieve, Nevinson continued to support him and persisted in publicly calling him 'my friend'. Indeed 'he lived the life of a man'.

Erich Maria Remarque's book about peace, *The Road Back*, was reviewed in the *Cape Times* on 4 June 1931. It was 'an even more damning indictment of war and the results of war' than his earlier *All Quiet on the Western Front*. A compassionate book and artistically powerful, it spoke of the last days of the First World War when all rumours of peace were unsettling and painful: 'every hour has gained in weight a thousandfold, every minute under five seems harder and longer almost than the whole time before'. And before the armistice was declared tragedy struck again: yet another man from the battalion was killed.

The men who were left – a small proportion of those who had arrived at the front – faced the difficulties of returning to civilian life. They were ill-adjusted to the life they tried to re-enter; could not bear the trivial conversations to which they were subjected; resented the need to pass school examinations to get on with their civilian lives. Ernst, who tells the story, became a teacher in a village school and found his work irrelevant. Others from the group were disorientated. Some died in the uprisings that spread across Germany or killed themselves in despair. Only the less sensitive could find a place for themselves.

Ernst, one of the luckier, perhaps, summed up his experiences:

> One part of my life was given over to the service of destruction; it belonged to hate, to enmity, to killing. But

> life remained in me. And that in itself is strength, of itself almost a purpose and a way ... There are many things to be built and almost everything to repair; it is enough that I work to dig out again what was buried during the years of shells and machine guns.

But his words were hardly those of hope. The dead would be silenced and the past would not pursue him any more. The road would be like other roads, 'a road to toil. And I shall be alone.' However as Ruth quoted these lines the road was being churned up again and nobody was left alone. Ruth might have had a glimmer of what the future held, a future grimmer than anything that Remarque could have envisaged. But the book was gripping, to a point where the reader was overwhelmed by the atmosphere created in the novel. Remarque could offer little hope and what there was was far from reassuring.

Rabindranath Tagore – The Righteous Writer

Ruth was not a roving journalist moving from country to country, seeking out newsworthy events. Situated in Cape Town, she relied on newspapers, journals and imported books for her knowledge of world events and, as a reviewer, relied on a sub-editor for the allocation of books – although she obviously received many books she wanted. It is therefore not possible to detect in her articles and reviews her thoughts on all contemporary events.

In the light of her admiration for Gandhi there might have been some comment on what was happening in that vast sub-continent – but I have found little. It seems likely that the visit to South Africa by the Rev C F Andrews led to her article on Nobel Prize winner Rabindranath Tagore, whose philosophy was close to that of Gandhi. Whatever the cause, her sketch of this saintly man, and the appearance shortly after of an article by Andrews were noteworthy.

In the works reviewed by Ruth entitled 'An International Writer' (*The South African Nation*, 20 February 1926), there is nothing but praise for Tagore. In addition to describing his activities, she expressed her appreciation of the universality of his role as writer, moralist and teacher. The central thrust of her piece is summarised in the following extract:

> But it is not merely as a great artist, not merely as the poet, playwright, essayist, lecturer, story-writer, and exquisite translator of his own works in English that Rabindranath Tagore is revered and sought. Nor is it merely for the sake of his gracious personality, nor even for the sake of his simple, lofty and beautiful philosophy of life. To the writer and the teacher and the thinker is added the internationalist, the man who, while he has rendered and is rendering incomparable service to his own country, is the friend and champion of all lands, the enemy of none.
>
> In story after story and novel after novel Tagore describes for his people the evils of jingoism, the struggle of a fine nature away from it towards the wider love, the deeper patriotism in which the boundaries of caste and race disappear.

Her article was complemented by the article on Tagore by C F Andrews in the same journal on 22 January 1927. Concentrating on Tagore's book of lectures, entitled *Nationalism*, Andrews commented on his writings about the Japanese attempt to force a protectorate upon China in 1915; the militarisation of Japan itself; and his opposition, in 1926, to fascism in Italy.

'The ultimatum to Serbia, he said, which had precipitated the war in Europe, was obviously the model on which Japan took action. China, in her utter helplessness, was obliged to give way.' The only weapon available was passive resistance 'to avoid the impending doom of submission to Japan'. When Tagore visited Japan in 1916, and was fêted by the administration, he refused to approve what Japan had done. Neither was he impressed by what he saw. He was horrified by the sight of little children of five and six strutting to school and back in military uniform; the schools 'decorated with blood-stained trophies of the Russo-Japanese War'; and the new ports of Kobe, Yokohama and Nagasaki, belching smoke and bristling with hideous corrugated-iron sheds. When he spoke 'he lashed out quite fearlessly'. He did so again in Italy where he went as the guest of Mussolini. The lectures he gave formed the basis of his book on nationalism:

> These lectures on Nationalism struck not merely at Japan. They struck at Japan's teacher in frightfulness – Europe. For while expressing, in the most full and generous terms, the East's gratitude to the West for its magnificent search after scientific truth, he scorched the West with his poet's wrath for being the first to infect Japan herself with the poisonous doctrines of militarism as a chief means of national aggrandisement.

This was a righteous, if not altogether accurate observation. But it was a 'poet's wrath'. Tagore also spoke out against Britain for the ruthless shooting in Amritsar in 1919. His was 'the agony of mental suffering' from which he only won relief with 'that tremendous letter – one of the masterpieces of English literature – in which he resigned his knighthood as a protest against the wrong done to humanity by such a deed of bloody reprisal.' Tagore was not a pacifist. He believed that force 'has its own limited sphere in human life ... But he is essentially a lover of freedom; his fundamental belief is this, that moral freedom and physical compulsion are incompatible inter-relations'.

On the USSR

After Olive's war-time declamation against Tsarist Russia and her delight when Denikin was defeated, Ruth kept her enquiring mind on events in the USSR. Official Russian books she declared were not of great interest to those 'outside the Marxian faith' and, although there had been good, clear and objective books on Russia many questions were seldom answered. Although critical texts were coming out of the left opposition in the USSR she still asked:

> What is life like for the ordinary people? What sort of teaching is done in the school? How has the new regime

> affected art and literature and the drama? How far have the illiterates, so large a pre-war proportion of the population, begun to educate themselves? How is it really with the churches? To what extent has the life of the villages been affected by the new regime?

To these and cognate questions, wrote Ruth in the *Cape Times* of 11 July 1929, the books *Dreiser looks at Russia,* and A Rhys Williams's, *The Russian Land*, both provided replies that 'have the stamp of truth' and were readable and lively. There was information to satisfy Ruth but too little space in her review to provide details for her readers. Also, as important as some of her questions were, she seems to have missed some of the most crucial points. What had led to the expulsion of leading members of the government? How had the Bolsheviks coped with the massive haemorrhage suffered in the war against the White Generals (so ardently discussed by Olive after the defeat of General Denikin)? Why had the Soviet leaders made such huge concessions to the peasants which partly restored the 'free market', and why had they then turned against the rural population, exterminating millions of people? What effect had this policy had on Russian society and where did the state acquire the food to feed the populace?

Ruth found very different answers from very different writers and did not always know enough to read the texts critically. Dreiser came as a stranger to Russia, with no knowledge of the language. Opposed to Communism, he was a very critical observer. He went as he pleased – but always with a translator who mapped out an itinerary. He found that the Communist press all over Russia carried the same news and that all commentators on the West were required to show their governments as oppressive and labour as oppressed 'and constantly seeking to free itself from the shackles of capitalism'.

He denigrated the colouring and twisting of all art: *The Robbers*, a play by Schiller, was edited and furnished with a prologue and epilogue to underline its message, and *Uncle Tom's Cabin* left out little Eva and showed Simon Legree 'shot by a young Negro specially introduced for this purpose, who considers it his duty to avenge the brutal treatment of Uncle Tom and Eliza'.

Ruth described Dreiser's comments on the militarisation of the country, where the people were being taught that 'a great war was inescapable' and that in the innumerable 'Lenin Corners' which were centres of industrial, educational and political instruction for adults, there 'is also a rack of guns, bombs, gas-masks, first-aid kits, etc, and courses of instructions in the use of such things'. Dreiser saw these with dislike or misgiving but he also saw much to admire and believed that the system was 'likely to endure in Russia, perhaps with modifications, and not only that but spread to and markedly affect, politically, all other nations'. He rejoiced in an educational system 'that taught children to think'; in the economic emancipation of women who must work if they were able but were cared for by the state if they were unable; in equal pay for equal work of the two sexes, and the opening of all jobs to women. There were many other laudable improvements: adult education, the entertainment of peasants who visited the towns, and factories were springing up around the country. Ruth was impressed although she complained that Dreiser repeated himself far too often.

Rhys Williams was also an American but one who had been in Russia since 1918 and 'has written several books on the Communistic movement'. In *The Russian Land* he presented a series of pictures 'as vivid and crowded and charming as a Russian ballet, and his valuable information is given by the way'. He wrote about villages across Russia, speaking of a woman of eighty, the last surviving epic singer who sang for more than half an hour a few of the hundred thousand verses she knew by heart; saw the village folk clustering with rapture around the new cream separator; heard tales of the household deity, to whom the old still pay tribute; the grain buyer who bought for merchants before the war and now bought for the Red government. There was a great deal more for Rhys Williams to say, wrote Ruth, 'and so charming, so artistic and so informing are these sketches, that it is earnestly to be hoped that he has more in reserve.'

Ruth's interest in events in Russia endured, and despite her later attraction to the Communist Party, much of what she recounted from the books she read was far from complimentary. That was not the case when she reviewed two books on Isadora Duncan in the *Cape Times* –

My Life on 17 January 1929 and *Isadora Duncan's Russian Days, and her Last Years in France* on 29 May.

The review of Isadora Duncan's autobiography, described as the 'most truthful book ever written by a woman, and one of the most beautiful' was extraordinary. Although it described the dancer, the review could, with minor changes, be read as a comment on Olive. In her opening paragraph Ruth wrote:

> Now and again there pass through the world certain men and women who live with an intensity unknown and undesired by the majority. Their joys and sorrows, their absorption in work or ideas or pleasure, are to the joys and sorrows and absorptions of others as wine is to water. A creative force burns within them, consuming them and often those nearest to them in the process. For they are usually gey [that is, considerably] ill to live with, except to those devoted tenders of the flame who would rather suffer their exactions and serve them than be themselves tended by the most considerate care. They are usually unpractical, difficult, if not impossible, in their daily encounters of life, and yet whatever beauty and inspiration, help and healing men have given to their fellow men in this strange world of ours from the beginning has been poured from their hands.

This great dancer who inspired artists and poets, and 'enchanted audiences in every great city of the world' with dancing which she originated and taught, suffered poverty and rejection by lovers – though she gave of herself 'riches of mind and body and spirit ... beyond those of ordinary mortals'. Her dream of building a school, a vast ensemble to present the dances that would consolidate her techniques, was shattered by the war as were the dreams of so many others. But perhaps, wrote Ruth, even if there had been no war she would not have succeeded. Isadora never recovered from the news that her two children, together with their nurse, had been drowned in the River Seine. This had been the 'last day of her spiritual life'. Since then her one desire had been (as she wrote) 'to fly from the horror of it'.

But that was not the end for Isadora. Before her death (her neck was broken when her scarf became tangled in the wheels of a car) Duncan had been invited to set up a school in Soviet Russia. As she wrote in her book, in words reminiscent of Olive (but not quoted in this review):

> On the night of the Russian Revolution I danced with a terrible fierce joy. My heart was bursting within me at the release of all those who had suffered, been tortured, died in the cause of humanity.

In the penultimate page of the book (which is still in print) there is an account of a cable received from the Soviet Government saying: 'The Russian Government alone can understand you. Come to us; we will make your school.' The closing words (of her unfinished book) when her boat arrived, were:

> Now for the beautiful New World that had been created! Now for the world of Comrades! The dream that had been conceived in the head of Buddha; the dream that had resounded through the words of Christ; the dream that has been the ultimate hope of all great artists; the dream that Lenin had by a great magic turned to reality, I was entering now into this dream that my work and life might become a part of its glorious promise.
>
> Adieu Old World! I would hail a New World.

There the book ended and she did not recount the Soviet experience. Instead it was recorded by Irma Duncan, her pupil, friend and companion during her last years, and Allan Ross MacDougall, her secretary and then companion in 1916-17 in Paris and Nice. The trips to Russia were marked by failure – a tragic and ill-considered marriage to get the poet Essenine [Yesenin] out of Russia – a sacrifice which he treated with contemptuous boorishness. Often drunk and often more than half insane he interrupted her dancing, swore at her, filched her belongings and destroyed her picture album.

The account of what Isadora experienced in the new Russia was quite unexpected.

> Petrograd, dirty, dingy, with empty, unwashed shop windows and people standing in queues for food ...; a room found with difficulty, which contained one bed without sheets and pillows, and was infected with vermin; and no food but black bread and dark greasy-looking soup, eaten in company with grimy, unshaven 'comrades' who would not talk to her ...

There was no school for dancers and no plans for one, but she was only really upset when she was taken to a party to meet prominent Communists. She was distressed to find 'comrades, well-dressed, listening to a lady warbling a French Bergerette'. When the woman began a second song Isadora rose in anger and harangued the audience, accusing them of being bourgeoisie in disguise, of throwing out the old leaders 'only to take their place and indulge in the same ridiculous antics as they used to do here in this very room'.

Yet she was happy. Hungry, neglected by the government, and tormented by Essenine, she was still convinced, despite her disappointment, that she had seen the dawn of a new era. Departing for America to get money for the children of Russia she met only hostility and, in Boston, carried away by the coldness of her audience, she waved her red scarf around her head and cried 'This is red! So am I! It is the colour of life and vigour. You were once wild here. Don't let them tame you!' That ended her American tour. European countries did not treat her much more kindly. Greeted with calumny in the press, refused a visa in Austria, she was ostracised and reduced to penury.

Isadora gave one last successful performance in Paris in July 1927, dancing her dance of maternal love to Schubert's *Ava Maria*, leaving many of the audience sobbing aloud. Two months later came her tragic death. Only then did her friends and admirers return, to bury her with eloquent words, with heaped flowers and beautiful music. Her unfinished autobiography, when it appeared, was greeted with acclaim. But it was not Russia that was glorified. Rather it was the story of a woman who gave her all for the art she created.

In the *Cape Times* of 12 March 1931 Ruth reviewed two novels set in Russia: *The Dogs*, by Ivan Nazhivin, and *Three Pairs of Silk*

Stockings, by Panteleimon Romanof. These two books said Ruth, '[supplement] each other, cancel each other, check each other, comment on each other, so that ... taken together they form one picture of fresh and unusual interest.'

The story of the last generation of landowners under the old regime and then under the beginning of the Bolshevik era is told through the lives of a group of dogs who shared the fortunes and daily lives of their owners. The story proceeds from the stability and graciousness of the Prince's country house to its graceless invasion by the Grand Duke and its gradual degradation and then destruction. After scenes at the war front the action shifts to a famished and hysterical Moscow of the early Soviet days. The dogs of the Prince's estate have been killed by the Grand Duke and at this stage fearsome gangs of dogs, relapsing into savagery, roamed the outskirts of the city, snatching at food and terrorising the hungry inhabitant.

Despite its unflattering portraits of the Royal family, *The Dogs* was neither written nor published in Soviet Russia. *Three Pairs of Stockings* which was, tells the story of an intellectual bourgeois and his circle, confronted with the social change after the revolution, who degenerate in their newly found cramped quarters, lack of privacy and feeling of social outlawry. The collapse of all moral values, the betrayal of long-time friends, the toadying to anyone of goodwill was set against the children in the building 'who are banded together solemnly into a complete Communist organisation'. Ruth found this 'refreshing by contrast' – a mark perhaps of her coming political affiliation.

Feminist Viewpoint

It is hardly necessary to seek writings by Ruth on the question of feminism. Her essays are permeated with glimpses of her preoccupation with the subject. In a review entitled 'The Gentle Crusader' in *The South African Nation*, 9 January 1926, she wrote about the *Letters of Constance Lytton*, selected and arranged by Lady (Betty) Balfour. This volume, which covered the story of a British suffragette, was made more dear to Ruth because both the editor and Lady Lytton had been close friends of Olive.

'One important factor in reconciling people to the anguish and savagery of war-time ... is the joy, infectious and not ignoble, which informs the daily life of those who have dedicated themselves to some crusade,' wrote Ruth in her introduction. The crusade in which Constance Lytton was engaged was the struggle for the enfranchisement of women. In that struggle the militants faced imprisonment, brutality, enforced feeding, and death itself.

Lady Lytton had spent four years of her life as an activist, followed by eleven years of invalidism and an early death as a result of the mental strain and physical ordeal to which she had been subjected. The tactics of the militants – bloodless and using minimal violence – were met with barbarous, vindictive and stupid retaliation by the authorities. The women met this with 'utter selflessness and heroism and ... endured physical torture, nameless indignities ... and estrangement from their nearest and dearest.'

The story of her prison experiences had appeared in *Prisons and Imprisonment* in which she told of her two successive imprisonments. When she had given her own name she had, despite repeated requests, been treated with special care and attention. On the second occasion, when she had given her name as Jane Warton she had been force fed eight times by a doctor who left her prostrate after the first awful experience and slapped her on her cheek. Her letters fill in the picture of a shy, fastidious, humble woman, loving solitude, disliking functions, devoted to flowers, animals and children, ill at ease with strangers. And yet, paralysed and invalided, she had given help to passive resisters, Germans who were boycotted, war babies, ex-prisoners of all sorts. She had given the whole of her legacy from her great-aunt to the suffrage cause and had sold nearly all her possession to have more money for distribution. She died in 1923.

More generally, Ruth confronted feminism in an omnibus review in the *Cape Times*, 18 April 1931, under the heading 'Women Must be Given a Life Pattern'. In using this review as a medium to advance her views on this subject she was over ambitious. The books she used did not offer the canvas that she sought. Starting with Chekhov's story, 'The Darling', she moved to Tolstoy's criticism (printed below the Chekhov story), to *Women and Children Last* by Beverley Nichols, and on to *Ragged Banners* by Ethel Mannin, with a reference to D H Lawrence to underline the arguments. It is an unwieldy discussion, putting together contrasting views on feminism (as seen in the early years of the century).

'The Darling', perhaps the best of the writings, tells the story of Olenka, widowed twice and married a third time who, on each occasion echoed her husband's interests. Married first to the manager of a provincial theatre the 'darling' sat in the box office and talked gravely to all comers of the matters that bothered her husband: the capriciousness of public taste; the importance of fine weather; and so on. When he died, and after a period in which she was inconsolable, she married a timber merchant. Henceforth she talked, and even dreamed, of the price of timber, the different kinds of planks, the cost of freight. But he too died. She was lost and wretched until she married a veterinary surgeon. Again she learnt a new set of conversational openings until he was transferred to Siberia and she felt that she was living in a vacuum. He returned after an interval, bringing with him his schoolboy son. Life returned as she turned to mothering the boy, getting him up in the morning and hearing his lessons. She repeated after him: 'An island is a piece of land which is entirely surrounded by water'. This, wrote Chekhov, 'was the first opinion to which she gave utterance with positive conviction after so many years of silence and dearth of ideas'.

Although Chekhov told the story without comment Tolstoy believed that Olenka was being ridiculed, but he found 'her faculty of devoting herself with her whole being to anyone she loves ... not absurd, but marvellous and holy'.Chekhov was criticised for presenting the image of a new woman 'mentally developed, learned, working independently for the good of society' This, wrote Tolstoy, was wrong: 'a woman's fundamental work was to cherish others, and the ideal of feminine perfection must remain different from that of masculine perfection'.

Not much is to be gained by quoting from the other books included in this omnibus. The ideas are dated and could not have expressed Ruth's own, even if they do throw some light on D H Lawrence, who said that women 'must have a pattern of themselves by which to live, furnished to them by the men' – and only gave of their best when they had a satisfactory pattern 'to play up to'.

Women and Children Last is by Beverly Nichols who was antagonistic to the 'liberated woman'. Women, he wrote, were either hardened masochists 'who yearn to be bullied by their men or sticky sentimentalists, expecting all men to be ready to make love to them on every occasion'. Women were dishonest about money and were bad housekeepers. The only exceptions, and of these he approves, were mothers: 'whenever a mother talks to her son there is the echo of a lullaby there, even though you may not hear it'. Nichols maintains that he is 'discarding a sort of chivalry the occasion for which has vanished': 'If women insist on demanding equality, it is only fair that they should have equality of criticism'. And he does criticise, insisting that women cannot be vamps and independent human beings all at the same time.

Ruth gave Chekhov the last word. In a letter to his brother he wrote that what he wanted in women was: 'Freshness, elegance, humanity, the capacity for motherhood'. 'A woman possessed of these qualities,' wrote Ruth, would quite possibly be an improvement both on the 'New Woman' and on the 'Darling', not to speak of the 'Vamps'. 'But there are not likely to be many of the Tchekov sort for some generations to come.'

The Essayist

In considering the body of Ruth's essays I am again confronted by the dilemma of what it is possible to cut without spoiling the original text? Some of the books Ruth wrote about are no longer readily available, others are so dated that only the scholar might be tempted to search for them. I found my interest awakened (or reawakened) by Ruth's reviews, either because I had read them long ago or because there seemed to be urgent reasons for reading them now. At times I could only regret that she was not able to include the fullest information available when she was writing, at others I exclaimed at the extent of her knowledge of world events. I set out to write a biography and eventually felt that if I was able to transmit Ruth's ideas even partially my project would be fuller and more fruitful.

On South African Authors

The review of Sarah Gertrude Millin's railway guide: *The South Africans* in *The Nation*, 27 July 1927, begins gently: 'with its chatty diction, its breezy descriptions of its principal towns, people, political parties, social problems and racial conflicts of the country, it is an admirable guide-book'. If at this point the reader has missed the irony, he/she might be tempted to put the article aside. Further on, though, it becomes obvious that the review has altered course. 'For all its flair and attractiveness,' wrote Ruth:

> there is something fundamentally superficial, impenitently trivial, which forbids its criticism except at that level. Mrs Millin's knowledge of three-fourths of South Africa is that of the well-to-do tourist; her knowledge of the South African natives, Asiatics, and coloured people is that of the average European in South Africa who has never come into social contact with any of them save as employer.

Taking Mrs Millin to task for her statements on class she wrote, 'There are no idle rich in South Africa. There are no leisured classes. There are no upper classes. There are no lower classes,' Ruth maintained: 'This is just not true. Mrs Millin is speaking about the whites (the whole ... of which could be housed in a fifth part of New York)'. Her contention, wrote Ruth, was 'unsound and at best half true'. Her summing up of the position of the African with the statement 'But in the end, of course, they will do as they are told to', was hopelessly wrong:

> This simply is not true. There was a time when it was so, but it came to an end some years ago. From the passing of the Land Act of 1913 the native ceased to trust the white man's good intentions with regard to himself; during the Great War he learned that his respect for the power and wisdom of the white man had been exaggerated. Since the Act of Union [in 1910] one piece of harsh legislation after another has forced him into race-consciousness and into an embittered, determined independence. During the coming year Kadalie ... who has organized the natives into trade unions and made of them a large and powerful

> organization [the ICU], is to lecture in America, as well as in England. Those who hear him will have an opportunity to realize for themselves how little likely, from now on, the natives of South Africa are to do as they are told – unless, of course, they are told with machine-guns.

In a country in which there was so little protest from the white electorate against the government's racist legislation this was a perceptive statement; years ahead of the spate of stories and novels in which the African was portrayed. In an essay entitled 'The Literary Exploitation of the Native', published in *The South African Nation*, 25 September 1926, Ruth exposed the pretensions of some would-be writers and condemned the mediocrity of much of the work that appeared in the daily papers and weeklies. Nor could it be otherwise: the writers had no first hand knowledge of the African. All that the whites knew were 'the citified errand-boy or kitchen-boy of the big towns, or the semi-slave dependant of the farms'. They knew nothing or had no understanding 'of the customs, laws, religious beliefs or moral and social values of those whom they describe'. More specifically Ruth turned on Mrs Millin's sketches of an African servant, stating that despite some 'truthful observations and shrewd judgment' the writer herself would 'probably agree that neither observation nor judgment could be other than fairly superficial'.

Mrs Millin aside, she wrote, there was a large bulk of such work being produced and published in South Africa which augured ill for the future of literature of the country. 'For if the effect on the writer of untrue work is bad, the effect on the reader is even worse.' She queried who might want to read these stories and why they would want to do so.

> With honourable exceptions, we are not as a population interested in the life of the native. He is a convenience or a problem as the case may be, and when he is being neither in any marked degree he is well out of the picture. No; it is probably just because the reader knows so little of the native and is so unconcerned to know more that he or she finds these tales, rich in local colour and adventure of the moving-

> picture type, and well-finished with dark-skinned marionettes whose feelings and experiences we need not take over-seriously ... Any reader who really thinks of the natives as a race of human beings treading along a way of which the end is not in sight, and on which their feet were set not by themselves but by the white men, must deplore on social as well as artistic grounds the foolish grotesqueness of these presentations ... Is not the economic exploitation with which long ago we gaily sowed the dragon's teeth enough? Must we add to it the more than slightly vulgar frivolity of literary exploitation?

Continuing her criticism, Ruth wrote again – this time under the title 'Literature and Patriotism' in *The South African Nation*, 31 July 1926. On this occasion her subject was the fate of anything written in South Africa earlier in the twentieth century. 'It used to be extremely unusual to take any approving or even critical interest in anything written in this country':

> A South African writer who was very often mentioned in overseas periodicals began gradually, because of that fact, to be talked of on this side. Long after *The Story of an African Farm* had been accepted as a classic in Europe it remained unknown and unread in this country, and its writer, who to Europeans not interested in gold or diamonds seemed the one important figure in South Africa, remained for the majority of her fellow countrymen merely an eccentric invalid with unpopular views.

The change of heart which had resulted in enthusiasm about local literature was commendable. It was 'the outward and visible sign of an inward self-respect.' Yet it was also a manifestation of a 'staggering indiscrimination'. Readers, determined to find a national literature, had surrendered any critical appraisal. All standards had been debased:

> The same humourless enthusiasm is lavished on insignificant essays, inferior stories, artistically non-existent

> work of all the genres. Every conscientious reviewer in the country knows by heart the sinking feeling with which he opens each new local effort.
>
> This parish-pump criticism will have to go if South African literature is to live.

Ruth declared that South Africa had produced only two writers – Olive Schreiner and Roy Campbell – who were discussed by lovers of literature the world over, and only three others who had written works of great talent. They were William Plomer, 'for whom greatness may well be in store'; Sarah Gertrude Millin, who had arrived with her 'competent, economical, clever stories', but whom Ruth thought could never produce a work of genius; and Pauline Smith, 'with her single volume of Karoo stories, one of which is an exquisite thing'.

The review of Pauline Smith's *The Beadle* appeared in *The South African Nation* on 30 October 1926. Ruth describes it as an account of 'a handful of men and women' in a small town in the Karoo, their sweetness, or their smothered lives or, in one case, a man who comes to stay and whose 'easy selfishness' leads him to cruelty. In this case he uses his gaiety and charm to seduce Andrina, the central figure in the story. It was her ignorance and innocence, her obedience, her lack of feeling and shame, wrote Ruth, which made this loveable woman (as portrayed) unbelievable. Her impossible innocence 'strikes a jarring note'. Nevertheless the book is 'beautifully written from end to end':

> it is rich in description of a life now all but vanished with the coming of the railroad, not to mention the motor-car and the wireless set. But the ideas and ideals behind this life have not died out. They inform to this day the existence of a large part of the country, and go far to condition its present history, as they did its past.

If the review had been written without a word about Pauline Smith it would have been interesting but unremarkable. Not so! The article is introduced with a brief resumé of the life of Miss Smith whose childhood had been spent in South Africa before she accompanied her parents to

Britain. She had visited South Africa as an adult but in *The Little Karoo* and in *The Beadle* she wrote as she remembered it, as she knew it, as the daughter of a country doctor.

> It is perhaps this that gives to her work a strange quality, not so much of unreality as of remoteness. She is remembering rather than recording the atmosphere, the setting, the types from which she must draw to create. And things remembered, almost inevitably, become more or less sentimentalised. The glamour of the past is round them; to look at them objectively is well nigh impossible ... All her figures, men and women, are a little sentimentalised, a trifle out of focus.

Finally, Ruth's appreciation of this fine writer is captured in this short extract. Suggesting that the writer has 'a bond of inner sympathy between her own spirit and that of those simpler, more isolated folk of whom she writes', she writes of Miss Smith:

> Has genuine talent of a rare order; her really lovely English, with its untortured, limpid sentences, her artistic truthfulness that is not afraid of emotion, not obsessed by ugliness, not ashamed of beauty ... would make of any scene she chose some picture worth studying for the sincerity of its presentation and the ordered, gracious clarity, like a Vermeer interior of its detail.

Turning her attention to William Plomer and Roy Campbell, Ruth wrote that it was essential to outline the background to their recent dismissal from the journal *Voorslag*. There had been a time when the journal had showed promise but within a year after the bitter dispute after which the management had dismissed Campbell and Plomer the 'pathetic, bantling, lamentable, unregretted' journal had collapsed. The rights and wrongs of the dispute had been 'noisily and unedifyingly' disputed by both sides. She remarked caustically that the two men were 'intransigent, foul-mouthed, and probably quite impractical', but it was shameful to drive them out of their jobs and out of the country, 'to the accompaniment of abuse as shrill as their own'.

In leaving they 'had good reason to think and to write of South Africa as "a country in which artists cannot live"'. The pair, she wrote in her review of Plomer's compendium of stories, *I Speak of Africa*, were not alone among local youth in displaying in print, a 'crude bumptiousness'. But apart from their crudity and their tirades they were engaged in the production of sincere and non-commercial literature. Ruth praised Campbell's 'The Flaming Terrapin' as a poem 'of vigour, of beautiful undisciplined richness', the 'stamp of a true poet in the making'. Since then, among a handful of short pieces, there had been one sonnet and one lyric 'which for beauty and for power may be ranked with the finest in the great treasury of English poetry'. She described Plomer's *Turbott Wolfe* as rough, disconnected and sketchy, but vibrating 'with a force and with a deep truth which has been silent in South Africa since Olive Schreiner left off writing'.

Turning to *I Speak of Africa*, Ruth praised the novelette 'Ula Masondo' as 'the most complete, the most finished, the most important thing he [Plomer] has yet published'. Commenting on this tale of an African who went to the mines on the Witwatersrand (or 'Goldenville') Ruth wrote:

> It is the unvarnished story of a native African to whom contact with the white man's civilisation means only slow, deep, complete degradation and destruction ... as it stands it forms a terrific and an unanswerable indictment of that civilisation as it manifests itself in 'Goldenville'.

Campbell won an accolade when Ruth reviewed *The Wayzgoose* in *The South African Nation* on 10 March 1928. Under the heading 'Mr Campbell Wins', Ruth wrote that for two years she had despaired at the' patronising, slanging admonishment and vilification' of Campbell and at his extravagant responses in letters in some paper. 'But with the publication of his satirical *Wayzgoose*, he has silenced both admirers and enemies. This work, which owes so much to Pope's *Dunciad*, still stands on its own by its brilliance and originality.'

> It is a question whether there is any poet of to-day writing in English fit to stand beside him. Indeed it is the outstanding feature of *The Wayzgoose* that amid its passage of witty abuse, and far from ignoble and equally witty wrath, there are interspersed couplets and whole passages of pure poetry, poetry which though didactic in thought is lyric in its gay outpouring of rhymes and images.

Expressing her own beliefs, she wrote that she found herself among those 'who find themselves in agreement with most of [Campbell's] opinions and sympathies'. She also thought that:

> In many a little village, in many an ultra-respectable clique or household, a phrase from *The Wayzgoose* shall fall with quickening power on some young heart, and kindle within it the good laughter of rebellion against what is narrow, mean, provincial, muddled and muddy in the life of the country.

South African readers recognised an affinity with novels that came out of race-bound America. For that reason it seemed quite natural to cite a book on colour in the US alongside some South African novels.

According to Carl van Vechten, who introduced a new edition, James Weldon Johnson's book, *The Autobiography of an ex-Coloured Man*, was not always true to Johnson's life. Nonetheless Ruth found a universality in this account of a near-white boy who discovers that he is not white, but the illegitimate son of a famous white man and a coloured woman. 'He is forced to take his outlook on all things, not from the viewpoint of a citizen, or a man, or a human being, but from the viewpoint of a *coloured* man.' And as he has already said: 'this is the dwarfing, warping, distorting influence which operates upon each and every coloured man in the United States'.

The boy is transformed by his new knowledge after a sojourn in New York where he earns money and leisure both as a coloured and as a white man. Having a knowledge of music he travels to the Southern states to collect and compose from Negro melodies. There he sees a black man burnt and lynched. He returns to the north, neither disclaiming his black race nor claiming to be white. He changes his name and decides it is not necessary to go about with a label of inferiority pasted across his forehead.

> 'All the while I understood that it was not discouragement or fear or search for a larger field of opportunity that was driving me out of the Negro race. I knew that is was shame, unbearable shame. Shame at being identified with a people who could with impunity be treated worse than animals. For certainly the law would restrain and punish the malicious burning alive of animals.'

But, wrote Ruth, 'the shame of which he writes is also an emotion well-known to other persecuted races, and it is in essence merely a side of the slave mentality engendered by persecution.'

Miscellany

Ruth's reviews in Cape newspapers appeared almost every week for many years and sometimes included surveys of several books. She occasionally reviewed reprints of older works, but more generally wrote about new publications. The output was truly vast, and the total number of reviews she wrote must have run into the hundreds. She prided herself on her knowledge of contemporary literature – and she seems to have emulated her father's reading habits – he claimed to read a book a day. To have read all the books and then written reviews was a labour of love which may have prevented Ruth from succeeding in her ambition to write her own books. But had the reviews not appeared the readers of the Cape Town daily press would have been the poorer.

Some information on her working day was provided in a letter written to Ben in March or April 1932. There is no indication in the letter of the book or books to which Ruth was referring.

> I think my lecture went well. I gave the whole day to it, with the usual incidental interruptions, and as I read here

> and there my admiration grew all over again. What artistry, what power, what sense as well as courage the man had. 'The great danger,' he says, speaking of war-time, 'lies not in the power of the wicked but in the weakness of the good', and he's got a lovely story of a missionary on the Gold Coast, who was told by the natives that God asked the Europeans 'What hast thou done with thy brother?' and the Europeans *turned white with fear*. My audience were impressed and cordial, though I think they jibbed at the end.

And on 19 March 1932 she wrote saying that she was to lecture on Romain Rolland:

> I've been reading today his book on Beethoven and Goethe. It's really an account of their meeting – and parting, for they did not get on. He analyses the two with great skill and no sort of sentimentality, admiring both, but seeing both.

The review of *Goethe and Beethoven* appeared in the *Cape Argus*, on 26 March 1932. Goethe rejected the composer's music as part of 'a decaying world, a world returning to its elements' although he was impressed by the man and they saw one another socially. In a letter to his wife Goethe wrote 'Never before have I met an artist of more powerful concentration, more energy or deeper sincerity'. But the gulf between the two men reopened when Beethoven berated Goethe for kowtowing to the local dignitaries. The rift was not bridged even when Beethoven, 'ill, poor and harassed', asked Goethe to interest the Grand Duke in publishing his 'Missa Solemnis'. The 'unbeautiful silence that followed displayed a meanness of spirit. Did Goethe perhaps hear again Beethoven's words: "I have waited for you because I honour and esteem you, but you have honoured these people [the dignitaries] far too much"?'

One of Ruth's most lyrical reviews was of *The Letters of Katherine Mansfield*, edited by Mansfield's husband, J Middleton Murry. Ruth, for whom Mansfield was 'beautiful, indomitable K.M.' said of the collection:

> These letters are in truth remarkable and beautiful as are very few that have been given to the world. In literary quality, in vividness and delicacy of perception, in courageous and tireless truth-seeking, in felicity of expression, they are of a piece, cut from the same cloth, as 'her finest stories'. And in them she does indeed, as he [Murry] says, live again, unfolding to the reader a personality so rare, so exquisite, that it is with a mingled sense of actual personal loss and deep personal privilege that he closes the record.

She quotes from several of the letters, but one extract, with an introduction, must suffice:

> Of an unusual honesty and articulateness, the enforced solitariness and restrictions of her daily life allowed her to concentrate on the problems of her own art, and of art in general, and the results of her cogitations ... are as valuable as they are delightful reading. She writes, for example to a painter friend of hers: 'When you paint apples do you feel that your breasts and your knees become apples, too? Or do you think this is the greatest nonsense? I don't. I am sure it is not. When I write about ducks I swear that I am a white duck with a round eye, floating on a pond fringed with yellow-blobs and taking an occasional dart at the other duck with the round eye, which floats upside down beneath me.

Mansfield continued with that exploration of the process of becoming the duck – 'what Lawrence would perhaps call the consummation with the duck or the apple! It is so thrilling, that I can hardly breathe, only to think about it ... There follows the moment when you are more duck, more apple ... than any of these objects could ever be, and so you create them anew ... That is why I believe in technique'.

> I do, just because I don't see how art is going to make the divine spring into the bounding outline of things if it hasn't

> passed through the process of becoming these things before recreating them.

Some books were dealt with cursorily, others given more considered treatment. Whether one agrees with Ruth or not there was usually much wisdom, and much information, in what she wrote. She was impressed by G Jean-Aubry's two volume *Joseph Conrad: Life and Letters*, which she reviewed in *The South African Nation* of 24 March 1928. 'The outline narrative is so well written, and the letters so admirably chosen and arranged, that the work can never be superseded,' she wrote. Conrad's sincerity was so absolute 'that it seems to inform and even mould the very language he uses, of a piece with his writing'. Every adult day of his life was 'lived in the cold light of a singularly brave and convinced disillusionment that yet retained as its complement a profound reverence for the heroic element in man'. His disillusionment extended to his belief that socialism was the curse of the age and that internationalism was a mad and bad ideal. He had written to Cunningham Graham:

> Life knows us not and we don't know life – we don't even know our own thoughts. Half the words we use have no meaning whatever and of the other half each man understands each word after the fashion of his own folly and conceit. Faith is a myth and beliefs shift like mists on the shore: thoughts vanish: words once pronounced die: and the memory of yesterday is as shadowy as the hopes of to-morrow – only the string of my platitude seems to have no end. As our peasants say: 'Pray, brother, forgive me for the love of God'. And we don't know what forgiveness is, nor what is love, nor where God is. *Assez*! [Yet, wrote Ruth, he was certain that God was somewhere.]

Every step in his life, she wrote, had had something of the romantic: his devotion to England in which he lived as a naturalised person, the affinity he felt for the English temper, his immersion in the English language [even if 'half the words have no meaning!'], the generous and ardent friendships bestowed on those he loved. Yet the material world had brought few rewards. He had lived in financial want, earning paltry royalties for books that did not sell; his Congo adventure [as described in *Heart of Darkness*] ended his career as a sailor, and crippling attacks of gout made him bedridden for days on end. Because he was determined 'to give to the world only what he believed to be his best' Ruth could say with conviction: 'M Jean-Aubry has understood the benefit such letters as these confer upon a world not overcrowded with noble souls. It might be said truly enough of them is to have received a liberal education of the spirit'. She gave the last words of her essay to Conrad.

> One thing I am certain of is that I have approached the object of my task, things human, in a spirit of piety. The earth is a temple where there is going on a mystery play, childish and poignant, ridiculous and awful enough, in all conscience. Once in, I've tried to behave decently. I have not degraded any *quasi*-religious sentiment by tears and groans, and if I have been amused or indignant, I've neither grinned nor gnashed my teeth. In other words, I've tried to write with dignity, not out of regard for myself, but for the sake of the spectacle, the play with an obscure beginning and an unfathomable dénouement.

Colette's writings were very different. Reviewing the translation of her novel *La Vagabonde,* Ruth wrote:

> It is either a happy achievement or Providence that has chosen the present juncture at which to introduce Colette to English readers. At a time when ponderosity is at a premium, when wordiness is a fashion, her light-handed treatment of complex situations, her neatness of characterisation that is never superficial, may have a salutary influence upon the younger generation. Her readers, moreover, though they will for the most part enjoy her pervasive charm and the subtlety of her character-drawing, will be apt to find their taste for the more

> amorphous, heavier novel of psychological interest seriously impaired, and this in time may also produce desirable results.

Or writing about evil in Walter de la Mare's, *Seaton's Aunt*, ('The Modern Manner', *Cape Times*, 14 April 1928) Ruth said of him that his technique was 'an affair more of atmosphere and of the accessories incidental to the creation of atmosphere than of language'.

> Over almost all his stories lies a sort of spellbound horror, eating its way like a canker into the heart of the familiar sunshine-drenched things of every day. He likes to use the hot, white summer days and summer aspect of country houses and gardens to make darker and more sinister by contrast the shadowed rooms and opaque ponds and dusky-hearted trees necessary to his tale of witchery. *Seaton's Aunt* is quite typical.The reader is then prepared for 'a furtive, frightened, unwholesome small boy, growing into an equally unnatural and unwholesome youth, gradually witched out of existence by his wicked, creepy old aunt'.

For those who liked the genre, this would make it essential reading.

All too often Ruth saw in novels, plays and biographies, works that she praised excessively. They were the 'best', the 'most masterly', and so on. But, whether they did not stand the test of time, or were lost out of neglect, they have all but disappeared. The reader is entitled to ask whether Ruth erred in her judgement, or whether a fickle public failed to recognise quality when it appeared.

Thus it was, in 1931, that Ruth enthused about a trilogy written by Henry Handel [Edith] Richardson, who had started life in Australia, and wrote *The Fortunes of Richard Mahony*. She praised the three volume book in both the *Cape Argus* of 10 January 1931 and the *Cape Times* of 26 February and accorded it the highest rating in her selection of 'Noteworthy Novels of 1931' in the *Cape Times* on 31 December that year. In the same piece she named Richardson as one of 'three brilliant writers', the other two being Virginia Woolf and Sigrid Undset.

> Of the most artistically important novel of the year there can be no question. Henry Handel Richardson's *The Fortunes of Richard Mahony* stands above any other written in English during more than the current year [the third and final volume was published in 1927] for sheer creative power and depth of understanding. It is a great novel, taking its place of right with the classics of our language.

Why is this a great novel 'one to be set beside *Middlemarch*?' Ruth asked in the *Cape Argus*:

> To answer this question is to define the peculiar elements necessary to a work of artistic importance. Style is much in a novel; the angle of approach is much; the technique is much. But all these are equally necessary to the essay or the short story of artistic importance. The peculiar glory, however, and the peculiar field of the novel is its tracing of the development of character in one or more individuals, and of the fate imposed upon them by that development.

It is by the 'comprehensiveness, the subtlety, the truth of this history of the inner lives of his [her?] characters that the novelist stands or falls,' and Richardson's delineation of the inner lives of Richard Mahony and Mary his wife, and their impingement on the people among whom they lived, led Ruth to affirm that 'Richardson takes her place by right beside the great names of English letters'.

The novel did not achieve the prominence that Ruth foresaw. Was she wrong, or had she failed to reckon with the provincialism that controlled the taste of readers? Germaine Greer, in an introduction to the reprint of an earlier novel by Richardson, *The Getting of Wisdom*, wrote in 1980 that:

> Richardson's Australian epic remains her chief claim to fame, because the Australians, who are the only people to study it, share the common misconception that breadth

> equals profundity, especially when it is accompanied by seriousness of tone and turgidity of style.

Greer cannot be taken as the arbiter of literary greatness, nor of the discernment of the Australians, but she is correct in saying that the novel only has currency in Australia.

It is a sobering reflection on reading tastes that the South African writers acclaimed by Ruth are hardly read by their compatriots. Perhaps she was carried away in finding greatness where it was not warranted. But Henry Handel Richardson is at least studied by the Australians. She is surely big enough to have earned Ruth's enthusiastic praise in 1931.

A list of authors or of the titles of books Ruth reviewed would not necessarily inform the reader. Many of them are unknown today. Among the more prominent authors were Virginia Woolf, Erich Maria Remarque, Colette, Theodore Dreiser, Osbert Sitwell, Ellen Wilkinson, George Gissing, George Bernard Shaw (*The Intelligent Woman's Guide to Socialism and Capitalism*), Anatole France, Karel Capek, Ludwig Lewisohn, and books about Joseph Conrad, Isadora Duncan and Emily Hobhouse. Ruth also reviewed books of social interest such as Mrs Cecil Chesterson's *In Darkest London*, an account of doss houses for impecunious or homeless women.

Ruth's article on 'Noteworthy Novels of 1931 discussed, among others, the novels of Virginia Woolf, A J Cronin, Pearl Buck, George Moore, William Plomer and Sarah Gertrude Millin. She also mentioned or appraised works in translation of Sigrid Undset, Franz Werfel, Vicki Baum, Maxim Gorki, Colette, and many others.

It was perhaps no wonder that Lancelot Hogben, exposed to Ruth's reviews (and those of a coterie of like-minded reviewers), could say that during his stay in Cape Town he was as well read as his contemporaries in Britain. He was also fortunate in having access to the bookshop run by Paul Koston with its stock of *avant garde* works. For the discerning reader (as directed by the reviews) there was a treasure house to be explored and sampled.

10
A NEW BEGINNING AND THE END

The files on Ruth Schechter Alexander are coming to an end. They cover the last twelve years of her life and, apart from a small collection, most are unfortunately empty. The years that followed 1929 are marked by a scattering of short reports of activities amid long silences.

One important episode in Ruth's life that is undated but was probably taking place as she distanced herself from Morris and from her past was her rejection of religion and, with that, her withdrawal from the Jewish community.

It is only in her novel that I have found direct reference to the synagogue and to Ruth's severing all bonds with it. There had probably a loosening of the bond over several years, at least partially influenced by Hogben, who revelled in his attacks on all forms of mysticism (with religion as the keystone) and by Ben, who had long shed any religious beliefs he might have acquired as a young man – although he accommodated himself at a later stage to his daughter's adherence to the Friends (Quakers). These influences are not recorded and can only be guessed at from reading *The Exiles*. Given the assertion that the incidents described in the novel are based on actual events the rejection of the synagogue by Miriam, Ruth's *alter ego*, must correspond, at least symbolically, with Ruth's own break with religion. What remains in doubt is the year in which the severance took place.

Ruth's account of the breaking point is described casually, with no attempt at justification. On an impulse Miriam joins a congregation which is about to enter a synagogue. She climbs the stairs to the segregated women's gallery filled with childhood memories which take her back to the 'sense of purification of the smell of fresh clothes, of new shoes, of freshly washed hair'. This is in sharp contrast to the heavy atmosphere of perfumes and powders; the portly women 'rustling in silks and satins ... repeating the prayer that was being chanted by the cantor at the desk below'. Miriam observes the younger women whispering throughout the service, more concerned with the apparel of those around them than the prayers being intoned, and inspecting the males below who attract their attention. Nor is it very different among the men – although there is less looking about and less whispering. Many recite the prayers at their own pace, seemingly unconcerned about the portion reached by the cantor; while other groups sit together and speak of matters that have nothing to do with the service.

Among the congregation are men and women devout and devoted to the spirit for which the gathering has met. In a passage which evokes her past Ruth writes that there were those for whom:

> The service clearly held something of the reality it would have held for her father. These stood unmindful of their surroundings, rapt, and though their lips moved over the words of the ritual with the speed of long familiarity, there was nothing perfunctory in their utterance of them. They shook with the force of their own response to the ancient prayers; every sentence of praise, of admonition, of petition, struck on their hearts direct, moving them as though it had been newly penned by themselves.

The older women praying in this synagogue attract Miriam's particular attention. They are among the few who have learnt in Europe how to read the prayers intelligently:

> Last leaves on a tree, lingering representatives of an era as remote from the lives of their South African grand-children as if it had belonged to the sixteenth century instead of the middle of the nineteenth, they prayed with a devout intensity, in exaltation, in terror, and the tears stole down their worn faces as they prayed.
>
> She was ashamed of watching them, ashamed of her inescapable speculations as to what they looked forward

> to, what they dreaded, those women with their long pasts behind them, their long sleep so near. She closed her eyes, and let the sounds of the place wash over her.

The sounds merge with the strong baritone of the cantor into 'a medley of sound that rose and sank, sank till it was more a vibration in which she heard the uncrushable voice of "the Chosen People".'

> She thought with awe and with something like horror of the long centuries during which it had assailed the skies with its changeless arrogance, its changeless humility. And she thought, within the ghetto the Jew moved with a free mien; down the centuries he has lived enclosed in the prison palace of his own building; the ghetto opened, and he was still enclosed.

She realises that she has parted 'from the temper of the race as well as from its dogma'. Until others 'had raised the question, she had felt no barrier, no faintest barrier, on the score of her Jewish origin … This marked the end of her connection with the synagogue, of the tradition of her forefathers'. This is the catharsis in which she feels that the prayers have brought only torture, maltreatment and death. 'The Jews were not alone. Other nations also prayed anew for the success of their armies in battle.' She thinks of the Boers in South Africa who read into the Bible that they were the Chosen People, led by the Lord to the land of milk and honey, for whom the children of Ham were to be servants in perpetuity.

With these thoughts in her mind as she prepares to leave the synagogue, she gives thanks to the few in every generation 'who have known that the Life Force is not to be bottled up for local consumption, that patriotism is not nearly enough, and who had the courage to live their knowledge'.[1]

These pages were Ruth's clearing of the way for her marriage with Ben. But they were not merely a solution to her own intimate problem – the break with her religion and her rupture with the Jewish community had had a long gestation and included her disenchantment with Morris, her growing awareness of the plight of the blacks in South Africa and her acceptance of Gandhi's world view. There were obviously other factors as she faced the seemingly immovable stranglehold of Afrikaner nationalism in South Africa – which was merged with her fear and abhorrence of Nazism.

Events crowded in on Ruth in 1930 and culminated in the Enfranchisement Act. In a letter to the *Cape Times* on 5 March 1930 she, together with Caroline Murray, Anna Purcell, F H Schreiner, Lyndall Gregg and Rose Movsovic, all former members of the Cape Enfranchisement League committee, protested against the Bill.

> The Constitution of that organization pledged itself to work for the securing of the franchise to the women of the Cape Colony on the same terms as the men of the Cape Colony. May we point out that if *white* womanhood suffrage is given in the Cape Colony, the whole franchise basis of the Cape will have been altered before the contemplated joint sitting, and that while the European women will be represented as compared with the men, the Coloured and Native women will have no representation whatsoever?[2]

The tensions between Ruth and Morris Alexander became uncontainable when he voted for the Bill. After it was passed all white women had to register on the electoral roll. This was too much: she signed under protest and said that she would leave the country – although her departure was delayed by the need to support Morris in his despair and arrange matters for the three children.

Before she left she had to face some embarrassing functions. Perhaps the most difficult arose from the determination of some Jewish notables to mark the silver wedding of Morris and Ruth with an official reception. Both put on a good face and attended. Speaking about Morris, Rabbi Bender said:

> Mr Alexander had, for the past 25 years and more, done work which proved over and over again his desire for the social and political advancement of every section of the community.

> In whatever he had done, whether in public life, or in the smaller spheres of service to individual Jewish organisations, he had worked not for himself, but for the community, and his thought had ever been to do what was best.

There was also a commendation for Ruth:

> Mrs Alexander, too, had made her contribution to the community, particularly in her distinguished contributions to the press and in her lectures on literature, in which she displayed her wonderful gifts as a writer and critic.[3]

Ruth addressed the gathering, saying, among other things that it 'gave her great pleasure to know that he had the trust and affection of so many friends'.

Despite preparations for her departure Ruth did not stop reviewing books or submitting articles to the local press. What is surprising is that she offered some of her writing to the *Cape Argus*, a paper that had not previously carried her pieces. The probable reason for this is that Laurens van der Post had been appointed editor of the reviews page, an appointment which coincided with Ruth's decision to earn more money. She wrote for both the *Cape Argus* and the *Cape Times* from 1931-1933. It was a tribute to Ruth and a mark of her stature as a writer that two newspapers in competition with each other should both carry her reviews and articles.

The twenty-five pieces in the *Argus* were of uneven quality, many being little more than 'pot-boilers'. Some of these have been quoted in earlier chapters. In addition there were two articles about Joseph, the gardener, one revealing the misery caused when the minimal pension, given to him as a coloured, was stopped. A spiteful priest, whose congregation he had left, had denounced him as an African, who was therefore not entitled to draw such relief. She was the first to expose these iniquities but did not achieve any redress for the gardener or for the millions who reached old age without any income.

Among her reviews published by the *Argus* was an appraisal of Mrs Cecil Chesterson's book, *My Russian Venture*, on 31 October 1932.

The author, in line with other journalists at the time, was enthusiastic about Russia, finding 'bright, alert, happy young men and women content utterly to go short of food and clothing, to go without luxuries, to work extra hours' to build a better Russia. She had visited a collectivist farm and found a society that 'lived in a simple comfort and a mutual helpfulness, a pleasant combination of corporate labour and individual earning, of public spirit and private life, that seemed to her both delightful and stable.' The eulogies were taken at face value. Mrs Chesterson believed that she had seen 'a new and terrific chapter in the history of mankind', and Ruth believed that the author was 'altogether right'.

At the end of 1933 Ruth departed for the United States. If farewell parties were given they were not publicised, although many people must have been saddened to bid her farewell.

It was to be almost two years before she sailed again – this time to Britain. Once again the details of that time are lost. Ray Levy supplied some information in his informative letters, but he could only speak from his personal experience and Ruth did not see him all that often.

It is known that she occupied an apartment near the Hudson River in New York; that she saw Amy and undoubtedly got more details on the strike in Gastonia, heard about Amy's work in the Communist Party, and discussed events in South Africa and the threat of war in Europe and Asia.

It was inevitable that Amy should speak in glowing terms about the USSR. The unpleasant arrests and purges of Bolshevik leaders might have been discussed but, in line with party policy, they would have been accepted by this loyal member. Although there might have been some misgivings about the accusations levelled against such men the evidence could only have been unravelled by specialists. Saboteurs were everywhere and this settled all arguments. There is only one document available, and it is instructive. In the *Nation*, on 4 July 1934 under the heading 'The Factory as Hero', Ruth reviewed the novel *Driving Axle*, by V Ilyenkov. It was, as she observed, a work of 'frank propaganda mainly for home consumption'. Yet it was commended because it did not 'in a single instance sentimentalize the workers it describes'. Ruth welcomed Ilyenkov's description of the work as 'A Novel of Socialist Construction', writing that it was 'a just description'. Many novels of factory life had appeared on both sides of the Atlantic, all filled with gloom and doom, some better than others. A few were very good, 'but not one of them is cheerful reading'.

> *Driving Axle* is not by any means unremittingly cheery either. It too is a history of ceaseless struggle – against the stupidity of some, the laziness and indifference of others, the deliberate sabotage of a wicked few. But the fruits of the struggle are clear. Men are broken, die, come to promotion, quarrel, are reconciled, but the life of the plant goes on, and through all these happenings, tragic and otherwise, the knitting together of men of diverse character and education into one cooperative unit turning out first-class work for the Soviet proceeds steadily.

It was not a great novel, wrote Ruth, but she believed that 'workers in engineering shops all over the Soviet Union' would read it and 'find their own problems, their own crises, their own types mirrored there', and undoubtedly watch out for 'the sinister group of saboteurs' about whom Ilyenkov so dutifully wrote. In conclusion Ruth wrote of the real power conveyed by the book 'that self-forgetting devotion to an impersonal idea which is the basis of Communist life'.

It is an illuminating review, more for what it says about the changes taking place in Ruth's life than about a politically correct novel that left little or no mark in the annals of Russian literature. Ruth was either moving towards the Russian controlled Communist movement, or had already accepted its basic premises. The several meetings with Amy in New York undoubtedly helped her decide her future course.

Ben returned to Britain in 1935, briefly as a temporary lecturer in Bristol and then as Professor of Classics at Swansea University College from 1936 until his retirement in 1956. In August 1935, a few days before Morris's second marriage, Ben and Ruth married. In a letter to Raphael and Florence Levy on 9 February 1936, giving information about the marriage and the job in Swansea. Ruth wrote:

> Swansea is a tinplate and mining centre we've got to. Not a big town; most of the students very poor, but good

> students, Ben says. The speech, look, manner, of the people is as different from the rest of England as it we'd crossed the channel instead of the Severn. It's interesting. And its queer to be again in a bilingual country. All round is wilder common and forest than I've seen yet over here, and within a few miles a chain of great wide empty beaches, most lovely. Oh dear me! If only I could send you bathing on them, to come home to supper with me afterwards...
>
> My only personal grouse at the moment is that I'm not ten years younger, so that I'd free time ahead of me for writing.

Ruth also inquired after Amy who had not replied to several letters sent care of *New Masses*. Similarly, Frank had not answered her letters. 'Perhaps he thinks after all ... that for father's sake he ought now to disown me, cut me off. He's capable of it.' The letter contained the sad tale of her novel being turned down by publishers – even though her revised version was better than the first.

Ruth had invested so much energy in writing *The Exiles* that the rejection slips she received had been a sore disappointment. Try as she might the book could not succeed. She had neglected one of the rules she had laid down for a good novel: the characters had not developed and, despite some brilliant writing, the catastrophe that overtook the main characters had left them strangely unchanged. They were faced with an intractable tragedy – love across the colour line and the ending of Emanuel's career – but apart from affirming their love and seeking help from a new-found friend, they did not evolve. Was there perhaps a reason that defied any alteration? Was this, consciously or otherwise, a protracted love letter, in which Ruth and Ben confronted whatever problems they had together, in which they were seen to march together, to grow together, but not to change appreciably?

Ruth joined the Communist Party in Britain – the logical outcome of her growing despair of anything ever happening through parliamentary processes in South Africa. She had moved away from the parochial affairs on which Morris Alexander thrived. What concerned her thereafter was the increasingly difficult situation in South Africa – the extension of the oppressive colour bar, the whittling away of any protection from those laws.

Although there are no documents to chart the course she took, the Italian invasion of Ethiopia and the remilitarisation of Nazi Germany had made war inevitable and, like so many others, the only hope she saw lay in the Soviet Union which appeared to present the one gleam of sanity. They accepted the propaganda coming out of Moscow uncritically, and wandered into a wasteland, thinking they had found salvation for society. In that lies a tragedy that affected tens of thousands of people. Their aims and activities, however devoted, helped conceal the barbarism of the Stalin regime and, added to the glorification of the USSR – they destroyed the very revolution to which they aspired.

Ruth's decision to join the Communist Party was not precipitate. According to Ben, she was finally persuaded when she read the 'Stalin constitution' of 1936 (his phrase). This document, which persuaded (or fooled) so many people outside the USSR, proclaimed the full equality of women and men, of races and nationalities 'in all spheres of economic, state, cultural, social and political life ... ' Ben, who also accepted the truth of the document and joined the Communist Party, quoted in full at Ruth's commemoration service Articles 122 and 123 of the 'constitution' which, he said, had been taken by Ruth 'to be an epoch-making event'.[4]

It is only from the commemorative service that it is possible to discover the extent of Ruth's activities. In Swansea she spoke to members of the Workers Educational Association, the National Council of Labour Colleges, the Left Book Club, the National Council of Civil Liberties, the Women's Co-operative Guilds, and the British-Soviet Unity Committee. She spoke about the struggle in Spain as the beginning of the transformation of all Europe and she travelled to Scotland and to the valley towns of Wales, where her talks won her many friends.

If she heard any critical comments about what was happening in the USSR, she stopped her ears. Accepting Communist Party propaganda, Ruth turned to the crude literature that was emerging from party functionaries. But she was also steeped in British literature and prepared a course 'treating of Langland and Thomas Moore, of Milton and Shelley, of Cobbett, William Morris, Dickens, Olive Schreiner, and Ralph Fox, who in our day made light of his promising life if by the sacrifice of it he could prevent the triumph of Fascism in Spain'.[5]

In a more considered vein Ben was to write in a letter to Julius Lewin:

> I often feel very sad that Ruth did not have some higher field for the exercise of her talent and her influence. She was on the grand scale. But, although she was always so full of courage and activity, in truth her life broke her. I can see now, what I did not want to see so plainly before, how very much of an invalid she was all the time we were together. She was so alive, so busy, so interested, touched so many people's lives, and did so much that her failing health was less obvious than it might have been. She went from illness to illness, and suffered pain so continuously, that, had she been a more ordinary person, she would have been an acknowledged invalid. Instead life poured out of her. She never complained. She never lost interest. She never lost touch. She thought of her old friends and welcomed new ones. A little thing I never ceased to wonder at, and now never cease to miss, was the way she filled the house with cheerful laughter. She had the amazing capacity of laughing down the telephone. People would ring her up a lot, and whether Ruth was in her bed, with the phone beside her, or up and dressed, immediately the house would be full of laughter. She was the most serious of people and the most gay. She had more capacity of flowing out to others than anyone else I ever met.
>
> In her years with me her failing health made regular study difficult. But it was a grand thing to feel that, being together, we were developing together. Our lives were fuller and richer than ever before, not only because we were together, but because we could now really talk things out and live out our conclusions together, and because we made important decisions together. And Ruth showed a surprising capacity for new ideas. She was only part of what she

> should have been, had she had health and strength. But it was wonderful to have had those years.
>
> I have had the sense often since her death that I only knew her incompletely. I do not mean that there was any reserve between us. But I owed her so much, she upheld and supported me for so many years, and she was so much wiser in living than I, that I could not know all she had to give. The more I grew up, the more there was to discover in her, and the process had not ended.[6]

Ben wrote about the friendship he and Ruth had always felt for Julius and Eleanor Lewin. He said he was well and not unhappy. 'I don't think I was "viable" when I first met Ruth. But I am now. I wondered at first what would happen to me – whether I would slip back to the poor creature I was before I met her. But that is not so. So I get along very well. I am still in the last home she made for me.'

Ben's revelation that Ruth had been ailing for some time is the only information on her physical condition. A photograph taken shortly before her death shows that she had grown stout – something about which she was most unhappy – but the underlying pathology is unknown. She died at the comparatively young age of 53, in March 1942.

In one respect, at least, Ruth lived on. She had been privy to Ben's writings and had encouraged him to complete his works. After he left South Africa he published extensively. In an obituary it was said:

> Almost all his considerable writing gravitated around two themes (the connexion between 'science and practical life' and 'the rationalism of Epicurus and Lucretius'). He saw the ultimate weakness of ancient science in its divorce from practical life – it became a way of knowing, not of doing – and that led him to Francis Bacon, about whom he wrote two books, one with the revealing sub-title, 'Philosopher of Industrial Science'. Similarly his humanism engendered a work on Darwin in addition to his life-long work on Epicurus ...[7]

Over the years, he published many books:

Science in Antiquity (1936); *Science and Politics in the Ancient World* (1939); *Greek Science: Its Meaning for Us* (1944), *Head and Hand in Ancient Greece* (1947); *Francis Bacon: Philosopher of Industrial Science* (1949); *Francis Bacon: Pioneer of Planned Science* (1963); *The Philosophy of Francis Bacon: Its Development from 1603-1609* (1964); *Aristotle: Founder of Scientific Philosophy* (1965); *The Faith of Epicurus* (1967). Many of these works were translated into European languages and Japanese and several went into two or more editions.

He also contributed more than a dozen articles to journals or collections of essays, and was general editor of the *Past and Present* series – eight volumes produced between 1964 and 1969 and *Marxism Today*- nine booklets published between 1943 and 1952.

After Ruth's death Ben married Barbara Sell. They had one daughter, Jane. Ben left the Communist Party in 1956 after the invasion of Hungary by Soviet troops. He died in November 1974 at the age of eighty-three.

EPILOGUE

It is fitting to give the last words to Ruth or, if not all the last words, at least the penultimate ones. Writing in the *Cape Times* on 19 July 1924 about the 'Living Past', she compared the writing of biography with the creation of a novel. Extolling novelists for their 'creative imagination', she went on to say:

> the historian rescues for us the dead, who, however mighty, splendid or lovely they may have been in their day, from beyond the great silence can tell us as little of their real selves, their real lives as if they had been the most colourless, the most insignificant of their own times. From the grey oblivion of the years, from the dust-covered obscurity of forgotten archives and uninteresting compilations, the chronicler of genius gives back to us a living, laughing, suffering fellow-human so that we are at once startled and cheered by our fresh realisation of the changelessness and variety of humanity. To make these dry bones live, indeed, with a patient, faithful regard for the facts, and yet to achieve the dramatisation which is necessary to place the man or woman before the reader is a gift as rare as it is precious.
>
> The secret is, of course, that those so rescued must live for the chronicler as intensely as they are to live for the reader.

I can only be grateful that Ruth is not here to review this book. The genius she sought is, unfortunately, not present. Yet, throughout this labour (obviously of love) I have hoped to offer the portrait of a human being who lived intensely and hoped to find, or to inspire, the same intensity in those she loved. There are no 'forgotten archives' on which to rely, no compilations, interesting or otherwise. But, for me, Ruth has lived intensely. If my readers have caught even part of that intensity I will consider the work good enough to have passed her critical eye.

There are some, living now, who may object to my having written about people who did not seem ever to join groups or organisations involved in the struggles against discrimination or oppression. Besides the fact that there were few effective organisations in Cape Town during the period that Ruth lived there, or certainly none outside the trade unions which recruited only whites, such considerations do not enter my story. The fledgling Communist Party was ineffectual, and the Trotskyist groups only organised meetings in the early 1930s. Attempts were made 'to win Ben to the Spartacists', one of the Trotskyist groups, and he did speak to the small circle of adherents but he was not the joining type.

This book is, consequently, not about the left groups, and not about the few working class struggles of the time. Nor is it about the national movements, which were not very active in the Western Cape. What it does include is in many ways more important: Ruth's descriptions of District Six and the people who were crowded into its confines, and her growing reactions to the repressive legislation being introduced by the leaders of the National Party. More theoretical analyses of the problems facing the African people were offered by two Trotskyist groupings, but by that time Ruth had departed.

I have discussed these issues in some detail in the journal *Searchlight South Africa* and there has been no need to repeat them here. Indeed, had I done so they would have been redundant to the subject that happened to develop into this book. It was a book I never meant to write, but having done so I feel that I entered a period of history about which I knew far too little. For this knowledge I can only extend my thanks to Ruth Schechter, who so presumptuously attached herself to Morris Alexander at the age of twelve.

Postscript

Just when I thought that no more information could be found a further search by the librarian of the University of Cape Town, Mrs Lesley Hart, revealed a letter and an article on woman's enfranchisement (delivered in New Jersey) in the Morris Alexander files. Diaries, plays and poetry left by Muriel (Bobbet) that were stored in the files of Louis Hermann were found by Shula Marks but were not relevant to this work. Articles in the *Cape Argus* that Ruth mentioned in her letters to Ben have been retrieved and inserted into the text. This raises hopes that more may be discovered to supplement my story – or even to challenge some of my conclusions. That I leave to other researchers.

NOTES

CHAPTER 1

1. Mel Scult, pp 4-5; N Bentwich (1931), pp 24-25 quotes only part of the passage.
2. Lecture on Olive Schreiner, 1929, subsequently expanded and printed in instalments in the *Cape Times,* 26, 28 and 29 April and 1 May 1930. This is in strange contrast with the religious zeal of the 'wanderers'. As Ruth wrote in her review of the previously unpublished novel *Undine*, in the *Cape Times*, 30 March 1929: '*The Story of an African Farm* was a story lifted to splendour by the lyrical passion of its revolt against the conventional life and religion of its time, and it was the wild sweet nobility of that revolt which roused an answering cry in thousands of hearts.'
3. Bentwich (1938), pp 79-80.
4. Frank Schechter (1922).
5. Ibid.
6. Ibid.
7. Bentwich (1938), pp 83-84.
8. Bentwich (1931), p 15.
9. A copy of this letter is included in Ruth's papers. The text is quoted in Bentwich (1938), p 88.
10. M Scult.
11. Bentwich (1938), p 90.
12. Quotations and descriptions from Meir Persoff, 'Hidden Treasures of Cairo', *Jewish Chronicle* Magazine, London, 27 November 1977. Raphael Levy (1982) adds material on the Genizah which is incorporated into my text. In his letter to me of 25 June 1992, Levy notes that Judeo-Arabic was Arabic written in Hebrew characters, the *lingua franca* of Jews living in the Moslem world from the 10th through the 13th centuries. The Hebrew literature was largely sacred, or religious literature.
13. Frank Schechter.
14. The letter is reprinted in *Genizah Fragments*, October 1996. H Jenkinson's role is described by Stefan Reif.
15. Raphael Levy (1982), 'First Dead Sea Scrolls', p 65.
16. Ibid.
17. *Times*, 20 November 1978.
18. Quoted in Bentwich (1931), p 30.

19. Frank Schechter
20. Bentwich (1931), p 40. Bentwich also says that Schechter bought every book that appeared about Lincoln for 'the Puritan and mystic element in the American President.' Ibid, p 49.
21. Memorial service, thought to be written by Benjamin Farrington.
22. Bentwich (1938), pp 92-93.
23. Enid Alexander, p 18. I quote with some reservation from a text that is filled with errors of detail, but it seems that this passage, if not the words, is accurate.
24. This community carried with it some of the enthusiasms of the Hassidic sect and differentiated itself from the Orthodox communities and from the Reform (or Liberal) communities.

CHAPTER 2

1. Bentwich (1931), pp 32-33.
2. Ibid, p 34.
3. Quoted by Bentwich (1938), pp 218-19.
4. M Shain, pp xvi, 56. (Cape Town had a Jewish population of 8 114, and its suburbs 2 568).
5. For Goldblatt's role, see Shain, p 57.
6. Details of the test, including the passage used for translation are in Shain, pp 27 ff and Appendix II, pp 130 ff
7. G Saron, pp 16-18; E Alexander, pp 26-36.
8. E Alexander, p 38.
9. E Alexander, p 50.
10. *New York Times*, 10 June, 1907.
11. E Alexander, pp 51-52.
12. *New York Times*, 10 June 1907.
13. Olive Schreiner, *Cape Times,* 1930.
14. Sent to me by M Scult.
15. Information about the family was received from Raphael Levy in a letter dated 25 June 1992.
16. The letters written en route home from a visit abroad in 1913 are those of a devoted wife. (Found in M Alexander papers, University of Cape Town.)

CHAPTER 3

1. Bradlow, pp 133-34.
2. Bradlow, op cit.
3. Bradlow, op cit, pp 135-137.
4. Ibid, pp 139-141.

5. See Swan, p 2. It is estimated that those Indians organised in Gandhi's campaigns never numbered more than 2 000 in Natal (or 3,5 per cent of the non-dependent male population), and half that number in the Transvaal (or 15 per cent of the non-dependent male population). No numbers are available for the Cape.
6. Swan, pp 114 ff, p 240.
7. The copy of this letter was sent by E S Reddy, New York, to Yousuf (Joe) Rassool who has written a history of the Gool/Rassool family. Thanks to the latter for the loan of this document.
8. Communication from E S Reddy, 22 January 1998.
9. There was no definitive definition of Theosophy. According to Helene Petrovna Blavatsky the Theosophical Society's 'aim was a) to form the nucleus of the Universal Brotherhood without distinction of race, creed, sex, caste and colour; b) to encourage the study of Comparative Religion, Philosophy and Science; c) to investigate the unexplained laws of Nature and the powers latent in man.' Quoted by Chatterjee, p 3.
10. From a precis of a talk (c 1905) by Gandhi, found in H S L Polak's papers, as quoted by Phyllis Dean in her history of the Johannesburg Lodge and requoted by Chatterjee, pp 172-73.
11. Shimoni, p 5, quoting from Gandhi's autobiography.
12. Ibid, p 7.
13. Indians were not allowed to purchase land in the Transvaal. It is also unlikely that the Indian movement had enough money for such a venture.
14. Reprinted, with minor cuts, in Sarid and Bartolf, pp 34-61.
15. Quoted in Sarid and Bartolf, taken from Gandhi's *The Story of My Experiment With Truth*, part 1, Chapter 20.
16. E Alexander, p 116. There is no indication in Mrs Alexander's account of what was said that night nor, indeed, of whether Morris travelled with Gandhi and Gokhale as they toured the country.
17. Reprinted in *Indian Opinion*, 7 January 1914, and quoted by E S Reddy. Dr W E B DuBois, who inspired and organised the Pan-Africanist movement, is more correctly quoted as saying in 1900 'The problem of the twentieth century is the problem of the colour line.'
18. Quoted in E Alexander, p 119.
19. Ibid.

CHAPTER 4

1. Letter to Lily (Guinsberg), 22 September 1959.
2. Dora Taylor, 'Olive Schreiner - A Challenge to Today, II', *Trek*, 3 February 1942.
3. See First and Scott, p 59.

4. Address to the Social Democratic Federation, February 1905.
5. Address to the Jewish community after their successful campaign to have Yiddish accepted as an European language.
6. An undated cutting from an unknown newspaper, found in Julius Lewin's papers.
7. E.H. [Ethel Herrman], 'Personal Recollections of Olive Schreiner', *The South African Nation*, 9 August 1924.
8. A tribute by Ruth on the second anniversary of Olive Schreiner's death. It is not known whether this was meant for publication.
9. Louis Herrman(nd), 'Olive Would Have Led Permissive Society', newspaper cutting of unknown origin.
10. First and Scott, p 260.
11. Ruth Alexander, 'Talk on Schreiner, Part III', 29 April 1930.
12. Claudia Roth Pierpont, p 79; First and Scott, p 254.
13. First and Scott, p 258; Dora Taylor, op cit, 13 March 1942.
14. First and Scott, p 188.
15. Reprinted in Norman Herd.
16. Schreiner's letter to the meeting called to protest against the massacre in Johannesburg in 1913. Quoted in Hirson and Williams, p 128. The protest meeting was reported in the *Cape Times*, 21 July 1913. The letter to Carpenter was reprinted in the British *Labour Leader*, 28 August 1913. No copy was found among the Carpenter papers in Sheffield.
17. Thanks to Karel Schoeman, archivist at the South African Library, who sent me this copy.
18. The International Socialist League was the precursor of the Communist Party of South Africa.
19. Kallenbach was in Britain and, although he was a convinced pacifist, was interned because he carried an Austrian passport.

CHAPTER 5

1. Hogben (1998), p 93.
2. Ibid.
3. Vera Brittain, p 62.
4. Ibid, p 205.
5. A corrected typescript is held by Jane Straker. A copy has been deposited in the South African Library, Cape Town.
6. Typescript (nd), 'Coloureds: A Bye-Product of Empire'.
7. The occupations of coloureds living in District Six are not easily available. However there are some figures which provide an overview of social differences. In 1921 less than one per cent were employed in white-collar

or professional occupations, while fewer than three per cent were employed in retailing, commerce and recreation. Of the women, 87 per cent were classified as domestic servants, less than five per cent were in skilled or semi-skilled jobs. The numbers of skilled and semi-skilled men dropped sharply after the passing of the Apprenticeship Act in 1922. (Figures in Goldin, pp 41-42.)

8. Shain, quoting from *The Cape*, January 1906, p 90.
9. After Morris's disagreement with Rabbi Bender over the establishment of the Board of Deputies the Alexanders attended this independent synagogue.

CHAPTER 6

1. This information is in a taped interview with Farrington held by Mrs Straker
2. Lestrade achieved prominence in his field as an ethnologist. He is said to have mastered thirty-four languages and Farrington referred to his skill in mastering the African languages and recording their sounds phonetically.
3. Quoted in Geoffrey Haresnape, p 113. Ruth's reviews of the *Voorslag* group appear in chapter 9.
4. A scrapbook found in her loft by Jane Straker is both a treasure and a source of endless exasperation. Hundreds of reviews and essays written by Ben or Ruth were pasted into the back of this book, but over the years many had been ripped out. In some cases all that was left were fragments, some of unknown origin, others with a heading (from which the titles can sometimes be discerned). Some are dated, others are glued into pages that give only the month and year of printing. Furthermore, with no signatures it was not always possible to determine authorship. Because there is a surfeit of material several pieces that might have been worth salvaging were abandoned. Pasted into the front are articles on Ireland, some written by Ben, and cuttings from the press in Europe and South Africa. These include the articles in *De Burger*.
5. The letters to Ben from his family in Ireland are in the possession of Jane Straker.
6. Ibid. Few of the letters to Farrington discuss the contents of his letters home. However, one correspondent, 'Q', writing on 16 August 1920, took Ben to task for having come to these conclusions.
7. The translations from the Afrikaans were made with the assistance of Isabel Hofmeyr.
8. Copies of *The Republic* and the article on the IRA(SA) were obtained from Donal MacCracken at the University of Durban Westville and from Donel Lowry at Brooke, Oxford University.

9. The letters are in the possession of Jane Straker.
10. Letter to the author from Howard Phillips, University of Cape Town, 4 June 1992

CHAPTER 7

1. A copy of a page from the *Review* published by the *Oheb Shalom Congregation*, in 1913, was sent by Dan Schechter to Elsie Alexander (Australia), and in turn sent to me. Unfortunately there was no indication of what Ruth had said. Accompanying the report was a column-long poem, 'The Yellow Badge', by Ruth. Although written so long before it portended the 1930s.
2. At a meeting in March 1927 of the South African branch of the English Association the Chairman, a Professor Notcutt, described it as a branch of a world-wide association that had been founded in England in 1906. The South African branch was small and had fewer than fifty members. Notcutt stressed that the Association 'had nothing whatever to do with politics; it aimed at the promotion of good English and the encouragement of good literature only'. When John Galsworthy visited the Cape in 1926 five hundred people had to be turned away (*Cape Times*, 19 March 1927). The first available set of minutes of the branch was dated 7 April 1922. The only matters minuted were proposals for forthcoming lecturers, and annual recommendations to the Matriculation Board of set works.
3. The correspondence between Ruth and lawyers representing Cronwright during the period 4 May to 8 August 1929 is in the South African Library. Included in the papers is an opinion by Morris that the will did not allow Cronwright to publish Olive's letters!
4. This account of Goodlatte was extracted partly from letters written to John George Chapman, a former pupil, deposited in the South African Library; from obituaries by HO [Helena Olendorf], from the College Magazine in 1942; and from its final issue in 1975. I wrote an initial article, '*Spark* and the "Red Nun"', in *Searchlight South Africa*, No 2, February 1989.
5. Adrian and Anne Hogben, p 99.
6. Quoted in a letter to me dated 18 January 1994, from Frances Liebenberg, who presented a dissertation on Boonzaier. Ms Liebenberg also sent me copies of pages 64-67 from Boonzaier's diary No 21 (Msc 4) – with the permission of the South African Library – in which there were references to Wenning and Ruth.
7. Ibid.
8. Adrian and Anne Hogben, pp 113-4.

9. Roux, pp 90-92.
10. Roux, pp 103-104. Roux's account, which I summarise above, was appreciably different from that of Hogben, pp 114-5.
11. Compare my book, *Year of Fire, Year of Ash*. I found this pamphlet many years after I wrote the book.

CHAPTER 8

1. Irving Howe and Lewis Coser, pp 257ff. The stretch-out reduced the labour force by requiring workers to attend additional machines without a commensurate increase in pay. That is, weavers were stretched from 24 to 48 looms and up to 96 looms. See also the history of the strike as described by F Beal, *Proletarian Journey*, 1934. Amy's function in Gastonia did not take her into direct contact with Beal and there is only a passing reference to her in his book.
2. *Labour Defender, USA,* September 1929, in an article headed 'Who are the Gastonia Prisoners?', with subheading 'The lives and activity [sic] of the sixteen men and women – union organizers and textile workers who are being tried for murder in Gastonia, North Carolina.'
3. Christina L Baker, 'Gastonia Strike'. In *The American Left Encyclopaedia*.
4. Howe and Coser, op cit.
5. Yellen, p 306.
6. Ibid, pp303-305
7. William F Dunne, quoted in Howe and Coser, p 261.
8. Letter from Raphael Levy to the author, 25 August 1993.
9. John was a grand-child of Ruth's brother, Frank. The letter provided a short account of the descendants of Solomon and Mathilda Schechter. Although John tried to provide as much information as was known to him, he was not able to offer much detail. The letter, unfortunately, contains many inaccuracies and I cannot be certain that what I copied was correct. Thanks to Elsie Alexander for a copy of the letter.

CHAPTER 9

1. There is a short reference to Cissie Gool leading a campagn against the proposed Enfranchisement of Women Act in an unfinished biography of Ray (Alexander) Simons in Uppsala.
2. The history of the strike and the agitation among the Indian community is described in Baruch Hirson and Lorraine Vivian.
3. S van der Horst, p 236.

CHAPTER 10

1. *The Exiles*, pp 231-240.
2. The letter is reprinted in Enid Alexander, p 146.
3. Reported in the *Cape Times*, 10 June 1932.
4. 'Memorial Service for Ruth Schechter Farrington', 5 March 1942.
5. Ibid.
6. Letter from Ben Farrington to Julius and Eleanor Hawarden Lewin, 8 July 1943.
7. Professor M I Finley, *The Times*, 21 November 1974.

BIBLIOGRAPHY

Primary Source Material

In the search for documents I am indebted to the South African Library and the Library at the University of Cape Town, Eleanor Hawarden, Stefan Reif, Raphael Levy, Tikvah Alper, Jane Straker, Adrian and Anne Hogben, Brian Farrington, Hannah Kantor, Elsie Alexander, E S Reddy, and many others who have been so co-operative and willing to assist me.

JULIUS LEWIN PAPERS

Obituary to Ruth (memorial service), 5 March 1942.

Articles on the Cairo Genizah (*Jewish Chronicle* and others).

Book reviews by Ruth S Alexander in the *Cape Times* and *South African Nation*.

Printed version of the lecture on Olive Schreiner, *Cape Times*, 1930.

Two letters from Benjamin Farrington.

Obituary of Farrington, *Cape Times*, 21 November 1974.

SOUTH AFRICAN LIBRARY

Letters from Clare Goodlatte to John Chapman.

Letters from Olive Schreiner to Ruth and other letters relating to possible publication of letters.

Correspondence with Cronwright.

Lecture on Olive Schreiner (typescript and *Cape Times*).

Several articles on Olive Schreiner.

Copies of articles from the *Cape Times* and other Cape papers.

Letters from Ben Farrington to Lily Guinsberg and to Julius Lewin.

University Forward, March 1942. (MSC 26). My thanks to Karel Schoeman for encouragement and assistance in securing documents.

UNIVERSITY OF CAPE TOWN

Letters from Ruth to Morris Alexander, 1913.

Accounts of Ruth's talks in the US.

Extracts from H M Robertson, 'The University of Cape Town, 1918-68', typescript.

Letter from Patrick Duncan to Ruth: thanks to the librarians, Leonie Twentyman-Jones and Lesley Hart.

British Library Newspaper Collection

Articles and Book Reviews by Ruth Schechter Alexander in newspapers and journals.

Articles by Amy Schechter in journals from New York.

Farrington's Papers in the possession of Jane Straker

Photographs of Ruth and of Farrington.

Unpublished novel *The Exiles* c1936.

'Cape Coloured: A By-Product of Empire' c1938. Fourteen pages devoted to a description of District Six, typescript (21 pages).

Letters to Ben from friends and relatives, mainly 1920/21, and from Ruth in 1932.

Typescript (3 pages) by Farrington meant to introduce the publication of three essays by Ruth.

Scrapbook with cuttings – see below.

Scrapbook with Cuttings

Articles and reviews in Cape Town papers, some of them destroyed or torn out, commencing in September 1920 with articles on Ireland, including an historical survey, by Ben Farrington in Afrikaans.

Articles and reviews, at the other end of the scrapbook, by both Ben and Ruth, from October 1922 to December 1924.

Hogben's Papers

'An Unauthorized Autobiography of Lancelot Hogben', edited by Adrian and Anne Hogben, typescript, 1989.

Lancelot Thomas Hogben 1895-1975 by GP Wells (Bibliographical memoirs of Fellows of the Royal Society, Vol 24, November 1978).

L Hogben, 'Preface on Prejudice'. In Cedric Dover, *Half Caste*, Secker & Warburg, 1937.

Articles by Olive Schreiner

Address to the Social Democratic Federation of Cape Town, 5 February 1905, following the strike wave in Russia in January 1905. Reprinted from S A Rochlin, 'They Helped to Shape Our Future', *South African Jewish Frontier*, September 1946.

From the 'Address by Olive Schreiner', presented by S C Cronwright-Schreiner to the Jewish Territorial Organisation, Cape Town, 1 July 1906.

Letters to Ruth Alexander, 1909-1920, from the Ruth Alexander collection, donated to the South African Library.

OTHER PAPERS

Ruth's letter to Gandhi.

Raphael Levy's letters to the author.

Two letters from Ruth to Raphael Levy.

Three letters from Ruth to Hermann Kallenbach.

Two memoirs of Olive Schreiner by Ethel and by Louis Herrman.

Genizah Fragments, a newsletter edited by Stefan Reif.

SELECTED BOOK REVIEWS AND ARTICLES BY RUTH SCHECHTER ALEXANDER (ENTERED CHRONOLOGICALLY)

'Capetown Cafe Girls: How they are Paid', *The Cape Times*, 19 November 1915.

'Women's Work after the War', *SA Lady's Pictorial*, December 1915.

'A Living Wage', *SA Lady's Pictorial*, January 1916.

'The Girl of Tomorrow', *SA Lady's Pictorial*, April 1916.

'Perilous Economy', *SA Lady's Pictorial*, February 1916.

Stories, Dreams and Allegorie by Olive Schreiner, edited by S Cronwright-Schreiner, *Cape Times*, 24 February 1923.

The Story of John Paul by V R Emanuel, *Cape Times*, 2 June 1923.

Thoughts on South Africa by Olive Schreiner, edited by S Cronwright-Schreiner, *Cape Times*, 23 July 1923.

'Yiddish', *Cape Times*, 11 August 1923.

'The Jewish New Year', *Cape Times*, 11 September 1923.

Olive Schreiner, S Cronwright-Schreiner, *The Nation*, 4 June 1924.

Olive Schreiner, S Cronwright-Schreiner, *The South African Nation*, 9 August, 1924.

'Olive Schreiner and the Brontës: A Note', *The Educational News*, September 1925, mimeographed.

The Letters of Olive Schreiner, 1876-1920, edited by S Cronwright-Schreiner, *Cape Times*, December 1924.

The Letters of Olive Schreiner, 1876-1920, edited by S Cronwright-Schreiner, *The Nation*, 14 October 1925.

The Letters of Constance Lytton, edited by Betty Balfour, *The South African Nation*, 9 January 1926.

'An International Writer' (Rabindranath Tagore), *The South African Nation*, 20 February 1926.

'The Colour Question in South Africa', *The Nation*, 23 June 1926.

'Literature and Patriotism', *The South African Nation*, 31 July 1926.

'The Literary Exploitation of the Native', *The South African Nation*, 25 September 1926.

From Man to Man by Olive Schreiner, edited by S Cronwright-Schreiner, *Cape Times*, 28 October 1926.

The Beadle, by Pauline Smith, *The South African Nation*, 30 October 1926.

Journals of Katharine Mansfield, edited by J Middleton Murry, *The South African Nation*, 24 September 1927.

The South Africans, by Sarah Gertrude Millin, *The Nation*, 27 July 1927.

I speak of Africa, by William Plomer, *The South African Nation*, 5 November 1927.

The Autobiography of an ex-Coloured Man, by James Weldon Johnson, *The South African Nation* , 25 February, 1928.

'The South African Native Worker', *The Nation*, 29 February 1928.

The Wayzgoose by Roy Campbell, *The South African Nation*, 10 March 1928.

Joseph Conrad: Life and Letters by G Jean-Aubry, *The South African Nation*, 24 March 1928.

Seaton's Aunt by Walter de la Mare, *Cape Times*, 14 April 1928.

'The Colour Line in South Africa', *The Nation*, 19 November 1928.

H W Nevinson, *Cape Times*, 4 January 1929.

My Life by Isadora Duncan, *Cape Times*, 17 January 1929.

The Letters of Katharine Mansfield, edited by J Middleton Murry, *Cape Times*, 14 February 1929.

'The South African Native Trade Union', *Nation*, 29 February 1929.

'*Undine*: Olive Schreiner's Lost Novel', *Cape Times*, 30 March 1929.

India- Stepmother by Sir Claude H Hill, *Cape Times*, 14 May 1929.

Zaka Ullah of Delhi by C F Andrews, *Cape Times,* 14 May 1929.

Isadora Duncan's Russian Days and her Last Years in France by Irma Duncan & Allan Ross MacDougall, Cape Times, *29 May 1929.*

The Letters of Sacco and Vanzetti, edited by Marion Frankfurter and Gardner Jackson, *Cape Times*, 28 June 1929.

Boston by Upton Sinclair, *Cape Times*, 28 June 1929.

Dreiser Looks at Russia by Theodore Dreiser, *Cape Times*, *Cape Times*, 11 July 1929.

The Russian Land by A Rhys Williams, *Cape Times*, 11 July 1929.

Letter on 'flu epidemic of 1919, *Cape Times*, 25 July 1929

'Is Charity Over-organised – And Too Easy?', *Cape Times*, 8 January 1930.

'Olive Schreiner' (in 5 parts) 26/28/29 April, 1 May 1930, *Cape Times.*

The Fortunes of Richard Mahony by Henry Handel Richardson, *Cape Argus*, 10 January, and *Cape Times*, 26 February 1931.

The Dogs by Ivan Nazhivin, *Cape Times*, 12 March 1931.

Three Pairs of Silk Stockings by Panteleimon Romanof, *Cape Times*, 12 March 1931.

The Darling by Anton Tchekov, *Cape Times*, 18 April 1931.
Women and Children Last by Beverley Nichols, *Cape Times*, 18 April 1931.
Ragged Banners by Ethel Mannin, *Cape Times*, 18 April 1931.
'A New South Africa', *Nation*, 27 May 1931.
The Road Back by Erich Maria Remarque, *Cape Times*, 4 June 1931.
Goethe and Beethoven by Romain Rolland, *Cape Argus*, 26 March 1932.
'The Girl who was Malay Tricked', *Cape Argus*, 14 May 1932.
'The Penny Bank: A Little Known Side of District Six', *Cape Times*, July 1932.
My Russian Venture by Mrs Cecil Chesterson, *Cape Argus*, 31 October 1932.
'In the Twilight of Liberty', *Cape Argus*, 26 November 1932.
'The Intruders', *Cape Argus*, 18 March 1933.
Driving Axle by V Ilyenkov, *Nation*, 4 July 1934.
'A Very Great Woman', published under the name Ruth Farrington, *University Forward*, March 1942.

BOOKS AND ARTICLES

Alexander, Enid.1953. *Morris Alexander: A Biography*. Juta, Cape Town.
Alexander, Ruth S (nd). *The Exiles*. Typescript.
——— (nd), 'The Coloureds: A By-product of Empire'. Typescript.
Anon [Benjamin Farrington]. 1942. Memorial Service for Ruth Schechter Farrington, Swansea.
Baker, Christina L. 'Gastonia Strike'. In *The American Left Encyclopaedia*.
Bentwich, Norman. 1931. *Solomon Schechter*. George Allen and Unwin, Woking. [Reprint of a talk by Bentwich]
——— (1938). *Solomon Schechter: A Biography*. Cambridge University Press, London.
Bradlow, Edna. 1979. 'The Cape Community during the Period of Responsible Government'. In *Pachai*.
Brittain, Vera. 1981. *Testament of Friendship: The Story of Winifred Holtby*. Fontana, London.
Buchanan-Gould, Vera. 1949. *Not Without Honour*. Hutchinson, Cape Town.
Chatterjee, Margaret. 1992. *Gandhi and his Jewish Friends*. Macmillan, London.
Chaytor, Miranda and Lewis, Jane. 1982. 'Introduction' to Alice Clark, *Working Life of Women in the Seventeenth Century*. Routledge & Kegan Paul, London.
First, Ruth and Scott, Ann. 1980. *Olive Schreiner*. Andre Deutsch, London.

Goldin, Ian. 1987. *Making Race*. Longman, London.

Haresnape, Geoffrey. 1983. 'The *Voorslag* Movement and Olive Schreiner. In Van Wyk Smith and MacLennan. *Olive Schreiner and After: Essays on South African Literature in Honour of Guy Butler*

Herd, Norman. 1974. *Counter Attack: The Story of the South African Shopworkers*. National Union of Distributive Workers, Cape Town.

Herzberg, Bernhardt.1998. *Otherness: The Story of a Very Long Life*. Lehavot Publications, Israel.

Hirson, Baruch. 1979. *Year of Fire, Year of Ash: Soweto, Roots of a Revolution?*. Zed, London.

——— 1989. '*Spark* and the "Red Nun"'. In *Searchlight South Africa* No 2. and Lorraine Vivian. 1992. *Strike Across the Empire: The Seamen's Strike of 1925, in Britain, South Africa and Australasia*. Clio Publications, London and Gwyn Williams. 1995. *The Delegate for Africa: David Ivon Jones, 1883-1924*. Core Publications, London.

Hogben, Adrian and Anne (eds). 1998. *Lancelot Hogben: Scientific Humanist, An Unauthorised Autobiography*. Merlin, London.

Hogben, Lancelot. 1937. 'Preface on Prejudice'. In Dover, Cedric, *Half Caste*. Secker & Warburg, London.

Howe, Irving and Coser, Lewis. 1957. *The American Communist Party: A Critical History (1919-1957)*. Becon Press.

Levy, Raphael. 1982. '"First Dead Sea Scroll", Found in Egypt Fifty Years Before Qumran Discoveries'. In Shanks.

McCracken, Donal P (ed). 1996. *Ireland and South Africa in Modern Times: Southern African-Irish Studies, 3*.

Pachai, Bridglal (ed). 1979. South Africa's Indians: The Evolution of a Minority. University Press of America, Washington.

Persoff, Meir. 1977. 'Hidden Treasures of Cairo'. *Jewish Chronicle* Magazine, 25 November.

Pierpont, Claudia Roth. 1992. 'A Critic at Large: A Woman's Place'. *New Yorker*, 27 January.

Reddy, E S. 1993. 'Gandhiji and some Remarkable European Women who helped him in South Africa'. Typescript, 25 January.

Reif, Stefan. 1992. 'Jenkinson and Schechter at Cambridge: An expanded and updated assessment'. The Jewish Historical Society of England, XXXII, 1990-1992.

Roux, Eddie and Win. 1972. *Rebel Pity*. Penguin, Harmonsworth.

Sarid, Isa and Bartolf, Christian. 1998. *Hermann Kallenbach: Mahatma Gandhi's Friend in South Africa, A Concise Biography*. Gandhi-Informations-Zentrum, Zelbstverslag.

Saron, Gus. 1966. *Morris Alexander: Parliamentarian and Jewish Leader.* South African Jewish Board of Deputies.

Schechter, Frank I. 1922. 'Schechteriana'. *Menorah Journal.* New York, Vol 8.

Shanks, Hershel (ed). 1982. *Understanding the Dead Sea Scrolls.* Random House.

Scult, Mel. nd. *The Baale Boste Reconsidered: The Life of Mathilde Roth Schechter.* No publication details.

Shain, Milton. 1983. *Jewry and Cape Society: The Origins and Activities of the Jewish Board of Deputies for the Cape Colony.* Historical Publication Society, Cape Town.

Shimoni, Gideon. 1977. *Gandhi, Satyagraha and the Jews: A Formative Factor in India's Policy Towards Israel.* Jerusalem Papers on Peace Problems, No 22. Hebrew University, Jerusalem.

Swan, Maureen. 1985. *Gandhi: The South African Experience.* Ravan Press, Johannesburg.

Taylor, Dora. 1942. 'Olive Schreiner – A Challenge to Today'. Three articles commencing 30 January, *Trek*, Cape Town.

Van der Horst, Sheila. 1971. *Native Labour in South Africa.* Frank Cass, London.

Van der Poel, Jean. 1934. *Education and the Native.* 'Paper read at the Conference of the South African Teachers' Association at Cape Town on June 28th, 1934'.

Van Wyk Smith, M and MacLennan, D (eds). 1983. *Olive Schreiner and After: Essays on South African Literature in Honour of Guy Butler.* David Philip, Cape Town.

Walker, Cheryl. 1979. *The Woman's Suffrage Movement in South Africa.* Centre for African Studies, University of Cape Town.

——— (ed). 1990. *Women and Gender in Southern Africa to 1945.* David Philip, Cape Town.

Yellen, Samuel. 1985. *American Labour Struggles, 1877-1934.* Monad Press.

INDEX